Nobody Ever Tells You These Things

Nobody Ever Tells You These Things

About Food and Drink

by Helen McCully

Holt, Rinehart and Winston
New York   Chicago   San Francisco

Published simultaneously in Canada by Holt, Rinehart
and Winston of Canada, Ltd.
Library of Congress Catalog Card Number: 67–12647
Published, May, 1967
Fourth Printing, February, 1972

Portions of this book have appeared
in *House Beautiful Magazine*.

Grateful acknowledgment is made to the following for permission to
quote from their works:

House Beautiful Magazine in which portions of this book have appeared.
Liquor Store Magazine.
American Heritage Publishing Co., Inc. for: THE AMERICAN HERITAGE
COOKBOOK, copyright © 1964 by American Heritage Publishing Co., Inc.
Harper and Row Publishers, Inc. for: THE NEW YORK TIMES COOK BOOK
by Craig Claiborne, copyright © 1961 by Craig Claiborne; AN HERB AND
SPICE COOK BOOK by Craig Claiborne, copyright © 1963 by Craig Claiborne;
THE NEW YORK TIMES MENU COOK BOOK by Craig Claiborne, copyright ©
1966 by The New York Times Company; and FRENCH PROVINCIAL COOKING
by Elizabeth David, copyright © 1960 by Elizabeth David.
Hastings House, Publishers, Inc. for: ENCYCLOPEDIA OF WINE by Frank
Schoonmaker, copyright © 1964 by Frank Schoonmaker.
Alfred A. Knopf, Inc. for: ITALIAN FOOD by Elizabeth David, copyright
© 1958 by Elizabeth David; and MASTERING THE ART OF FRENCH COOKING
by Simone Beck, Louisette Bertholle and Julia Child, copyright © 1961 by
Alfred A. Knopf, Inc.
Charles Scribner's Sons for: GROSSMAN'S GUIDE TO WINES, SPIRITS AND
BEERS by Harold J. Grossman, copyright 1940, 1968 by Harold J. Grossman.
Simon and Schuster for: THE ART OF FINE BAKING by Paula Peck, copy-
right © 1961 by Paula Peck; THE CHEESE BOOK by Vivienne Marquis and
Patricia Haskell, copyright © 1964, 1965 by Vivienne Marquis and Patricia
Haskell; and THE PLEASURES OF CHINESE COOKING by Grace Zia Chu, copy-
right © 1962 by Grace Zia Chu.
David White Company for: THE SPICE COOKBOOK by Avenell S. Day and
Lillie M. Stuckey, copyright © 1964 by Avenell S. Day and Lillie M.
Stuckey.

Designer: Ernst Reichl
ISBN: 0–03–063750–3
Printed in the United States of America

For James A. Beard,

dear friend, dear mentor,

who can tell you these things

and everything there is to know

about food.

Preface

Stalking the answers to the endless questions that come to a cook's mind is a fascinating and, as often, frustrating experience. *Nobody Ever Tells You These Things About Food and Drink* is a direct result of my own curiosity. I really wanted to know how split peas got split; how come oysters had crabs boarding with them; why angel cakes must hang until cold. In the course of my own explorations I discovered that numbers of my friends, especially the good amateur cooks, were equally puzzled by mysteries of the kitchen: "Why don't egg whites beat up properly at certain times?" "Do you or don't you wash omelet pans?" "Is a hen turkey more tender than a Tom?"

To someone who has cooked during the better part of her lifetime and has been fortunate enough to know and work with some of the best food professionals in the world, these questions often seem naïve. But, even the most experienced of homemakers have blanks in their culinary knowledge. It was the awareness of how many blanks there are that sparked the column in *House Beautiful* on which this book is based—an idea that would have remained in limbo if Sarah Tomerlin Lee, my old friend and *House Beautiful's* talented Editor-in-Chief, hadn't proposed to establish it as a regular monthly column in the magazine. To her, I am more than grateful.

My gratitude, however, also extends to more people than I could ever name—among them, Lillie Stuckey who, for almost three years, patiently answered endless questions about herbs and spices, fruits and vegetables, drawing from her inexhaustible knowledge; John von Glahn, of the Fishery Council, whose interest and enthusiasm have been a constant spur; Dr. Frank V. Kosikowski, Professor of Food Science at Cornell, and one of the world's most distinguished cheese authorities, who was generous enough to edit my cheese questions; Jacques

Pépin, good friend and brilliant chef, who has taught me much of what I know about *haute cuisine*, and was kind enough to edit my references to French cooking; Dan Hecht, Editor of *Liquor Store*, who has put me forever in his debt by checking the accuracy of my material on distilled spirits; both Reba Staggs and Jacques Filiatreau (Secretary of the Sausage Council), of the National Livestock and Meat Board, who supplied me with vast quantities of information on meats and sausages and checked my facts; and Eleanor Bateman, of the Poultry and Egg National Board, who has been a constant source of help in an area in which she is extremely knowledgeable. I would be remiss, indeed, if I did not publicly thank William Belkin, Dennis Belkin, and Henry Heinsohn (of the Mid-City Market) for their endless patience with an often impatient editor.

HELEN McCULLY
New York, 1967

Contents

Nobody Ever Tells You These Things

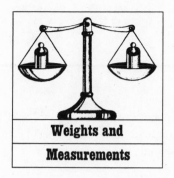

Weights and Measurements

Weights and Measures

A pinch is as much as can be picked up between the thumb and forefinger

3 teaspoons equal 1 tablespoon

4 tablespoons equal ¼ cup or 2 ounces

5 tablespoons plus 1 teaspoon equal ⅓ cup

8 tablespoons equal ½ cup or 4 ounces

1 gill (liquid measure) equals ½ cup or 4 ounces

10 tablespoons plus 2 teaspoons equal ⅔ cup

12 tablespoons equal ¾ cup or 6 ounces

16 tablespoons equal 1 cup or 8 ounces

2 cups equal 1 pint or 16 ounces

2 pints equal 1 quart or 32 ounces

4 quarts equal 1 gallon

8 quarts (dry measure) equal 1 peck

4 pecks (dry measure) equal 1 bushel

16 ounces (dry measure) equal 1 pound

Butter, Lard, Margarine or Shortening

1 ounce equals 2 tablespoons or ¼ stick

2 ounces equal ¼ cup, 4 tablespoons, or ½ stick

4 ounces equal ½ cup, 8 tablespoons, or 1 stick

½ pound equals 1 cup, 16 tablespoons, or 2 sticks

1 pound equals 2 cups or 4 sticks

Cheese

½ pound Cheddar cheese, grated, yields 2 cups

½ pound cottage cheese equals 1 cup

1 3-ounce package cream cheese equals 6 tablespoons

3

Cream

  1 cup or ½ pint of heavy cream, whipped, yields 2 cups

Eggs

  4 to 6 whole eggs, depending on size, equal 1 cup
  8 to 10 egg whites, depending on size, equal 1 cup
  12 to 14 egg yolks, depending on size, equal 1 cup

Flour

  1 pound all-purpose equals 4 cups sifted
  1 pound cake equals 4¾ cups to 5 cups sifted
  1 pound whole wheat equals about 3½ cups

Fruit

  3 medium apples, or 1 pound, equal 3 cups sliced
  3 medium bananas, or 1 pound, equal 2½ cups sliced
  1 medium lemon yields about 3 tablespoons juice
  1 medium lemon yields about 1 tablespoon grated rind
  1 medium orange yields about ⅓ cup juice
  1 medium orange yields about 2 tablespoons grated rind
  1 8-ounce package pitted dates equals 1¼ cups, cut up
  1 15-ounce package raisins equals 3 cups (not packed down)

Pasta

  1 8-ounce package macaroni, or 2 cups, uncooked, yields about 4 to
    5 cups cooked
  1 8-ounce package noodles, or 2½ cups, uncooked, yields 3 to 4 cups
    cooked
  1 8-ounce package spaghetti, or 2½ cups, uncooked, yields 3 to 4
    cups cooked

Rice

  1 cup uncooked long grain rice yields 3 cups cooked
  1 cup parboiled or converted rice yields 4 cups cooked
  1 cup precooked rice yields 2 cups cooked
  1 cup brown rice yields 4 cups cooked

Sugar

  1 pound brown, firmly packed, equals 2½ to 2⅔ cups

1 pound confectioners', unsifted, equals about 4½ cups
1 pound granulated or superfine equals 2¼ to 2½ cups

Vegetables

1 pound dried white beans, or 2 cups, uncooked, yields 6 cups cooked
1 pound dried kidney beans, or 2⅔ cups, uncooked, yields 6¼ cups cooked
1 pound dried lima beans, or 3 cups, uncooked, yields 7 cups cooked
3 medium tomatoes equal 1 pound
3 medium sweet potatoes, or 1 pound, equal 3 cups sliced
3 medium white potatoes, or 1 pound, equal 2⅛ cups sliced

Housekeeping

What kind of beaters do you use? In addition to my *fouets* or whisks, which I use for whipping up sauces, egg whites, and so on, I have a rotary beater, an electric hand beater, and an electric mixer. Of the three, I probably use the electric hand beater and the mixer the most. The hand beater for creaming butter, beating a small number of eggs, beating over hot water; the big electric mixer when the recipe calls for a quantity of eggs (angel cake, for example), or a mixture that requires prolonged beating. I also use it, with the hook, to knead certain breads. However, when I only want to beat up a couple of eggs, I reach, more often than not, for my rotary beater or fouet. I consider fouets, the rotary, and the electric hand beater essential; the electric mixer, a modern miracle I would part with reluctantly.

How can you cut down the racket when beating something? Put a damp dishcloth under the bowl (not a sponge, it won't work), which not only eliminates much of the noise, but also keeps the bowl from bouncing around.

How do you use the electric blender? To grate nuts; to grate chocolate pieces; to grate hard cheeses, such as Parmesan; to crumb bread; to crumb crackers; to purée fruits, vegetables, meats, fish, poultry; to mince parsley; to chop vegetables; to make Hollandaise and mayonnaise. Once you learn to use the blender, you'll agree it's one of the greatest inventions since the wheel. Any cook who knows and loves the blender keeps it right on her work table so that it's always at hand.

Why are boxes of crackers, cereals, potato chips, etc. half empty when you buy them? Half empty is an exaggeration. The manufacturers of such foods pack them with the greatest possible care to minimize breakage in transit but, by "the very nature of the beast," they settle in shipping, leaving air spaces at the top of the box. The point to remember is that you pay by weight—not space—and you get every ounce you pay for. The U.S. Government sees to that.

How can you keep fresh bread crumbs fresh? Put the fresh crumbs in a polyethylene bag, squeezing out all the air, tie the bag securely, then refrigerate. They stay really fresh an amazingly long time. Incidentally, when a recipe calls for bread crumbs, unless it specifies "dry" be sure to use fresh crumbs. The end result is infinitely better. Ready-made bread crumbs in packages are available in all food markets, but you can always make your own. To make soft bread crumbs, crumble day-old bread then rub between your hands until crumbs are fine and all of about the same size. This can also be done in the electric blender if you want extremely fine crumbs. To make fine, dry bread crumbs, dry out slices of stale bread in a 250° F. oven, then roll crumbs with a rolling pin, grate on a grater, put through a grinder, or grate in the electric blender.

Is it possible to prevent brown sugar from hardening? Sugar experts recommend removing brown sugar from the package and storing in an airtight container such as a large-mouth pickle jar with rubber rings (usually available in hardware stores) and buying only as much as you can use up in a comparatively short time.

What is a bulb baster? A metal or glass tube, with a rubber bulb, used to siphon off juices and to baste meats. Extremely handy.

Is there any easy way to measure bulk butter or other solid fat? Let's assume you want half a cup. Fill a measuring cup half full of cold water, then add the fat, bit by bit, until the water fills the cup completely. Violà! Half a cup of fat. (Don't forget to pour off the water.)

Is it safe to use the contents of a can that has bulged? If bulged or swollen, it is certainly suspect and should be discarded. However, cans that have stained labels, rust, or dents, so long as there is no leakage, are perfectly okay. Just not attractive.

Where do you hang your wall can opener? On the wall beside the sink, for the obvious reason that if any liquid is spilled, it will go into the sink.

Can food be left in the can once it has been opened? Yes. But it must be securely covered and refrigerated. As the National Canners Association points out, "Modern cans are lined with a thin layer of pure tin that can in no way affect the food."

What's your opinion of the cast iron enameled cooking ware? Having once cooked with it, I can't imagine any knowledgable cook (with a fat bank account—they're costly) using anything else. It's heavy, but that's its great advantage—the heat is evenly distributed, which means perfectly cooked food. They are made of cast iron with a heavy enamel finish, in brilliantly beautiful colors. The size range and shapes are all-encompassing, so there's a "pot" or pan with a cover (don't ever buy cooking ware without covers) for every possible need. Because of the enamel, they can be cleaned easily and perfectly—a signal improvement over the old, plain cast iron utensils our grandmothers had to cope with. One additional virtue, the casseroles are so attractive they can go straight to the dinner table.

How do you keep cast iron pans from rusting? Wash thoroughly, then dry quickly over a high heat. Rub with paper toweling.

Are all non-stick cooking wares alike? No. There is a marked difference in the finishes—some are much more durable than others. Since it is inclined to be rather costly, because of the special lining, you would be wise to shop around, compare, and ask pertinent questions, before making a purchase.

Is fat ever used in cooking with non-stick pans? You do not actually need fat to cook in non-stick cooking ware but, as any good cook will tell you, a little fat, and especially a little butter, adds to the flavor of whatever is being cooked. With or without fats, foods will not stick in non-stick pans.

How do you clean non-stick cooking ware? It's as easy, as they say, as pie. Just wash out with good, soapy water and a soft cloth. Or use one of the detergents made especially for this type of cooking ware. *Don't* use abrasives of any kind or soap pads.

Is it true non-stick pans are ruined if scratched? No. Obviously, scratches affect the appearance of the pans, but they in no way affect the performance. The first examples of this type of cooking ware, at that time mostly imported, had not been perfected and even small scratches could, and often did, counteract the effectiveness of the lining.

Do you consider cheesecloth an essential kitchen "tool"? Definitely. You use it in innumerable ways. To line sieves for straining foods; to tie up fish to be poached; in some cases, to cover fowl during roasting; to hold the *bouquet garni* in soups and stews, etc. It's available everywhere (in variety stores, department stores, supermarkets), very inexpensive, and should be standard equipment in every cooking household.

Can Pyrex custard cups be used in place of ramekins? Broadly speaking, they can. Pyrex custard cups are somewhat different in shape, although about the same size as ramekins, having a rounded bottom rather than the flat bottom and straight sides of traditional earthenware or porcelain ramekins. The latter are somewhat more elegant to bring to the table. Ramekin (sometimes spelled ramequin) also means the mixture baked in a ramekin: hence, ramekin soufflés.

What utensils should NOT go in the dishwasher? Very few. The extremely hot water is hard on antique or hand-painted china; rubber and wood will lose their new look quickly; heat-resistant hard plastics are safe, but soft ones get distorted; certain colored aluminums with special finishes are apt to fade; some aluminum may discolor, which doesn't hurt its working ability; pots and pans with attached wooden handles; and, importantly, fine knives or silverware with separate, attached handles.

Is it necessary to hand-rinse dishes before putting them in the dishwasher? In up-to-the-minute dishwashers, no, although common sense would indicate you scrape off any large food and bones.

How can you dry freshly washed berries or vegetables quickly and easily? Drain as well as possible. Then place on a tray—large enough so the berries or vegetables are not crowded—lined with paper towels. Shake the tray gently to encourage any water lurking around to drop off. Or, place paper towels on top and pat with a light hand. Leave on the tray until perfectly dry. Refrigerate only if you are not going to use them in a comparatively short time.

Should you wash a flour sifter? It can be washed, but because it is such an intricate contraption, it should be dried in a warm oven.

What are freeze-dried foods? Foods in which all but about 2% of the water has been removed. They are rehydrated in liquid. Mr. Kermit Bird, of the U.S. Department of Agriculture, illustrates it graphically in terms of the clothes line. "In the North, in winter, housewives hang their laundry outside to dry. If below-freezing temperatures exist, their sheets and shirts freeze and get stiff as boards. Later, as the wind blows through them, the ice crystals transform to water vapor. There has been no dripping or melting. After the laundry dries, they still look hard and frozen, but actually are now soft and porous."

This same process happens to freeze-dried foods. Once the ice has disappeared, they are sponge-like, porous, and look somewhat like the initial products, in shape and size, weigh much less, are so dry as to be brittle, and somewhat lighter in color. There are a limited number of freeze-dried products on the market: cereals packed with freeze-dried fruits, shrimp and crab (available only at this time to restaurants), a number of meat items, primarily for campers, and freeze-dried instant coffee. One of the great advantages to freeze-dried foods is that they do not need refrigeration and will keep as long as two years without spoilage.

What foods cannot be frozen? The list is very short: bananas, cream fillings and puddings, custards, gelatin dishes, hard-cooked eggs, cooked potatoes (in or out of a salad), raw vegetables, such as celery and radishes, soft cheeses.

What materials do you use for packaging and freezing foods? The following, but not necessarily in this order: foil, plastic bags, plastic wrap, moisture–vapor-proof wrappers, plastic tubs, freezer glass jars. Be sure to mark the package because the food, once frozen, rarely looks like the original model.

Do you approve of the garlic press? With reservations. Based on the fact that garlic when pushed through the little hand press is infinitely more pungent than when chopped or minced or crushed. Cooks should use the press with caution since one clove of garlic, pressed, with every bit of the volatile oil released, is the equivalent of three cloves of the same size minced or chopped.

Why do glass bottles sometimes smell musty? Undoubtedly, because they've been sealed and no air can circulate. It is always a good idea to sniff a bottle before using and if there is some mustiness, to rinse it out in boiling water, then dry before using.

Do you wear gloves when cooking? No. They are too cumbersome to work with efficiently. To protect your hands, we suggest you keep a good hand lotion right by the sink and try to remember to use it after every washing-up bout. At night, lather your hands with a heavy hand cream, working it in well, then put on paper-thin polyethylene gloves (available in drugstores) which will not only protect your bed linen but warm your hands and hold the cream tight to the skin until as much as possible is absorbed.

Should you store liquid honey in the refrigerator? No. It will granulate. Actually, it is best to store it in a dry place. If, however, the honey does granulate, place the jar in a pan of warm water until all crystals have disappeared and honey has reliquefied. What is true of honey is also true of preserves, marmalades, etc. They, too, become granular in the refrigerator, and can be restored by the same method.

Is it true that high humidity affects cooking? Yes. Very often recipes made with egg whites, such as meringues or frostings and, particularly, brown sugar. Pastry, especially a very rich one, can also act up in hot weather. Best to avoid these when the weather is against you.

Is there any way to build a backlog of ice cubes? Sure. Empty ice trays and place cubes in a polyethylene bag at once—before they have begun to melt and while they are still dry. Place in the freezer or freezing compartment of your refrigerator. This won't work, by the way, if you haven't a freezer that maintains zero temperature.

What knives do you consider essential in a kitchen? To work efficiently, the very minimum I think you can get along with are these: two single-blade paring knives, two chef's knives, 7-inch and 9-inch (also called butcher's knives or French knives), and a ham slicer. They should be carbon steel (stainless steel won't keep an edge) and with them you need a "steel" (the rod used to sharpen knives) to give them an edge each time they are used, remembering they should be sharpened professionally several times a year. In addition, you should have a vegetable peeler (also called a swivel-bladed paring knife) and a serrated bread knife. If the carving is done at the table, you also need a carving set. But here, too, I recommend carbon steel rather than stainless, though for fruit and vegetables stainless steel is practical.

How do you clean carbon steel knives?   Scotch-Brite scouring pads. Reusable, washable, rustproof, splinterproof. Just wet and scrub. It's a good idea to clean them as soon after using as possible, especially if you've been cutting anything acid which discolors them. Psychologically, it's good to clean them because you feel more efficient when you work with a bright, shining, sharp knife. Whatever, always wash and dry thoroughly as soon after using as possible to avoid rust.

What type of knife should you use when frosting cakes?   If it's a large cake, a fairly broad, medium length, flexible metal spatula—frosting the sides first, then the top. For small cakes, a palette knife such as artists use (available in any art store), because it's short, narrow, flexible, and just the right size.

What are dry measuring cups?   Metal cups in four graduated sizes: ½-cup, ⅓-cup, ¼ cup and 1-cup measure. They are used to measure dry ingredients such as flour, sugar, etc. To measure liquids, use a glass measuring cup with a rim above the 1-cup line. Place cup on a level surface and fill the cup to the point called for in the recipe.

What are measuring spoons?   They come in sets (¼ teaspoon, ½ teaspoon, 1 teaspoon, and 1 tablespoon) on a ring. To measure any dry ingredients, such as salt, flour, sugar, baking powder, in these small quantities, fill the spoon very full, then level off with the edge of a knife or metal spatula.

What is the accurate way to measure pans?   All pans should be measured at the top to get width and length or diameter.

Do you use a meat thermometer?   Yes, for meat only. A very special type of thermometer originally designed for food inspectors to use testing foods on docks, in markets, etc. Now used extensively by professional chefs, the best one seems to be a two-metal stem thermometer whose dial, only 1 inch in diameter, has a clear plastic window. Its 5-inch shaft is as slender as a knitting needle. The range is from zero to 220° F. and the thermometer is so sensitive and so accurate, you can determine the inner temperature of a roast instantly. Unlike standard meat thermometers, you do not plunge it into the meat at the beginning of the roasting period but, rather, test the temperature of the meat toward the end of the roasting period. This particular thermometer is expensive but worth it.

What can you do about the film that forms on opened bottles of olives?   Not much. It's perfectly harmless and doesn't affect the olives. It's just not very attractive. You can scrape it off or, if you have a half bottle or less, turn them into a clean, but smaller bottle, thus eliminating the air space which is the cause of the problem. Refrigerate, of course.

Should omelet pans be washed, or not?   Authorities differ about this. Rudolph Stanish, probably the best-known omelet chef in America, cleans his pans with soap pads. Narcissa Chamberlain, author of *The Omelette Cook Book*, says: "The pan should not be washed, but wiped out with paper after use to preserve the oily surface." Whichever school you follow, remember it is of the utmost importance to keep the surface of the pan smooth, so the cooked omelet will slide out easily. That is why it is a good idea to have a pan that is kept exclusively for omelets.

How can you eliminate onion odor from your hands?   Run your hands under cold water, then rub with salt. Rinse off. It's that easy.

In oven cooking, does it matter where you place the food?   Yes. Baked goods such as cakes, pastries, puddings, etc., with the exception of angel cakes and sponge cakes, should be placed in the center of the oven. Angel cakes, sponge cakes, roasts, and casseroles should go on the lower rack.

If you are using two racks, for example, and cooking a roast or a casserole and a pie, you should put the roast and/or casserole on the bottom rack, the pie on the top rack.

Don't ever crowd an oven, because free circulation of heat is very important. Allow a couple of inches at least between pans and between the pans and the walls of the oven. When you are using two racks, with pans on both, try to arrange them so one pan is not directly over another. Sometimes it takes some fancy juggling.

What can be done when oven racks stick? This is perhaps a more important question than appears at first glance, because a rack that won't slide easily on the "runner" can jar anything as delicate as a cake or a soufflé. Wipe the "runners" off to make sure they are clean, then dry, and coat lightly with a film of pure petroleum jelly—that old stand-by from your medicine chest—and racks will glide as if on skates.

What is meant by preheating the oven and why do you do it? It means to heat the oven or broiler, to the right temperature called for, before placing the food in the oven. Allow 15 to 20 minutes for the oven to reach the right temperature. If anything as delicate as a cake or a soufflé were put in the oven before it was heated up, chances are you would have a failure. In rare cases (an example is flank steak, or London broil, as it is designated on menus) food is started in a cold oven or broiler.

Is it true that some electric ranges clean themselves? Yes. Called self-cleaning, these high-quality ranges clean by baking at extreme heat, and all the housewife has to do is brush out the small amount of ash that accumulates.

What is the parchment paper used in cooking? A rather heavy parchment-like paper used to line pans for baking, also used by professional cake decorators to make a cone in which to hold the frosting. They prefer the paper to the commercial, cloth bags because they can make and discard them at will. The bags need washing, which is complicated if you are decorating with several different colors. Also called patapar, the paper is usually available in the housewares section of department stores.

Is there any really satisfactory pastry brush?   Pastry brushes are inclined to get stiff after continuous use and washing, making it somewhat difficult to brush pastry or dough with a light hand. Little
feather brushes are used by some cooks but they, too, will stiffen in
time. A good-cook friend had the ingenious idea of buying a good-
quality man's shaving brush which, she reports, works to perfec-
tion because it is very soft and remains both soft and pliable.

What is a pastry cloth?   One of the most useful "tools" in the cook's
batterie de cuisine but, unfortunately, not familiar to many cooks.
It is, in brief, nothing but a large piece of heavy canvas on which
to roll out pastry, cookies, etc. It is, or should be, accompanied by
a knitted sleeve that slips over the rolling pin. With a pastry cloth
and sleeve, lightly floured, you can roll pastry or cookies very thin
without ever having the problem of the dough's sticking. Look for
them in the housewares section of department stores.

How many will 1 pound of pasta serve?   If it's a first course, four;
if it accompanies meat, six; if it's the entire meal, about three.

Why does my peppermill stick so hard I can't turn it?   The oil from
the peppercorns rusts the thread on the screw. Unscrew the mill with
a pair of pliers, then clean the thread thoroughly with a piece of
steel wool—not soap pads. Rub lightly with a little petroleum jelly.
That should do the trick.

Is it true that refrigerating plastic wrap makes it unroll more easily?
Yes. When it's good and cold, it won't stick to you, the box, or itself.
An absolutely crazy idea that works.

Is there any trick to cleaning up a raw egg spilled on the floor?   Cover
all of it well with salt and allow to stand for 15 to 20 minutes, then
sweep it up with a broom. Easy?

What is the coldest part of the refrigerator?   This is an interesting
question because recipes and cook books sometimes specify storing
fruits or foods in the coldest part. If it's a large refrigerator with a
separate freezer (this means with its own outside door), there is no
"coldest part." The cold is evenly distributed throughout the storing
section, and it doesn't make one whit of difference where you place

the foods. However, in a refrigerator with an inside freezer section for ice trays and foods—which is not actually a freezer (a freezer must maintain zero temperature)—the coldest part is the shelf just below this compartment.

Should cooked foods be frozen while still hot, or cooled first?   Obviously, it's easier to package cooled foods than hot. Take chicken, for example. The practical way is to remove all the meat from the bones so it can be wrapped in the smallest package and occupy a minimum of space. This is a lot easier to do when it's cool or cold. However, it's a good idea to get it into the freezer as quickly as possible.

Can hot foods be refrigerated while still hot?   Today, they can. But in the old days of iceboxes and poorly insulated refrigerators, it was not advisable because hot foods would melt the ice or—and equally as unfortunate—raise the temperature of the storing section. Modern refrigerators are so well insulated and temperatures so perfectly controlled, these hazards no longer exist. However, unless immediate refrigeration is important, we would recommend a brief cooling-off period, because hot foods introduced into the cool depths of a modern refrigerator may cause some condensation on walls and containers— a minor inconvenience.

If cold meats are served with a hot vegetable, should the plate be hot or cold?   It depends. If the vegetable is in a sauce that would tend to cool quickly, our impulse would be to serve the meal on a warm plate. This is one of those questions best decided by the cook or hostess in terms of the food that is being served.

What's a quick, easy way to clean a roasting pan?   With the modern, hard-working liquid soaps, it doesn't seem to us much of a chore. Add some of the liquid, then hot water, and allow it to soak a good long time. Or, do as the old-time cooks did; put the pan, with the soap and water, over a moderate heat, and boil until all the incrustations come loose.

What is a salt cellar?   A dish, usually crystal, porcelain, or silver, in varying sizes, from which salt is served at the table. Salt cellars are common in England and European countries, but the salt shaker is

more generally used in this country. The accepted way of serving
salt from a cellar is to spoon a small amount on the edge of your
plate, then dip the food into the salt as you eat it. In the old days,
when salt was a rare and valuable commodity (it was sometimes
used as a means of exchange), salt cellars were large, extravagantly
elaborate gold or silver vessels placed at a specific point on the
table. Honored guests sat "above the salt" and lesser lights, below.
Once it was considered unlucky to spill salt and, to this day, people
aware of this omen will throw a little of the spilled salt over their
right shoulder to forestall bad luck.

Can you take the salt out of over-salted foods?   No. Old cook books
once suggested adding sugar to counteract the salt. It simply doesn't
work. Salting should be done by tasting. If a recipe calls for ingredients with a high salt content (anchovies, tuna, etc.), then it's
up to the cook to taste as she cooks.

How do you scald jars for jellies, jams, etc.?   As in the old days, the
jars are put in a big kettle with water and brought to a boil. You
cannot use a dishwasher because the water is not hot enough to
sterilize.

Is there an easy way to tidy up a serving dish once the food is on it?
With cotton swabs, available in your drugstore. Just dampen the
little cotton tips and "swab away" any spills, then discard. So much
simpler than a bulky, damp cloth. Also, they are especially useful
when frosting a cake and some of the frosting drips onto the cake
stand.

Should wooden salad bowls be washed, or not?   In our opinion they
should, because it seems inevitable that the oil soaked into the wood
will eventually turn rancid. By washing, this is not to suggest you
soak the bowls as you would dishes, but rather that you wash them
thoroughly with water and a mild soap, rinse, and dry well. You
may lose a bit of color in the wood (which is what the non-washers
say), but your bowls will be clean—a school we subscribe to. If you
don't agree with this principle, wipe the bowls out extremely well
with paper towels and keep them covered when not in use. Today,
many people are making their salads in crystal, porcelain, or silver
bowls.

What spatulas do you recommend? Three: the wooden spatula for stirring hot foods because it won't transmit heat and is easy on your hands; the rubber spatula with a wooden handle (plastic melts) for folding and cleaning the bowl of all ingredients; and the small, very narrow rubber spatula for extricating food from difficult places. Keep at least two of each on hand and replace the rubber ones as soon as the rubber gets chipped and discolored. They are so inexpensive you can always afford to work with fresh-looking ones.

Why are wooden spoons and spatulas so frequently recommended in recipes? Because the wooden handle is easier on the cook's hands; wood will not transmit heat, which metal will; metal, particularly aluminum, should never be used in making dishes that call for wine or eggs because it will discolor the food. French cooks use wooden spoons almost exclusively.

What carpenter's tools do you use in the kitchen? A pair of pliers, to loosen recalcitrant bottle tops, "stuck" peppermills, etc.; a screwdriver, to pry open boxes, to tighten a loose screw on an appliance, to lend to the repair man who turns up without one; a ruler, to measure pans, to use as a guide in cutting pastry or any dough that requires fairly precise measurements; a ball of soft, white string, to truss fowl, to tie asparagus in bundles before cooking, etc.; a pair of scissors for the obvious uses—cutting string, paper, and so on; a hammer to crack shells (lobster, nuts, etc.).

What's a good way to keep small kitchen tools right at hand? A crock with a wide, open mouth and a heavy base (so it won't tip over). Stick all your wooden spoons, spatulas, whips, your baster, kitchen forks, etc., into it and you won't have to fish in drawers when you need them. If possible, put up a magnetic knife holder in the same area and use it for your small knives, the vegetable peeler, screwdriver, etc.

How do you store fruits and vegetables when your hydrators are full? One of the blessings of the 20th century is polyethylene bags in which you can store almost any food. Carrots, celery, citrus fruits (you name it) can be put into bags, all air squeezed out, tied securely, then refrigerated. But don't limit their use to just fruits and vegetables, protect anything edible against drying out or picking up foreign flavors. Now available in three sizes—small, medium, and large—there's a size for every conceivable use.

Are aluminum cooking utensils poisonous to food? Don't be ridiculous. Heaven only knows how or where this canard got started, but it ought to be stopped. Aluminum is the third most plentiful element in the earth—the very same earth in which the foods we eat grow. Obviously, it is present in food, just as are all the other minerals that make up the nature of food.

Are copper utensils good for cooking? Excellent, but they should be lined with tin. Unlined copper will give the food an off-flavor. With constant use, the tin lining will eventually wear out. In this case, it should be retinned.

How do you warm plates these days without the dear old-fashioned warming oven? It can be done in the newest type electric dishwashers; in modern stoves that can be set at 140° F., or warming temperature; on hot trays; and electric "cosies" for plates.

How do you work on wax paper without its sliding around? Easy. Just dampen the work surface and the paper sticks like glue.

How can you remove wine stains from table linen? As soon as possible, soak the stains in hot milk that has been brought to the boiling point until they disappear sufficiently to be washed out with soap and water. If this can't be managed soon after the accident, soak the linen in cold water until you can get around to it. If the stain is unusually stubborn, sprinkle with salt and rub with half of a lemon. This should do the trick. Equally effective on lipstick stains.

Cooking Techniques

What is acidulated water? Cold water to which vinegar, lemon juice, or lime juice has been added in these proportions: 1 tablespoon of the juice to 1 quart of water. Acidulated water is used to prevent fruits and vegetables from discoloring.

What does allumette mean? It's French for match and is used in describing foods cut into thin, match-like strips. Strips of puffed pastry with a savory garnish and baked, or pastry finished with an icing are called *allumettes*. We're all familiar with potatoes, cut in thin strips which, in this country, we call shoestring.

What is the difference between an antipasto and an hors d'oeuvre? Essentially, they are the same thing—an appetizer, or first course. The Italian antipasto means literally "before the pasta," and the French hors d'oeuvre, "outside the work." The Scandinavian smorgasbord, meaning "bread and butter table," is also classed as an appetizer, although it is usually more formidable in scope than an antipasto or hors d'oeuvre and is often served as the main course.

What is aspic? The word is derived from the Greek, *aspis*, meaning shield. Originally aspic referred to a decorated dish coated with or molded in jelly. Today, it is used interchangeably with jelly (*gelée* in French) and it is called aspic or jelly, whether it is in liquid or jelly form. The finished dish is often called aspic: for example, chicken aspic; but the same dish can be called jellied chicken.

What is a bain-marie?   The translation is bath-marie, but in the food kitchen and laboratory it is known as a "water bath." In a sense, it is the equivalent of our double boiler, except that we cook foods over boiling water and with the bain-marie the pan is placed in another pan filled with water kept near the boiling point. Cooking over boiling water is considerably slower, but safer for those of us who are not professional chefs. The bain-marie is also used to keep foods warm much as we use the double boiler for the same purpose.

Where does the word barbecue come from?   The Oxford Dictionary, which dates it 1697, says it stems from the Spanish, *barbacoa,* meaning a rude framework, used in America for smoking or drying meat over a fire. By 1809, it had come to mean "open-air entertainment at which animals were roasted whole." Today, it generally means meat, fish, or fowl, cooked over an open fire (that is, direct heat), basted with a highly seasoned sauce, a barbecue sauce.

Is barding the same thing as larding?   No, but both serve the same purpose; to provide fat for lean meat so it won't dry out during cooking. To bard means to wrap meat with a fat such as fat salt pork, suet, or bacon. To lard means to insert thin strips of fat salt pork or bacon into the flesh of meat. This is done with a special larding needle.

Why does batter drop off food when cooked?   There are two reasons: one, the food was too moist when coated, which permits steam to form during cooking, separating the batter from the food; two, the temperature of the fat was too low.

Are bavarois and bavaroise the same thing?   No. Bavarois, or Bavarian cream, as we know it, is a combination of soft custard, gelatin, and whipped cream with various flavorings. Invented, we are told, in Bavaria in the 17th century. Bavaroise is a drink composed of strong tea, egg yolk, sugar syrup, boiled milk, and kirsch, rum, maraschino, or other flavorings.

Are beat and whip the same thing?   Yes, and both mean to mix foods or liquids or a combination with a whip or whisk (*fouet*), spoon, fork, spatula, rotary or electric beater, or an electric mixer. The extent to which you whip or beat, with what implement, and how vigorously, depends on the instructions given in the recipe.

What does bind mean?   To hold a mixture of foods together with egg, cream, mayonnaise, or other sauces.

Are blanch and parboil comparable?   In some respects. You blanch foods by plunging them into boiling water briefly, then draining, or you boil them for a few minutes (this is what we in the U.S. call parboiling). Nuts (such as almonds), fruits and vegetables (such as tomatoes and onions) are blanched to make it easy to remove the skins. Certain foods, like cabbage and onions, are blanched or parboiled to remove too strong a taste, and bacon to get rid of the salt and smokiness. Sometimes foods need to be partially cooked before proceeding with the recipe, and this also is the equivalent of blanching or parboiling.

How do you blaze foods?   You pour warm (they should be preheated) spirits (such as brandy or Bourbon) over a given dish and ignite with a match. It's a bright, flashy touch to do in front of guests. The term flame is sometimes used for this procedure, or *flambé*, the French word for blaze.

What is the difference between boil and a rolling boil?   Boil means, of course, when liquid has reached 212° F. on the thermometer at sea level. At this point bubbles constantly rise to the surface and break. However, as you will see from studying recipes, many specify slow, medium and fast "boils." The slowest of all is even below simmer, when there is only the barest movement on the surface of the liquid (the French call this *fremir*, "to shiver"). "Rolling" boil means to allow the mixture to cook at the fastest boil possible to speed up evaporation.

What does bone mean in terms of cookery?   It simply means to remove all the bones from a piece of meat or fish. It is comparable to, but not exactly the same as, fillet.

What does bonne femme mean?   Literally, "good woman," but in cookery it means food prepared "country style." In other words, simply, or unadorned. *À la bonne femme* and *à la paysanne* (country) are used interchangeably for innumerable dishes.

What is the meaning of Bordelaise?   Any dishes prepared with Bordeaux wines are termed *à la Bordelaise*, from Bordeaux, the French city famous as a wine center. Sauce Bordelaise, served with broiled meats, is a concentrate of chopped shallots, thyme, bay leaf, white pepper, red Bordeaux wine, mixed with a demi-glaze, etc. Since Bordeaux is also one of the important gastronomic centers in France, it does not necessarily follow that all dishes designated as Bordelaise call for wine, although it usually indicates that sautéed shallots were used in the composition of the dish.

Are braising and stewing identical?   No. Braising means to brown meat or vegetables in fat, adding a small amount of liquid, finishing the cooking by covering the pot tightly over low heat. Although normally done on top of the stove, braising can also be done in the oven. Stewing means to cook meat slowly in a fair amount of liquid for a long time until tender, which mellows and blends the flavors. Both methods are used to tenderize tougher cuts of meat.

What does "to bread" mean?   To coat a food (meat, fish, croquettes) in bread crumbs.

What is the meaning of brochette?   Literally, a skewer. *Shish* and *shash*, from the Turkish, also mean skewer. Meat, fish, fowl, vegetables, or fruits, or combinations, are threaded on skewers, then broiled. *En brochette* means on a skewer. Skewers can be long metal, wooden, or bamboo pins with or without ornate handles. Skewer also means to secure meat or fowl with a short metal pin before cooking. An *attelet* (from *hattelet* or *hatelet*, a small skewer), generally silver, with a very ornamental top, is used only to decorate roasts and other foods in the grand manner—never for the actual cooking process.

Are broil and grill identical?   Yes. Americans say "broil," the English, "grill." It means, of course, to cook under or over direct heat. Broiling can be done on a broiler, in the oven, under the heating unit; over a wood, coal, or charcoal fire; or in a portable electric or gas broiler. The word grill also refers to the rack on which foods are broiled.

Are brush and baste similar?   In some respects. Brush means to coat food with a liquid or fat, by dribbling it over with a spoon or by brushing with a pastry brush. This can be done before cooking or during the cooking process. Baste means to spoon or brush a liquid or melted fat over food while it cooks. Basting is one of the more important cooking techniques because it helps to keep food moist, to flavor it, and to glaze it.

What does "to candy" mean?   To cook citrus fruit in a heavy, simple syrup, roll in granulated sugar, and dry. It also means to glaze vegetables (particularly carrots and sweet potatoes) with a syrup.

How do you caramelize sugar?   Cook granulated sugar (sometimes a little water is added) over moderate heat, while stirring constantly, until it turns into a golden syrup. Take care, if you use superfine sugar, because it caramelizes in very little time.

What does à la carte mean?   *Carte* is the French for card and, in restaurant parlance, à la carte means from the bill of fare or menu on which each item is priced individually.

What is meant by clarification?   It means to remove any bits of food and all cloudiness from stock, broth, or bouillon so the soup is beautifully clear and sparkling. Butter is also clarified to eliminate the milk solids.

To clarify stock: First it must be free of all fat. Then beat egg whites (allow 2 whites to 4 or 5 cups of stock) into the cold stock in a heavy enameled saucepan. Place over a moderate heat and bring up to a boil slowly, beating constantly, with a wire whip. Reduce heat to simmer and stop whipping. At this point the whites will have risen to the surface. Allow the mixture to stay on very low heat barely moving, for 15 minutes. Line a colander or sieve with several layers of damp cheesecloth, place it over a bowl deep enough so the bottom of the colander will remain above the surface of the liquid. Pour the stock into the colander carefully so as not to disturb the egg whites more than is necessary and allow it to drain, undisturbed.

NOTE: In clarifying, you lose a good deal of flavor, so the original stock should be very well seasoned.

What does coat mean?   To cover food completely with seasoned flour, grated cheese, or crumbs (bread or cracker). Food is also "coated" with aspic or a sauce. Coating covers a multitude of sins in cookery.

What is a cocotte?   The name applied to cooking utensils, either round or oval, in which certain foods are cooked. Cocottes are made of earthenware, fireproof porcelain, tinned copper, etc. Foods cooked in one of these dishes, in which they are generally served, are described as *en cocotte:* for example, eggs en cocotte.

Are cool and chill the same thing?   No. Cool simply means to set a hot dish aside and allow it to stand at room temperature until it is no longer warm to the touch. Chill means to refrigerate until cold.

Is a cracker the same thing as a biscuit?   What we, in the U.S., call crackers, the English call biscuits—very thin wafers (commercial or homemade), plain or sweet. However, like us, the English call a dough made of flour, fat, liquid, and baking powder, baked in the oven, biscuits, too (our baking powder biscuits, for example). Cookies, as we know them, are sweet biscuits in England. Confused?

What does "to cream" mean in cooking?   To work fat and sugar together until light and fluffy. Use a wooden spoon, electric beater, or your hands.

NOTE: An electric blender does not work here.

What is the difference between cube and dice?   Cube means to cut food into precise cubes. Dice means to cut into very small cubes.

What do recipes mean by "cut in"?   To cut in, a term used in pastry making, means to work the fat into the flour with two knives or, better, a pastry blender.

Do dauphine and dauphinois mean the same in cooking?   No. Dauphine generally means any dish garnished with *pommes dauphine* (mashed potatoes and cream puff paste, shaped into croquettes, breaded and fried). *Dauphinois* means sliced raw potatoes with hot milk, seasoned with salt, pepper, garlic, and sprinkled with grated Gruyère cheese. Cooked and browned in the oven. Thus, *gratin dauphinois.*

What does al dente mean? Literally translated, "to the tooth." It is an Italian term used to describe food, especially pasta, that is cooked still firm to the bite. It is also frequently used in reference to vegetables.

What is meant by devil in cooking? To prepare food with sharp seasonings: deviled eggs, for example.

What does dredge mean? To cover food completely with a dry ingredient such as flour, cornmeal, or crumbs. Meat, chicken, and fish can be dredged easily by placing them in a bag of seasoned (allow about ½ teaspoon of salt and a few twists of the peppermill to ½ cup of all-purpose flour) flour and shaken until completely coated.

What does dress mean? To mix a food with some sauce or flavoring before serving. Salads are "dressed" with oil and vinegar, for example; vegetables, with melted butter.

What are drippings? The juices in the pan from roasted meats, fish, or fowl.

What does dust mean? To sprinkle food lightly with some dry ingredient. Cakes and cookies are sometimes dusted with sugar, for example; meat, with flour. Lightly is the key word here, in contrast to dredging, which means to coat heavily.

Is an entrée the main dish or the beginning of a meal? Entrée means entrance. In both American and English dictionaries, the meaning in cookery is given as, "a dish served between the chief courses or before the roast. Hence, a meat dish not classed as a roast, or a meat substitute, especially one served as the chief course." Time, however, has changed the "rules" and we now generally refer to the main course as the entrée.

Are fillet and filet the same thing? Yes. Fillet, with two "l's," is English and *filet*, with one, is French. In its simplest sense, it means a cut of meat or fish without bones. Fillet is also used as a verb: "to fillet" means to bone a piece of meat or fish. Note the difference between a chauteaubriand, tournedo, and a filet mignon.

What is financière in cooking?   From financier or banker's style. Hence, any elaborate garnish such as chicken mousseline dumplings, cockscombs and kidneys, sliced truffles, fluted mushrooms, etc. Also a sauce made with a demi-glaze flavored with truffle extract.

What does à la Florentine mean in cookery?   It means hot, cooked foods (usually fish or eggs) on a bed of seasoned spinach coated with Mornay sauce, sprinkled with cheese, gilded under the broiler.

What is forcemeat?   This is one of the oldest terms in cookery and is frequently used in foreign cook books. Forcemeat is what we, in this country, call stuffing—a mixture of minced or chopped seasoned ingredients used to stuff meat, fish, poultry, game, eggs, and the like.

What is a fouet?   The French name for a balloon-shaped whisk or whip which comes in many sizes up to the big balloon, so beloved by French chefs, for whipping egg whites. Once you've learned to work with a fouet, you'd almost as soon give up your right hand as do without it. Its uses are endless in cookery from beating up one egg to mixing a sauce. To work efficiently, you should have several sizes, though the big ones take a powerful right arm.

What is a fricassee?   The French word for "medley," but generally understood as meaning a stew. Chicken, lamb, or veal are cooked in a seasoned broth and served with a Velouté sauce.

Is a galantine the same thing as a ballottine?   Somewhat. Both are boned chicken, meat, game, or fish that are stuffed, rolled, and cooked in a rich bouillon. Originally, a galantine was made only with chicken and a ballottine only with meat. A galantine is always served cold glazed with aspic, whereas a ballottine can be served cold in aspic, or hot.

What does garnish mean?   It means to decorate and it also means the decorations. A bouquet of parsley on a platter is called a garnish. At the same time, cold fish or meat in aspic is garnished with herbs, pimientos, truffles, etc.

Is gelatin (without an "e") the same thing as gelatine (with an "e")? According to *The Oxford Dictionary,* the popular spelling is gelatine; the scientific, gelatin. But in cookery, in this country, gelatin means unflavored gelatin, and gelatine means flavored gelatine.

How do you dissolve unflavored gelatin properly? Unflavored gelatin must be softened first, then dissolved before it can be used. Sprinkle, do not dump, the granules over the liquid so the little grains will absorb the liquid, swell, and become soft enough to dissolve quickly and easily. The accepted methods are:

Over direct low heat. Sprinkle the gelatin over a cold liquid (water, wine, broth, or milk—no less than ½ cup) to soften the granules. Stir constantly, over low heat, until dissolved. If milk is used, it will take twice as long as with clear liquid.

With sugar. Since sugar "dry dilutes" the gelatin, mix the two thoroughly, then add the hot liquid specified in the recipe and stir until dissolved. Or combine the sugar and gelatin with the other ingredients and heat, stirring until dissolved.

By adding a hot liquid. Sprinkle the granules over cold liquid to soften. Add the hot liquid and stir until dissolved.

Over boiling water. Stir the gelatin-liquid combination constantly over boiling water until dissolved. A good, safe method that is especially useful when the stove does not have low-controlled surface heat.

Do glace and glacé have the same meaning? Glace means ice, and glacé, from *glacer,* to freeze as well as "to cover," means frozen or covered with icing or frosting or glaze. The French, with their customary logic, call ice cream, *glace.* Glacé or glaze in cookery actually means to give a glossy finish to food.

What is a glaze and how is it done? It's a glossy finish given to various foods and is done in various ways. Fish or vegetables, covered with a sauce or grated cheese, or both, are glazed under the broiler; onions and carrots, steamed in butter, are glazed the last minute with a little sugar; cold fish or meat covered with aspic are glazed; smoked ham coated with apricot purée or brown sugar, etc., is glazed. The handsomest glaze for ham we know is the apricot which is used by many professional chefs.

To glaze ham with apricot. A half hour before the ham has finished baking, take it out of the oven, cut off the rind, score the fat, diamond fashion, and place a whole clove in each diamond. Meanwhile, heat a jar of commercial apricot jam, push the warm jam through a fine sieve to purée, then spoon the apricot purée over the entire surface of the ham. Return to a 350° F. oven for half an hour or until glaze has set.

What is grenadine? One of the oldest, if not the oldest, of all flavoring syrups. Once made exclusively from pomegranates, today it is a combination of fruits and each maker has his own formula. It is available, both domestic or imported, with or without the addition of alcohol, and is used as an ingredient in cooking or as a sauce over ice cream, fresh or cooked fruits, unfrosted cakes, cupcakes, etc.

Are grate and grind synonymous? No. Grate means to pulverize food by rubbing it on, or putting it through, a grater. You grate the rind of citrus fruits, you grate nuts and cheese, etc. Grind means to put foods through a meat grinder, cutting it into particles—the size depending on the size of the blade used. Many foods can be grated or ground in the electric blender, but the finished texture will be different from either a grater or regulation meat grinder. You alone can determine which texture is best for the dish you are making, unless the receipe specifies.

What does gratin mean in cookery? The word, from the French, *gratter*, to scrape or grate, is the same in both French and English. The term generally means a dish sprinkled with bread crumbs or grated cheese, the surface then browned in the broiler or in a very hot oven. For example, onion soup. There are innumerable gratins including: *gratin de poisson; gratin languedocien* (eggplants and tomatoes); *gratin savoyard* (potatoes, cheese and bouillon); and its first cousin, *le gratin dauphinois* (milk takes the place of the bouillon). Gratins can be made with either raw or cooked foods, with or without sauces, and when a food is prepared in this manner, it is said to be served *au gratin* or *gratined.* Thus, *macaroni au gratin, sole au gratin.* A number of oval dishes are known as gratin dishes and in Provence the famous one is called a *tian.*

What is meant by grease? To coat with fat or oil, depending on the recipe.

Are julienne and shred identical? No. Julienne, from the French, means to cut foods into long, thin strips. String beans and chicken breasts are julienned. Shred, on the other hand, means to cut into thin slivers. Cabbage is shredded for cole slaw.

What does au jus mean? Jus means juice or gravy, and the term *au jus* means natural juices. In other words, the pan juices without any thickening. Meat *au jus* is meat served plain with its own juices.

What is a leavening agent? To answer you authoritatively, we quote from *The Handbook of Food Preparation*, published by the American Home Economics Association, "A leavening agent is a gas incorporated or formed in a batter or dough to make it rise, increase in volume or bulk, and become light and porous during preparation and subsequent heating." In the simplest terms, the leavening agents are: whole eggs; egg whites; egg yolks; baking powders; baking soda (used in combination with sour milk or cream and molasses); yeast (used in breads).

How do you translate maître d'hôtel? Literally, it means butler or head cook. Nowadays, it means the man in charge of the dining room in a restaurant. Gastronomically, it means a sauce prepared by creaming butter with chopped parsley, seasoned with salt, pepper, and lemon juice or vinegar. The sauce is served with broiled meat, broiled or fried fish, and other dishes.

Are marinade and marinate related? Yes. A marinade is a seasoned liquid in which meats or other foods are soaked for some time to impart flavor and, in some instances, to tenderize. Marinate means to soak in a seasoned liquid.

Are marinate and macerate the same thing? In this sense: they both mean to place foods in a special liquid to absorb flavor. However, marinate is generally used for meats and macerate, for fruits. Beef, for example, is marinated in red wine; fruits, in sugar and spirits.

What is marrow?   The soft, fatty substance contained in the leg bones of beef, considered a great delicacy. Poached, it is used as a garnish in soups, sauces, and on canapés.

Are marzipan and almond paste the same thing?   Yes. In France, it is known as *massepain,* also the name for little fancy biscuits (such as macaroons and some *petits fours*). It is more familiarly known as almond paste in this country, but in England as both almond paste and marzipan. Whatever, it is composed of ground, blanched almonds, confectioners' sugar, and egg whites. The English use it primarily to cover fruit cakes which are then "finished" with a decorative frosting. Both here and in France, it is used as an ingredient in pastries and to make candies. Commercial almond paste, which can be found in most good food shops, is apt to be finer in texture than homemade, but the two types can be used interchangeably in recipes calling for almond paste.

What is meant by mask?   In food terminology, it means to coat or cover food completely with a sauce or aspic. The eggs in eggs benedictine are masked with Hollandaise.

What does à la Milanaise mean in cookery?   To begin with, it means a garnish of meat (ham, tongue), mushrooms, and truffles, in a tomato sauce served over macaroni with a sprinkling of grated Parmesan cheese; cutlets dipped in egg, bread crumbs, seasoned with Parmesan cheese, and fried in butter; eggs à la Milanaise are fried in oil, arranged on a bed of macaroni, and surrounded with a ribbon of tomato sauce; asparagus, cauliflower, broccoli, and Brussels sprouts, sprinkled with grated Parmesan, brown butter, and finished with a fried egg are all prepared à la Milanaise.
As is obvious, Parmesan cheese is the common denominator.

What does à la mode mean in cookery?   The translation is, of course, "in the mode or fashion." To Americans it means fruit pie (usually apple), garnished with a scoop of ice cream (an American innovation, by the way, said to have originated in a New York State hotel). But there is a French recipe called boeuf à la mode which is a piece of beef rump that has been marinated for hours or days in brandy and wine, with seasonings, then braised with calves' feet. It can be served hot, or cold in a *terrine* with its own aspic.

Is a mousse a dessert or entrée?   It can be a sweet cold dessert (*entremet*) or hot or cold entrée. It can also be a *mousse glacée,* in other words, frozen. Dessert mousses are made in many ways, with and without egg yolks, with and without egg whites, with and without heavy cream, with flavorings such as chocolate or coffee, puréed fruits, or fruit juices. They are chilled and served in or out of the mold. Savory or entrée mousses are made of puréed fish, chicken livers, ham, chicken, turkey, duck, or game and are served hot, in the baking mold, or cold, out of it. Often the molds for cold entrée mousses are lined or *chemisé* with aspic, which can be a real spectacular when turned out.

Cold soufflés (*soufflés glaces*) are comparable to mousses in that they are made of eggs, sugar, flavoring, gelatin, etc., chilled until set, and always served from the mold. In general, they are not quite as velvety and creamy as mousses.

What is a navarin in French cuisine?   A *ragoût* or stew, specifically made with shoulder of lamb (mutton) and vegetables that include turnips, onions, carrots, and potatoes, garnished with minced parsley.

What are quenelles?   Dumplings made of forcemeats such as fish, crustaceans, veal, and chicken in various large and small shapes, poached, and served with a compatible sauce. Extremely delicate and, if made well, delicious.

Are pan-broil and pan-fry the same thing?   Yes. Both mean to cook food in a skillet with little or no fat added. Sometimes the pan is rubbed lightly with fat or oil, but note, the food is not cooked with melted fat.

Does it take as long to pan-broil as to broil in the oven?   It takes twice as long in the broiler as on the top of the stove. Pan-broiling is recommended for thin cuts of meat.

What does papillote mean? Papillote means frilled paper. Hence, the little frills on the ends of lamb chops, the tips of bone in a crown roast. But it also means meat baked in oiled paper: Veal cutlets en papillote, for example. Not be confused with *paupiette,* which means thin slices of meat, stuffed, rolled and wrapped in bacon, then braised or grilled. Filets of sole, en paupiette, are baked in the oven.

If you pare, do you peel? Yes, but curiously, and traditionally, you pare fruit but you peel both fruit and vegetables. They both mean, really, to remove the outer skin by means of a small, sharp knife or vegetable peeler or, as with oranges and tangerines, using your fingers.

Are pâtés and terrines the same thing? Pâté means pie and terrine, pie dish. Pâtés, when enclosed and baked in a pastry, become *pâtés en croûtes.* Terrines are simply meat pies without a crust and, except for certain details, all pâtés can be made into terrines. Common usage has made the terms synonymous, and they are used interchangeably. Pâtés or terrines are always served cold, while pâtés en croûtes can be served hot or cold.

What is the difference between pâté and pâte? Pâté is also the French word for a mixture of ground pork, pork fat, veal, liver, cognac or wine, spices, cubed meats such as ham or game and, sometimes, truffles baked in a terrine and served as a first course or as an informal meal. Pâte means dough, batter, or paste. Generally it is used to designate pastry, cooked or uncooked.

What does Périgueux mean in French cuisine? Specifically, garnished or made with truffles. Although the name Périgord (once the district of which Perigueux is the capital) is synonymous throughout France for fine food, the designation applies only to foods in which truffles play a dominating role. Thus, du Périgord or à la Périgourdine. Sauce Périgueux or à la Périgueux, brown madeira sauce with truffles, familiar to all of us, takes its name from the capital.

What does plank mean in cooking? To serve food, usually meat or fish, on a heavy wooden plank which is then garnished with bouquets of hot vegetables: planked steak, for example.

How do you poach food? Poach means to cook food in simmering liquid. Chicken breasts are sometimes poached in butter, which simply means gently. Food people will say "poached chicken," meaning chicken cooked slowly in simmering broth.

Is pralin (without an "e") the same as praline (with an "e")? No. Pralin is a "powder" made of caramelized sugar, flavored with vanilla, mixed with toasted almonds, cooled and pounded in a mortar until as fine as possible. Filberts, although not traditional, can be used in place of the almonds. Pralin is used in many French pastries. Praline (you probably know the famous pralines of New Orleans) is a French confection—essentially, almonds coated with colored, perfumed sugar. New Orleans pralines, undoubtedly a happy corruption of the original, are made in various ways, always loaded with pecans, and look like big, round, candy cookies.

RECIPE FOR PRALIN POWDER

Stir 1½ cups sugar with ½ cup water over medium heat with a wooden spatula until sugar is dissolved. Add at once, 2 cups blanched almonds or filberts (skins rubbed off) and cook until the syrup is golden. Take off the heat, pour onto a lightly oiled plate. When cold, break into pieces and pulverize in the electric blender.

This delicious pralin keeps well-stored in a screw-top jar and is lovely in desserts, sauces, over ice cream, or as a flavoring in frostings and cake fillings.

What is meant by purée and how is it done? Purée, from the French, means to mash solid foods to a smooth consistency (mashed potatoes, for example) by forcing them through a sieve or a food mill. Puréeing can also be done in the electric blender with, in some instances, the help of a bit of liquid.

Can a recipe be doubled? Certain recipes can be doubled or even tripled successfully but, in general, we would not recommend it unless you are an extremely experienced cook and thoroughly familiar with the recipes you are working with. Recipes calling for precise measurements—cakes come quickly to mind—can rarely be doubled. On the other hand, casseroles usually can if your baking dish will accommodate all the ingredients. It seems to us safer to make a recipe up twice rather than take a chance. However, if you try doubling, remember flavorings and seasonings should be added to taste—not in the quantities called for in the original recipes.

What does à la reine mean in cookery?   It very particularly means something elegant and delicate. *La bouchée à la reine* is a very small pastry shell; *le poulet reine,* a very small chicken. The essentials to a dish *à la reine* are chicken, truffles, and a rich cream sauce. The most famous dish is *potage à la reine*—soup made of puréed chicken breasts, combined with egg yolks, heavy cream, and seasonings.

Are reduce and "boil down" identical?   Yes. Both mean to reduce the quantity of liquid and concentrate the flavors.

What does render mean?   It means to cook solid fat slowly in a skillet or in the oven until the fat melts. The term "try out" is sometimes used for this process.

Is roasting the same as baking?   Yes and no. The original meaning of roasting was to cook meats on a spit in front of an open fire and the term is still applied, specifically to meat, cooked, uncovered, in the oven. Other food cooked in the oven is baked, such as cakes, cookies, bread, etc. Oddly, we always say "baked ham," although the method of cooking is roasting.

What is pot-roasting?   A method of cooking meat, usually beef, on top of the stove. The meat, like roasted meats, is cooked without the addition of any liquid except that which comes from the meat itself and the vegetables that accompany it. It differs from braising in that braised meats are combined with a liquid (wine and/or stock).

Is sauté the same as fry?   Technically, no. Sauté, from the French, *sauter,* means to cook or brown food in a very small amount of very hot fat. Fry has come to mean to cook in hot fat or oil deep enough to cover; in other words, deep-fat frying. Sautéeing is one of the most important primary cooking techniques and is often badly done because: (1) the fat is not hot enough before the food goes into the pan; (2) too much fat is used; (3) the food to be cooked is damp, which prevents it from browning and searing properly; (4) the pan is too crowded. Without space between pieces, the food will steam, rather than brown, and its juices will escape.

What is an after-dinner savory? A small portion of a hot, highly seasoned dish customarily served in England after the sweet course. Savories resemble cocktail fare, such as we know it in this country, except they are more substantial. Sardines on toast, toasted cheese, angels on horseback, devils on horseback, Welsh rabbit, etc., are typical.

What does scald mean? It means to heat milk or cream just to, but not above, the boiling point—or until a film shines or wrinkles over the surface. To be on the safe side, many cooks prefer to heat the milk or cream over boiling water rather than run the risk of its "catching," which can happen over direct heat.

What does sear mean? To brown meat quickly in or under high heat to seal in the juices.

What does shuck mean? To remove the shells from seafood, such as clams and oysters, and to take the husks off corn on the cob.

What exactly is simmer? A spread of 185° to 210° F. (on the thermometer) is considered simmering temperature. Actually, this is the stage when bubbles form slowly and collapse below the surface. When they reach the surface of the liquid and break, that is boiling temperature.

What is meant by sliver? To slice into long, thin pieces. Almonds are slivered, for example. It's not unlike julienne.

Do you steam foods in or out of water? You can do both. Originally, it meant to cook foods over, not in, boiling water in a tightly covered kettle. The steam from the boiling liquid does the cooking. Special steamers are available for just this purpose. But vegetables cooked very slowly in a little hot water or fat in a very heavy pan, tightly covered, are also steamed; steamed rice, for example.

What is meant by steep?   To extract the essence from a food by soaking in a hot liquid. Commonly used in reference to tea.

How does stew differ from poach?   They don't really. Stew is an old term and poach the word we use today for the same thing—to simmer, to cook slowly. The word stew also means the food itself: beef stew, lamb stew, for example.

Are stir and blend alike?   Essentially. They both mean to combine one or more ingredients with a spoon, preferably wooden, using a wide, circular motion so that all are completely incorporated. This contrasts with beating, which means to whip foods together vigorously.

What does stir-fry mean in Chinese cookery?   Just what its name implies, a technique for frying foods quickly over a high flame, stirring continuously. A small amount of cooking oil is used—only enough to cover the bottom of the frying pan, as in sautéeing. Anyone who has ever eaten in a Chinese restaurant must be aware of the crisp, delicious texture of the vegetables which are, of course, cooked by the Chinese stir-fry method.

What is castor sugar?   The English word for very fine granulated sugar—like our own superfine.

Is powdered sugar the same thing as confectioners'?   Yes. Old cook books say powdered sugar, and the English, icing sugar.

What is superfine sugar?   An extremely fine granulated white sugar that dissolves almost instantly. Ideal over fresh fruits and cereals. Many cooks prefer it for angel and sponge cakes, to sweeten whipped cream, etc. Bartenders swear by it because it dissolves so quickly and easily—an inside tip for home bartenders.

What is a simple syrup?   Sugar and water, cooked together until slightly thickened, in these proportions: 1 cup sugar to ½ cup water. It is used to glaze certain types of sweet breads, to sweeten fruits, etc.

Why does syrup sometimes crystalize on the sides of the pan? In all likelihood, the sugar was not completely dissolved before it came to a boil. When it happens, simply sponge the crystals off. A little corn syrup added to the mixture helps to prevent crystalizing.

What does "spin a thread" mean in cooking? It's an old-fashioned term rarely found in modern cook books. What it means is that the syrup (a combination of sugar and water) is cooked to the point where, when you drip it from the tip of a spoon, it makes long, gossamer threads. Candy thermometers are usually marked "thread" at 230° F. to guide you. If you don't own a thermometer, we recommend your buying one to take the guesswork out of your cooking.

What is the crack stage in cooking syrups? When a half teaspoon or so of the syrup dropped into cold water separates into hard, brittle threads which will actually crack, 270° to 330° F. on a candy thermometer.

What is the soft-ball stage in cooking syrups or candy? When a teaspoon of the syrup dropped in a bowl of cold water forms a soft mass that can be rolled between your fingers (234° to 238° F. on a candy thermometer). The hard-ball stage is sort of an extension of the soft-ball; the ball of syrup resists pressure slightly but is still malleable (248° to 254° F.).

What does table d'hôte mean? A lunch or dinner of several courses served at a fixed price for the entire meal—no matter how much is consumed.

How is food unmolded? Cold or hot puddings, aspics, mousses, jellied dishes, etc., are usually unmolded to serve. Sometimes it takes a bit of doing to release the molded food, especially aspics and mousses. One method is to invert the mold on the serving platter, then hold a hot cloth on the bottom of the mold, but not so hot or so long that the mold begins to melt. This is quite tricky stuff. The other method is to dip the mold in hot water until the food "gives." Again, it's a matter of judgment as to the length of time and the amount of heat. The point, obviously, is to break the seal without melting the food. This applies whether it's a hot or cold dish. Some French molds have a little screw cap on the bottom (this, of course, is the top when the food is unmolded) which, when unscrewed, allows air to enter, breaking the seal immediately.

What is the difference between sauce tartare and beef tartare? Sauce tartare is mayonnaise mixed with chopped dill pickles, seasonings, and fresh herbs. It is usually served with fish and is especially delicious with scallops. Beef tartare is highly seasoned, lean, ground, raw beef used as a spread on sturdy breads such as rye or pumpernickel, often served with cocktails. It was standard fare in the old days of the "free lunch" in bars. Beef tartare can also be served as a first course, in which case mounds of the seasoned ground beef are placed on individual plates, the yolk of an egg dropped intact into a little "well" in the center of each mound. It is generally believed the name stems from the fact shredded raw meat was very popular with the "Balts" of the Russian Baltic provinces (tartars, get it?): thus, steak tartare.

What is meant by "until set"? What it says; until the food is firm to the touch. Usually applied to aspics, jellies, custards, etc.

What does Véronique mean in cookery? Apparently, it comes from the name Veronica, or Veronika, and means garnished with white, seedless grapes. Although it is attributed to the French, they do not have white, seedless grapes in France. Sole Véronique with a rich sauce, glazed, is frequently seen on menus in French restaurants in this country.

Chicken and squab or chicken livers are also prepared Véronique, and many people make a fresh green salad, tossed in a vinaigrette sauce, with lots of garlic and white, seedless grapes. In Spain, they serve sweet, fresh grapes in the sauce with turkey. Good, too.

What is a wok? The all-purpose cooking pan of the Chinese kitchen. Madame Grace Chu, author of that splendid book, *The Pleasures of Chinese Cooking*, and one of the really great authorities on Chinese cuisine in the United States, says: "The wok resembles a salad bowl with handles. It comes in various sizes and is usually made of iron, aluminum, or copper. The Chinese cook uses his woks for everything from stir-frying (a Chinese cooking technique) to braising to stewing to deep frying." Because of its round bottom, designed to fit Chinese stoves, the wok cannot be used on gas or electric stoves without a metal ring on which it sits. These, and woks, are available in Chinese stores. Mr. Craig Claiborne, Food Editor of the New York *Times,* says the wok is "great for any quick cooking, but should not be used for anything that takes time because the food will burn."

Beverages, Wines and Spirits

What kind of coffee do you recommend? Here's what's available and only you can decide which you like best: whole roasted beans, ground (there are many grinds), instant, decaffeinated, and chicory- or spice-flavored.

How long can coffee be stored and where? Coffee, once opened and exposed to air, deteriorates rather quickly. The Pan American Coffee Bureau advises buying only as much as you can use within a week. At the end of ten days you have probably noticed that it has taken on an unpleasant staleness. Always store in a clean, airtight container in the refrigerator.

What's the best way to make iced coffee? If you like iced coffee with lots of authority, freeze coffee in your ice-cube trays, then pour freshly brewed, but cooled, coffee over the coffee cubes. Incidentally, this is a thrifty way to use up any coffee left over from a meal.

What is decaffeinated coffee? Pure coffee from which nearly all the caffein (the mild stimulant that keeps some people awake) has been removed before roasting. Available in ground and instant forms.

What is café brûlot? An unfortunate concoction made with strong coffee, lemon and orange rind, spices, sugar, and brandy, ignited before serving, that originated, apparently, in New Orleans. Served after dinner. Joseph D. Vehling in *America's Table* calls it "an after-dinner stunt."

What is a demitasse? *Demi* is half and *tasse* is cup. In short, half a

43

cup. Today we use it to mean a small cup of strong, black coffee served after dinner.

What is espresso coffee?   Technically, it's strong, black coffee brewed in an espresso machine under steam pressure. You are undoubtedly familiar with the espresso coffeehouses in this country and in Italy. To make a comparable coffee at home, you must use either a French or an Italian dark-roast coffee, very, very finely ground, brewing it in an Italian drip coffeepot, a *macchinetta* (these are widely available in shops specializing in cooking equipment). If espresso is served with a twist of lemon in a demitasse or in a tall wineglass, warmed, it is known as Roman espresso. American coffee roasters pack espresso coffee in half-pound vacuum tins.

Small espresso machines that will make 2, 4, and 6 cups are available for home use.

With *café filtre*, the French method of making coffee, it is filtered rather than boiled.

What is Irish coffee?   A combination of strong, black coffee, a dash of sugar, and Irish whisky, with a dollop of whipped cream floating on top. Mrs. Elizabeth David, a great English food authority, wrote in *Wine and Food,* "We must not forget that it is to a public relations expert that we owe the invention of traditional Irish coffee laced with Irish whisky, which nobody will deny is a very great improvement on Irish coffee *tout court.*"

What does mocha mean in cookery?   A combination of coffee and chocolate. Whether a drink or used as an ingredient, it is especially delicious because the coffee accents the flavor of the chocolate. The name Mocha, from the town in Yemen on the Red Sea and from whence, at one time, the finest quality coffees came, still stands for top-quality coffee although its trade has declined. In all likelihood, the French were responsible for combining coffee and chocolate and serving it in cups with whipped cream, thus adding mocha to our culinary language.

Is it possible to prevent iced tea from clouding?   Yes. Cool the brewed tea to room temperature (do not refrigerate), then pour the cold tea over ice cubes. Tea that is to be served iced should be much stronger than normal because of the dilution by the melting ice.

Refrigeration will almost invariably cause clouding. Restore its amber color by adding a small amount of boiling water.

What spirits and wines should I have in my kitchen for cooking?   Dark rum, cognac or brandy, and, in the refrigerator, once opened, sherry, madeira, marsala, port, white and red wine (not cooking wine).

What is cooking wine?   So-called cooking wine is wine to which salt has been added to make it unpalatable to drink. A ridiculous idea that can be laid right at the feet of the late, unlamented prohibition era. Any cook worth his or her salt would laugh his head off at the very thought. You cook with the wine you drink. Obviously, no one would think of taking a great vintage wine and dumping it into a stew, but a good wine is definitely called for if you want a good dish.

Is there a correct wineglass?   There are many types of wineglasses. The tendency today, contrasted with Victorian times when glasses were small, is toward large glasses. As Mr. Frank Schoonmaker points out in his *Encyclopedia of Wine*, "All wine tastes better in thin-stemmed (crystal) glasses, preferably uncut, and as simple in design as possible. The color of the wine can be better judged when it is served, and the wine seems to taste better in thin rather than heavy glasses."

The glasses generally recommended are: 10-ounce for red wine; 9-ounce as a single, all-purpose glass; 8-ounce for white wine; 10½-ounce for the great Burgundies; tall, slender, 9-ounce for champagne and other sparkling wines; 6-ounce, flat-shaped, for Rhine, Moselle, Alsatian, etc.; the slender, 5-ounce typical sherry glass for sherry, port, madeira; and the 7-ounce "snifter"-type for brandy, cordials, liqueurs.

This, of course, is the ideal, but you can get along fine with a 9-ounce all-purpose glass, the proper sherry glass, and the snifter.

How do you dry your fine wineglasses?   First, they are washed by hand in hot, sudsy water, then rinsed in very hot water and drained thoroughly. While still hot (they dry better), wipe with two fresh, clean, dry towels—one around one hand inside the bowl, the other, outside. Rub gently, working both hands around the bowl, until glasses are bone-dry and shiny.

How much wine is correctly served in a glass?   One-third to one-half full. No more. This permits the wine to "breathe."

Why is a small amount of wine poured into the host's glass first? Principally, so that he can sniff or taste the wine and be sure it is good before it is offered to guests. In more rugged times, when heads fell freely, it was undoubtedly done to assure guests the wine had not been poisoned.

Is it correct to use a wine basket to serve wine?   In Frank Schoonmaker's *Encyclopedia of Wine,* a masterly work by the great connoisseur, he writes: "The purpose of a basket (wire, wicker, or straw) is to hold a bottle in nearly the same horizontal position it occupied in the cellar, thus permitting it to be brought to the table and served without disturbing the sediment. Cradles are useful and almost necessary for the proper service of many old red wines, but to use a cradle for a wine that has no sediment at all is sheer pretentiousness and snobbery."

Should wine bottles be wrapped in napkins?   Not unless you want to conceal the source of the wine—in which case it would be better to decant it. A chilled wine, that comes from a cooler, must be wrapped to absorb any water that clings to the bottle, and it's certainly comfortable for the "sommelier" to keep it wrapped while pouring the wine. With a red wine or a white, chilled in the refrigerator, it would be a foolish affectation.

What is the correct way to open a bottle of wine?   First, cut around the capsule at the ridge, half an inch below the mouth of the bottle. Wipe around the mouth carefully with a clean, linen napkin. Then position the tip of the corkscrew dead center of the cork and twist it through. With a "wing" corkscrew, use the same technique, allowing the wings to rise, then squeeze the two wings together to lift the cork.

Is it safe to chill a bottle of wine in the freezer?   It really shouldn't be done because, if left there too long, it will explode. However, in dire necessity, you can chill it briefly in the freezer, but only if you have your wits about you and remember to take it out in a short time.

Can wine, once refrigerated, be brought back to room temperature?
It is not recommended. It would certainly not spoil the wine, if it
became necessary, but there would be some loss of freshness, aroma,
or whatever the wine has to offer.

Can you keep a bottle of table wine that is partly used?   Yes. In the
refrigerator. If, as sometimes happens, you don't consume an entire
bottle of a dry red or white wine, cork it well and refrigerate. Red
wines should be taken from the refrigerator several hours before they
are to be served, uncorked, and brought to room temperature. Partly
used bottles of wine can always be used up in cooking.

How do you store sweet wines, once they are opened?   They should
be refrigerated, well corked, and drunk within a week at the most
because they deteriorate very quickly. If used for cooking, which
is another matter, they should be refrigerated and used within a
reasonable time—a matter of weeks. This poses a problem for most
of us, since refrigerators are not designed to hold wine bottles
standing upright, and a gaggle of wine bottles is almost impossible
to accommodate, what with the other things one needs to refrigerate.

*Should a table wine (dry red or white) be served after the main
course has been removed?*   At a formal dinner, no. But, *en famille,*
it is quite normal, perfectly permissible and, certainly, comfortable
to continue drinking the same wine right through the dessert.

Speaking of red wine, what is room temperature?   The term originated in the days before central heating when room temperature or
cellar was, at most, about 60°. Today, it doesn't make any sense
because room temperature can be anything up to 90°. To serve a
red table wine at room temperature, which should be 60°, you just
have to use your head—unless, of course, you are fortunate to have
a proper wine cellar. A brief interlude in the refrigerator will cool
it, but care must be taken not to cool it too much or the bouquet
will be "frozen." The cork from a red wine should be removed
sometime before serving to allow the wine to "breathe."

Is age important in vins rosés or pink wines?   "All wines," Mr. Frank
Schoonmaker reports in his *Encyclopedia of Wine,* "if properly stored,
tend to improve somewhat with age but, generally speaking, there

has been too much emphasis placed on age, as if age itself were a virtue. It can be, but often is not. All *rosés*, whether from California or France, or elsewhere, should be consumed by the time they are three years old, and certainly, before the age of five."

Is wine ever served with salad?   Correctly, no, because the vinegar in the dressing kills the taste of the wine. However, in France, except at formal dinners, Frenchmen will go right on drinking whatever-the-wine with the salad or whatever else comes along. With certain types of salads, such as jellied chicken, fish, lobster, etc., you could serve a dry white, rosé, or a light red wine, providing the dressing, if any, was made with lemon juice rather than vinegar.

What is an apéritif?   An alcoholic drink before a meal, designed to stimulate the appetite.

What is the difference between apple juice and apple cider?   Apple juice is the fresh, sweet juice from apples which has been heated to arrest microbial action—in other words, pasteurized—and hermetically sealed in containers; cider is the fresh, filtered or unfiltered, juice of apples to which a preservative may or may not be added. Cider is sold *au naturel* without heating and is not hermetically sealed; hard cider is cider which has attained some degree of alcohol fermentation. Other countries do not define cider as we do. In England, for example, cider is the juice from apples which has achieved some degree of alcohol fermentation. It cannot be, as here, simply the fresh juice from apples.

Is applejack the same thing as calvados?   In this respect: American applejack (or apple brandy) and the French calvados are both made from distilled apple cider, aged in wood. The main difference lies in the aging. Applejack is usually aged only from two to five years; calvados, ten years. Also, our apple brandies are bottled at 100 proof, while the French are under 90 proof.

What is the difference between pink and white champagne?   Basically, champagne is a white wine made from a combination of white and blue-black grapes. The wine is white because the skins are removed from the juices immediately after pressing. With pink champagne, the juices are left in contact with the skins to give the pinkish color.

In some instances, small quantities of red wine from the Champagne district are added to achieve the correct shade of pink. The sweetness depends on the amount of sugar syrup added by the grower (all champagnes have sugar added), and this factor determines the dryness or sweetness of the finished wine. A pink or rosé champagne would not necessarily be sweeter than other types. French champagne designated as *brut* has the smallest "dosage" (as the syrup is known), followed by dry or *sec*, with the largest dosage in a *doux* (sweet).

What is the proper way to chill champagne?   The most elegant way, of course, is in a wine cooler or silver bucket. Place the bottle of champagne in cooler or bucket with chopped or shaved ice (not ice cubes) and water for about an hour before serving. Twist the bottle slowly every once in a while so that all surfaces come in contact with the cold mixture. A less glamorous alternative is the refrigerator, though not in the freezer, of course.

What does Chartreuse mean?   Several things. First, a liqueur made by the monks of Chartreux; also the name of an elaborate, molded entrée made of root vegetables, an invention of the monks, strict vegetarians. Later, less rigid souls added meat, game, and poultry to the original recipe; finally, *oeufs en Chartreuse* (eggs Chartreuse): eggs cooked in molds, garnished with tiny balls of carrots, turnips, peas, and green beans, served on croutons with braised cabbage, sausage, etc.

Where did the word cocktail come from?   In *America's Table,* Joseph D. Vehling writes, "The word has nothing to do with a cock's tail feathers, but rather refers to the strong stuff that roughshod horse dealers give to old nags before parading them in front of a prospective buyer, to make the decrepid horse prance and 'cock its tail.' "

What is claret?   It comes from *clairet,* meaning "light in color." Fernande Garvin, author of *The Art of French Cooking,* and Director of the Bordeaux Wine Information Bureau, went to the trouble to explain its meaning for me in great detail, "Today, claret has become synonymous with red Bordeaux, although for centuries it was a wine very different from what we now know as a red Bordeaux. Until the 18th century, red wines were not aged at all, and as soon as the juice had reached fermentation the wine was considered made. Such extremely young wines, which were entirely consumed during the year following the harvest, began to appear on the English table two weeks after fermentation—the time it took for the ships to go from Bordeaux to the Thames. These wines were more pink than red and were called clairet, from which the English got claret." These days it is not, of course, unusual to find bottles 50 years old, and even older, but such a wine is still claret to the English and even to many people in this country.

Are cognac and brandy the same thing? Cognac is brandy but not all brandy is cognac. Only brandy made in the Cognac region of France can legally be called cognac. All brandy is made from wine and all wine-producing countries make brandy. The juices of the grape ferment into wine, which is then distilled. The result, initially, is a tough, fiery, colorless liquid which is aged in old casks (preferably oak) until the master taster determines by smelling, not tasting, when it is ready for bottling. American brandy is made in California by the same time-honored method. Once brandy is bottled, no matter where it's made, it will not age further. Cognac labeled *Fine Champagne*, which confuses many people, indicates blends from two districts: Champagne and Petite Champagne. Connoisseurs consider it the finest of all cognacs.

Is a cordial the same thing as a liqueur? Yes. Cordial stems from the Latin, *cordialis*, meaning of, or belonging to, the heart. First used centuries ago by monks who created *liqueurs cordialis* to heal and comfort the poor in monastery hospitals, they soon became the pleasure of the rich who served them as a digestive after heavy dinners. *The Oxford Dictionary* describes a liqueur as a strong, alcoholic liquor sweetened and flavored with aromatic substances. In the June, 1965, issue of *Liquor Store*, a trade publication, the editors say, "Based on the type of flavor, cordials (or liqueurs) can be grouped into five broad divisions. These include fruits, seeds, herbs, peels, and crèmes." Fruit cordials are easily identified since they are plainly labeled, in most instances, with the name of the fruit—blackberry, peach, cherry, etc. The formulas for seed cordials, like those of herb, blend together a variety of ingredients, but one seed flavor will predominate. Anisette, made from aniseed, is a familiar "seed" cordial; with herb cordials, unlike seed, no single herb is likely to dominate. Chartreuse and Benedictine are typical herb-type cordials. Some of the well-known cordials take their flavor from the rind of citrus fruits. The one most widely used is the peel of the Curaçao orange grown on the island of the same name in the Dutch West Indies. Hence, curaçao, the orange liqueur. Among the many cordials (*Liquor Store* lists nearly 100, including the *eau de vie* which, technically, are not cordials), the crèmes are the sweetest which, because of the high sugar content, result in a creamy consistency. The best known of this group is probably crème de menthe.

Cordials (or liqueurs) are served after dinner as digestives, in mixed drinks, as a flavoring in desserts, or over fruits.

Vins de liqueur, the name given to any wine which is both sweet and intoxicating, are dessert wines which include marsala, port, sweet sherry, and madeira.

What is eau de vie?   In France, the skins and pits of the grapes left from the vintage are called *marc*, which is distilled to make eau de vie (water of life—a very fiery liquid). Alsace, Switzerland and the Black Forest specialize in producing an eau de vie from highly scented fruit. *Kirsch* is the eau de vie of cherries; *fraise* and *framboise* that of strawberries and raspberries respectively; *mirabelle* of little yellow plums, and *quetsch* of purple ones; *slivovitz* (Hungarian or Rumanian) is also made from plums. The great one is the Swiss, *Poire William*, made of William pears. All eau de vie is colorless and generally used as a digestive after dinner, although sometimes the more flavorful are used to perfume fresh fruit.

What is aquavit?   A modification of the Latin, *aqua vitae*, meaning water of life, a Scandinavian liquor made of grain or potatoes with different flavorings, the most popular of which is caraway seeds. It is served ice cold, as an appetizer, usually followed by a beer chaser.

What is hock?   The name commonly applied, in England nowadays, to any white German or Rhine wine, but originally only to the true Hochheimer.

Are Holland gins like other gins?   No. Often referred to as Hollands, they are made quite differently from English or American gins and because they have a very pronounced taste of their own, do not mix well with other ingredients, but are drunk straight.

What is a jeroboam? An oversize wine bottle, holding as much as six ordinary bottles, in which clarets (in America, we know them as Bordeaux) of great years are sometimes laid away. The jeroboam is also used for champagne but, here, as Mr. Frank Schoonmaker points out in his *Encyclopedia of Wine* (a reference that should be in every wine-lover's library), "The wine is fermented in regular bottles and then transfused just prior to shipment; this, of course, has a tendency to shorten its life."

What is a magnum? A magnum, more familiar to most of us, is a bottle of doubled normal capacity. Again quoting Mr. Schoonmaker, "Since wines, red wines especially, tend to develop and age more slowly in large bottles than in small, clarets and Burgundies of great years are often put up in magnums for laying away. Champagne is occasionally fermented in magnums (*never* in bottles over magnum size) but, more often, transfused from standard bottles into magnums when disgorged—as with a jeroboam, tending to shorten rather than lengthen the wine's life; that champagne is better in magnums is a harmless myth. The use of magnums for lesser wines is in some cases a convenience, more often an affectation."

What is kümmel? A sweet liqueur made from distilled spirits, flavored with caraway seeds. Used as a digestive.

What is May Wine? In German, *Mai Wein,* a special May Day drink made with wine, infused with wild woodruff, which comes into flower in May and imparts a very special fragrance to the wine. Also called *Mai Bowle.*

What is ratafia? There is a sweet, fancy wine biscuit called ratafia, somewhat like macaroons, but there is also a cordial or liqueur called by the same name. Apparently it stems from the Arabic, *tafia,* meaning a spirit, but it has become a generic term for certain thick alcoholic syrups or sweet cordials flavored with the kernels and juices of fruits, particularly almonds, cherries, apricots, peaches, and with spices. Homemade cordials (fruits and other basic ingredients steeped in alcohol or spirits) are often called ratafias.

What are the different types of rum and how are they used? "Rum types, with one exception, are determined by geography, not by definition," *Liquor Store*, a trade publication, points out. The exception is New England rum, a straight rum (all others are blends of young and older rums) which can be distilled anywhere in the U.S. Exclusive of Cuban rums, no longer available to us, we have (*Grossman's Guide to Wines, Spirits, and Beers* is our authority) the following: Puerto Rican rums—those designated on the label as white or gold are dry with a very slight molasses flavor, the gold being slightly sweeter; in addition, Puerto Rico also produces full-bodied rums that may be labeled either "red" or "heavy dark." Bacardi, as a matter of interest, is not a type of rum, but the name of a distilling company. Jamaica rum, a heavy-bodied rum, is aged at least 5 years, but the general average is 7 to 8 years. "All Jamaica runs," *Grossman's Guide* says, "have a full rummy (molasses) bouquet and flavor. The depth of their color depends, however, on the amount of caramel used. The natural color is a rich, golden hue, but of recent years the very dark mahogany colored rums have increased in popularity in America. These dark rums are generally labeled 'For Planter's Punch,' as this is the drink in which they are used most widely." Jamaica rums matured and blended in England, known in the trade as London Dock rums, command premium prices.

Demerara rums (the rums many Canadians are weaned on) come from British Guiana. "The chief difference," again quoting *Grossman's Guide*, "between Jamaica and Demerara rums is due to the quality of the sugar cane. Demerara rums are much darker and slightly heavier than Jamaica rums, and do not possess the finesse or the bouquet of the latter." As one of the Canadians who knows them well, they are, nevertheless, marvelous when used as a flavoring.

Virgin Islands rum, neither light nor heavy-bodied, is used primarily in mixed drinks such as swizzles, punches, and coolers. Arak, a brandy-like rum produced on the island of Java, dry and highly aromatic, is usually aged a total of 8 to 10 years before being blended and bottled, which is then done in Holland. Extremely pungent and rummy, it is used as any other rum. In Sweden, however, its greatest use is for making Swedish Punch. In the countries where rum is produced, it is drunk straight, rather than in mixtures, such as we make in this country. Rum, however, is used extensively in cooking—in sauces, ice creams, cakes, and some savory dishes.

What is sake and how is it pronounced?   Sake, pronounced sa-key, is not, as is often thought, a Japanese rice wine, but a beer made from steamed rice which undergoes two fermenting processes. In Japan, where it is made and from which it is imported, sake (the name is probably derived from the city of Osaka) is served straight, warmed to about 100° F. (actually lukewarm), in tiny porcelain bowls before, with, or after meals. Americans who have adopted the sake habit use it to make cocktails or serve it cold, as an apéritif.

Are sangría and sangaree the same drink?   No. All they have in common is wine. A sangría, a combination of fruits and red or white wine, is served with the meal; a sangaree, made with spirits (brandy, gin, or whisky), sugar and port wine, is served as an apéritif.

What are schnapps?   The German word for a "nip" of spiritous liquor of any kind.

Should sherry be served cold or at room temperature?   When served as an apéritif, or at dinner, it should be drunk very cold, iced as you would champagne, served in clear, tulip-shaped wineglasses, poured generously—at least 3 ounces (2 jiggers). Simple hors d'oeuvre, such as olives, almonds, shrimp, smoked salmon—nothing elaborate— should always accompany a cold, dry sherry, which is designed to stimulate one's appetite for the dinner ahead. Never, under any circumstances, serve sherry "on the rocks." Serve sweet sherries at room temperature.

Does sherry keep well when not refrigerated?   No. It spoils less rapidly than table wines, but it will "wither" perceptibly within a couple of days, losing much of its bouquet. Once uncorked, a bottle of sherry should always be refrigerated.

What is a spritzer?   White wine and soda water over ice.

What is tequila?   The national drink of Mexico which is enjoying increasing popularity in this country. Since there is considerable confusion about tequila and its history, I asked Elizabeth Lambert Ortiz, author of the forthcoming *The Complete Book of Mexican Cooking*, if she would clarify it for me. Here is what she writes: "Before the arrival of the Spaniards Mexicans drank (in fact, still do) *pulque*, a fermented beer-like brew made from the sap or juice of the *agave*, the American century plant which is a member of the natural

order of the *amaryllidaceae*. Not to be confused with the natural order
of *cactaceae*, though both are water-storing plants. *Pulque* is a
very ancient drink going back to legendary times and was probably
invented by women of the Toltec civilization which preceded the
dominance of the Aztecs in Mexico. The best authorities believe that
the process of distillation was first discovered, in this part of the new
world, by the Spaniards who were the first to distill tequila from the
agave plant. Tequila is named for a small town in the State of Jalisco,
where the blue or *tequilana agave* grows in profusion. Other tequilas,
made from another species of agave, produced in the State of Oaxaca,
are known as *mescal*. It is a rather stronger flavor. Tequila is also
produced in the north."

Margaritas, the famous Mexican drink, are made like this: Combine a pony of tequila, a dash of triple sec, and the juice of ½ lime
or lemon with ice and shake well. Strain and serve in a cocktail
glass, the rim of which has been dampened and dipped in salt.

What is vermouth?   Leaning on that unfailingly reliable source, Frank
Schoonmaker's *Encyclopedia of Wine*, we find: "A fortified white
wine, flavored with various herbs, barks, seeds, spices, etc. The
principal aromatic agent in vermouth consists of flowers of the shrub,
Artemisia absinthium, also known as wormwood. Today, vermouth
is used principally as an apéritif and as an ingredient in cocktails.
There are two types: French and Italian. The pale French vermouth
is quite dry but its counterpart is, like the Italian, quite sweet. Both
types of vermouth are produced in many other countries, including
Spain, Argentina, and the United States. The better American ver-
mouths are substantially as good as the imported."

Is vodka made like gin?   To this extent only, they are both made from
grain neutral spirits and neither is aged. But with gin, the neutral
spirits are flavored with juniper and other aromatics. Nothing is
added to vodka. It is odorless, virtually tasteless, and colorless. The
name derives from *voda*, meaning water in Russian. Given the
diminutive, affectionate noun ending, it becomes "dear little water."

Is wassail a drink or a toast?   Both, really. Originally, it was a toast
or salutation to a guest meaning, "be in good health." To which the
traditional response was "Drinkhail." But wassail also means the
liquor in which, formerly, healths were drunk, especially the spiced

ale served on Twelfth Night (twelve days after Christmas—January 6). It can also mean riotous festivity and a carol or song sung by wassailers. The wassail bowl is not a punch bowl, such as we know, but rather a large bowl or cup in which wassail was made and from which healths were drunk.

What does proof mean on a bottle of whisky or gin?   Proof indicates the amount of alcohol in any distilled spirits (all whiskies, gin, vodka, brandy or cognac, rum, tequila, and aquavit are distilled)—a measure of the alcoholic strength, not of the quality. As a rule of thumb, 50% of the indicated proof is alcohol. Therefore, a bottle of whisky that is marked 86 proof is 43% alcohol.

After the meaning of proof was published in *House Beautiful,* Roy Andries de Groot, author of *Feasts for All Seasons,* sent me this fascinating follow-up. He wrote, "I notice in your November 'Nobody Every Tells You . . .' you dealt with the meaning of the word 'proof.' A few weeks ago I met a deeply-accented old Scotsman who has been in the Glasgow whisky blending and distilling business for more than 50 years. He claimed that the use of the word 'prrroof' (as he said it) originated there about 100 years ago, before the development of the modern, extremely accurate methods for determining the degree of alcohol. When a wholesale customer was about to buy a barrel of whisky, it was the custom to offer him 'proof' of its strength by allowing him to withdraw a small quantity, gently heat it in a silver bowl and then set it on fire. The color of the flame was the 'proof' of the percentage of alcohol. With the comparatively crude distillation methods of those days, the highest strength they could usually achieve was about 50% alcohol. When the flame showed this percentage by burning a bright blueish-purple, the whisky was said to be 100% perfect, or 100-proof. All lower degrees of strength were pro-rated below the assumed maximum. No one even dreamed that 'proof' would ever go above 100!"

What is "Bottled in Bond" whisky?   It is not, as you might logically think, a guarantee of quality but, rather, a guarantee that certain federal legal requirements have been met. To be entitled to the bottled-in-bond identification, the editors of *Liquor Store,* a trade publication, say, "the whisky must be at least 4 years old (most are older); it must be bottled at 100 proof; and the whisky in the bottle must be produced in a single distillery, by the same distiller, and be the product of a single season and year." When federal inspectors are satisfied that all these specifications have been met and the tax paid, the little green stamp, the bottled-in-bond designation, is applied. Although, as the above indicates, it is not a requirement, most of the distillers use fine quality, straight whiskies.

What distinguishes Canadian whisky from other whiskies? Although in some parts of the country people are of the opinion Canadian whisky is primarily a rye whisky, it is generally made from corn and lesser amounts of rye, wheat, and barley malt. In the eyes of the U.S. Government, "It is a distinctive product of Canada," and the Canadians themselves say, "there is no other whisky like it." It is a blend, never straight. "A mild whisky," the publication *Liquor Store* calls it, "with a delicate flavor and light body."

What is the difference between rye whisky and Bourbon? Straight rye is distilled from a fermented mash of grain, of which not less than 51% is rye grain; straight Bourbon is distilled from a fermented mash of grain, of which not less than 51% is corn grain.
A blend means that rye contains not less than 51% by volume of straight rye or in the case of Bourbon, 51% of straight Bourbon.

What grain is Scotch whisky made from? It is distilled from barley, either malted or unmalted or both. The two methods of distillation are the pot-still process (this is known as malt whisky) and the patent-still process (this is known as grain whisky). Both come off the still as whole whiskies, and nothing is added to them except pure water to bring them to commercial strength. After the whiskies have been distilled, they must legally mature for at least three years but, frequently, it is much longer—up to seven, ten, or even twelve years. Then comes the blending, which can be a mixture of any two or more different whiskies, whether malt or grain. Once blended they are kept in casks for long periods to "marry," before being bottled. Unlike fine wines, whisky does not improve in the bottle.

At what temperature should beer be served? Taste experts say beer should not be served colder than 40° F. Beer cooled to 38° F. would be "served at" about 40° F. Europeans think Americans serve beer much too cold to enjoy its true bouquet and flavor.

How do you store beer?   It is well to remember that light, especially sunlight, is the arch enemy of beer. So, beer that is not stored in the refrigerator should be stored away from light.

What is the proper way to pour beer?   It's up to you. If you want a head, tilt the glass on its side and fill the glass about ⅓, then straighten the glass and pour the beer straight in. The custom is partially aesthetic and partly traditional, and most beer drinkers have come to expect it. If a beer won't "pour" a head, it has lost its carbonation and gone flat. Beer experts say a moderate-size head is a flavor enhancer and traps the hops aroma—an important characteristic of beer.

Men who buy draught beer in bars don't want a head because they get less beer. With bottled beer, you can pour to suit yourself—without a head, just pour it all straight into the glass.

What is Bock beer?   Originally, a beer brewed specifically during the winter for the spring market. Apparently first brewed in Einbeck, Germany, as far back as AD 1200, the name has been corrupted into *ein Bock*, which also means "a goat." Hence, the goat that still appears in advertisements for bock beer. A heavy, dark, lager beer, it is sweeter than regular lager because it is brewed with a more fully roasted malt.

What is draught beer?   Beer that is not pasteurized, deemed unnecessary because the beer is used up so quickly. All bottled or canned beer is pasteurized.

What is the difference between imported and domestic beers?   Broadly speaking, the imported are all lager beers and, in general, have a somewhat higher alcoholic content than domestic.

Is lager beer light or dark?   It can be either. Lager, from the German, *lagern*, meaning "to store," was originally and traditionally a German brew. It came into use centuries before artificial refrigeration when monks discovered that beer stored in cool mountain caves would keep during the hot summer months when brewing had to be suspended. Actually, it's a method of processing—known in the trade as "bottom fermentation"—which includes 90% of all the beers produced in the U.S. today. The term lager is not used greatly these days. Most people simply ask for "beer."

Are porter and stout alike?   No, but both are variations of ale which is a top fermented brew, heavier and more bitter than beer. Porter, brewed with some dark malt, which makes it slightly sweeter than ale, is dark brown, full-bodied, and less "hoppy" than regular ale; stout, still sweeter than porter, as well as stronger, is very dark brown and heavier, with a marked malt flavor. Popular in Great Britain and the Dominions, they are less so in the United States.

What is a Black & Tan?   A popular English drink. Half ale and stout or ale and porter.

What is a Black Velvet?   Champagne and stout (half and half).

What is bitter ale?   Also known as "pale ale," it is one of two types of ale sold in England, the other being "mild." They are often mixed to make "half and half."

What is a Red-Eye?   A very old drink made with beer and tomato juice in these proportions: 1 12-ounce bottle of beer to 1 36-ounce can of tomato juice, seasoned with Worcestershire sauce and Tabasco. Alleged to be even better than "the hair of the same dog . . ." the morning after.

What is birch beer?   The *Encyclopedia of Food* says, "A summer beverage made from the fermented sap of the sweet, or black, birch trees." A very old, non-alcoholic, mildly sweet drink, it is reminiscent of root beer—similar in that it is made from roots, barks, and herbs. Birch beer is not readily available on the open market, but it is served at New York's Zum Zum restaurants. In certain regions, specifically Pennsylvania, birch beer can frequently be tracked down.

What is a Shandy Gaff?   A bottle of ginger beer mixed with a pint of ale.

Breads and Baking

What is the correct way to measure flour? You should use a dry measuring cup. Spoon the flour into the cup well above the top, then level or cut off with the edge, not the flat surface, of a metal spatula or knife. Do not shake the flour down. This applies whether the recipe calls for sifted or unsifted flour.

What is meant by sift? To shake through a fine sieve. More often and usually more conveniently, a mechanical sifter is used.

Why do some recipes call for sifting flour? The reason is logical. Sifted flour measures less, by weight, than unsifted flour. Therefore, in making cakes, for example, which call for precise measurements, it is essential to be exact. Otherwise your cake will have too much flour and the net will be a heavy, dry product.

What exactly is a lightly floured board? A film of flour over the area on which you are working with bread or pastry. The reason recipes specify "lightly floured" is because you want only as much flour as will keep the dough from sticking to the surface. Further, you do not want to work in any extra flour which will make the dough tough and dry.

How do you flour a cake pan or cookie sheet? Grease the pan well with shortening or butter, add a couple of tablespoons of flour, and shake the pan gently (working over the sink), tipping it as you work, so the flour makes a light film all over it. Dump out or off any excess.

What is the difference between cake flour and all-purpose? Cake flour is a soft wheat flour, and all-purpose, a hard wheat. Cake flour is

61

used specifically for making light cakes (angel, sponge, etc.) and all-purpose, as its name indicates, is generally used for other cooking. NOTE: They cannot be used interchangeably in cooking.

Can self-rising flour be substituted for regular all-purpose? Yes, but only if the recipe calls for salt and baking powder. In which case, omit the salt and baking powder from the recipe since the self-rising flour already contains these ingredients.

What is instant flour? It's a granular flour that pours through a sieve like salt. Its advertised virtue is that it will dissolve in hot or cold liquids without lumping and almost instantly. True. Allegedly, it can be used any place that all-purpose flour is used. The retail price is somewhat higher than all-purpose, and I, personally, do not like its performance (although many people do).

What is potato flour or potato starch? A flour made from cooked potatoes which is used as a thickening agent and also in many dishes. Potato flour sponge cake is one of the most delicate, and delicious, you ever tasted. In using potato flour for thickening, it should be remembered that, like arrowroot, it reaches its maximum thickness at 158° to 176° F. on the thermometer and further heating causes very marked thinning. One tablespoon of potato flour is the equivalent of 2 of flour.

Why do you flour fruits, nuts, etc. before adding to a cake or pudding? To keep them from falling to the bottom.

Are double-acting and single-acting (regular) baking powder interchangeable in baking? No. Unless a recipe specifically calls for double-acting, use the regular.

Can active-dry and compressed yeast be used interchangeably? Yes. One package of active-dry yeast equals one cake of compressed yeast. The envelopes containing active-dry are dated and the yeast should *not* be used after the expiration date; compressed yeast should be refrigerated and used within thirty-five days of purchase.

How should yeast be dissolved? Both active-dry yeast and compressed yeast dissolve best in water, or the water in which potatoes were cooked. If a recipe calls for milk, substitute ¼ cup water or potato water for ¼ cup of the milk. Then sprinkle or crumble in the yeast and stir until dissolved. But note well: the liquid (either water, or water and milk) must be warm, 105° to 115° F. on the thermometer, which is actually lukewarm. Lacking a thermometer, test milk as you would for a baby's bottle: a drop on the inside of your wrist should feel warm, not hot. To maintain this temperature, measure liquid into a warm bowl (rinsed in hot water, then dried) before adding yeast. Temperature is of the utmost importance when cooking with yeast, because it is a living organism; if the liquid in which it is dissolved is too hot, it will "kill" the action of the yeast; if too cool, it will slow it down.

Can you explain the difference between dough and batter? Dough is usually used when referring to bread; batter, to cakes. Dough comes from Old English, *dah*, meaning to knead. A mixture of flour and liquid with the addition of a leavening agent is, hence, bread. However, we also say dough in speaking of pastry which is a combination of fat, flour, sometimes egg, sometimes sugar, and a liquid. Batter, on the other hand, is thinner, contains more liquid, can be both poured and stirred. In some instances it, too, contains a leavening agent, as in cake, for example. Batter also means the coating used to cover foods either sautéed, fried, or deep-fat fried.

How do you roll out dough? Ideally, you should have a pastry cloth and a rolling pin covered with a "stocking" although they are not downright necessities. Dust the cloth (or board) and the "stocking" (or pin) lightly with flour.

   To roll pastry: roll out only enough for a single crust at a time, rolling from the center out to the edges in all directions quite thin—less than ⅛ inch thick. The rolled circle should be large enough to extend 1½ inches all around the edge of the pie pan. To transfer the pastry to the pan, roll it around the rolling pin or fold it into quarters. If you have time, it's a good idea to refrigerate the pastry shell.

   To roll cookies: follow the same method, rolling only part of the dough at a time, to the thickness desired, then cut with a cookie cutter. Refrigerate the dough in between.

How do you knead properly? Kneading is a means of mixing and blending, by hand (or with the electric dough hook), a dough that is too stiff to mix with the average implement. It also serves to stimulate the formation of gluten (gluten is the rubbery substance in all-purpose flour that forms an elastic framework capable of surrounding and holding the carbon dioxide gas bubbles formed by yeast). To knead, flour your hands and flatten the dough on a lightly floured board. Pick up the edge of dough farthest away from you and fold it toward you. Then press down two or three times with the heels of your hands, pushing the dough away from you. Turn the dough a quarter of the way around, fold it, press, and push again. Repeat the turning, folding, pressing, and pushing motion until the dough becomes satiny, smooth, and quite elastic. In general, this takes 5 to 10 minutes of good, energetic kneading. More cooks tend to underknead, rather than over-knead. Keep your hands and board lightly floured even though the total amount of flour used may be more than the recipe specifies. Flours vary in the amount of liquid they will absorb.

Where should you place bread dough for rising?   Once the dough has been kneaded to the right point, it should be placed in a greased bowl, covered with a fresh dish towel, and put in a warm place away from drafts and direct heat of any kind. The Wheat Flour Institute recommends the oven or a cupboard. If a gas oven, place the bowl of dough on the middle rack, pilot light on, door closed; if an electric oven, place on center rack with a pan of boiling water on bottom shelf, door closed; if a cupboard, place a pan of hot water beside the bowl, keep the door closed. The ideal temperature for dough to rise is 80° to 85° F.

How long should bread be allowed to rise?   It should have doubled in size for the first rising. Your eyes are a good judge, but you can test by pressing the dough with the tip of your finger. If an indentation remains, the dough is ready; if it springs back, it needs more time. Approximately 1½ hours is usually required.

After the first rising, punch the dough down to press out the gas and break up large air pockets, so that the baked bread will have a firm texture. It is at this point you shape the bread and allow it to rise a second time, until double in bulk. This takes less time than the first rising, about 50 minutes.

How do you know when bread is baked?   A good test for doneness is to tap the loaf with your knuckles. It should give off a hollow sound. (This does not apply to rolls.)

Where do you store bread?   No one seems to agree on this. I have the best luck with loaves wrapped in pliofilm bags, all air squeezed out, tied securely, refrigerated. It seems to me they stale and mildew less quickly than out of the refrigerator. If I see the bread is getting old, I butter it generously, then bake it in a preheated 300° F. oven until it's golden. Baked bread keeps extremely well and makes a delicious crisp bite with hors d'oeuvres, salads, or any dish where bread is called for.

Can you freeze bread?   Yes. Most successfully, although once thawed, it deteriorates more quickly than bread that has not been frozen. To freeze: always use foil, wrapping loaves completely so no air can reach them. To defrost: take from freezer and allow to stand at room temperature until thawed, about 2 hours. Otherwise, preheat oven to 200° F., place bread, still in foil wrap, in center of the oven. This takes 60 to 70 minutes, depending on the size of the loaf. Once thawed, bread should be consumed as soon as possible because it tends to stale quickly.

NOTE: If you are using homemade bread or an unsliced loaf for sandwiches, it can be sliced in the frozen state very, very thin, much more easily than fresh bread.

Why are muffins sometimes coarse-textured?   They were mixed too much before baking. Don't ever beat muffin batter. Just stir until all the ingredients are nicely moistened. Proper muffin batter is never smooth. Too low a baking temperature can make them coarse-textured.

What are bagels?   Handmade (and they must be made by hand, no machine can do it) water doughnuts. A mixture of yeast, eggs, flour, salt, water, sugar, and oil. Called *Bablitcki* in Russia and *Buegel*, meaning stirrups, in German, originally they were shaped like stirrups, unlike the present circlets. The name was Judaized as its most devout consumers moved from Central Europe to the United States. A New York wag, on tasting his first bagel and having heard that, on Sunday morning, all Brooklyn reads the New York *Times* while eating bagels with lox and cream cheese, suggested they would be advised to "Eat the New York *Times* and read the bagels."

Is a beignet the same thing as a fritter? Beignet [beñe] means fritter. Essentially, they are the same. In general, a beignet or a fritter can be a mixture, shaped, and fried in deep fat, or it can be fruit, vegetables, fish, shellfish, or meat, etc., dipped in a batter, then deep-fat fried. *Larousse Gastronomique* devotes more than four pages to fritters, starting with hors d'oeuvre and small entrée fritters, and ending with soufflé fritters.

Are blini and blintzes the same? They are both a type of pancake. Blinis are Russian, made with a yeast batter and either buckwheat or white flour; blintzes are a Jewish variation and made with an egg batter. Blinis, from time immemorial, have been served in Russia during Shrovetide. Cavier and sour cream are the classic accompaniments. Blintzes, very thin, like *crêpes,* are filled with a cheese (farmer's or dry cottage), then rolled and baked in the oven. Sometimes served as a main course in "dairy" meals, they are now more common as a dessert with sour cream and sugar or sweet fruit jams.

What are batter breads? The easiest and quickest of the yeast breads. The ingredients and mixing method are similar to standard yeast breads but the amount of liquid is higher in proportion to the flour. The result is a relatively soft dough that is soft enough to beat with a spoon or electric mixer. As a result, these breads do not require kneading.

What is "cool rise" bread? A revolutionary new method for making bread at home. The major advantages to this method are as follows: the dough is mixed, kneaded, and shaped in one operation; and, instead of letting the dough rise several hours in a warm, draft-free place, then baking immediately, it permits a leeway of twenty-four hours in which the bread can be baked.

   N O T E : This method cannot be applied to the old, standard bread recipes.

What are quick breads? We have two types: hot quick breads such as biscuits, corncake, muffins, popovers, etc., and quick "loaf" or tea breads, usually made with nuts and/or fruits baked in loaf pans. Unlike the hot breads, these latter types improve in flavor and texture if stored overnight. If, on your first attempt at making them, you find a deep crack on the top of the baked bread, don't shoot yourself, it's par for the course.

What is brioche? A delicious, slightly sweet yeast bread, rich with butter and eggs, that looks not unlike a big mushroom when baked. Usually served for breakfast with sweet butter and jam.

What are canapés? "Little pieces of bread," sometimes *brioche,* cut into rectangles, toasted or fried, spread with *pâté,* caviar, anchovy or shrimp pastes, or other mixtures of this nature.

What is a chapon? A small crust of French bread rubbed with garlic and tossed with salad greens to flavor them with garlic. After it has done its work, it is discarded.

What are crêpes? Very thin, small pancakes, either sweet or savory. Savory crêpes are used as a garnish in soups or sometimes filled with a cheese mixture rolled, glazed in the oven, and served as an hors d'oeuvre. The most familiar of the sweet crêpes is the *crêpes suzette* (named, it is said, for a "gay, little lady friend" of Edward the Seventh), which are heated in butter, with sugar, orange zest, perfumed with maraschino, curaçao, and flamed with kirsch.

What is a croissant? A very rich, buttery French roll shaped like a crescent, hence the name. Customarily served with butter, jam, and coffee for breakfast in France—the famous Continental breakfast. I buy the best croissants this side of Paris at a French pastry shop and freeze them, so I can always have a Continental breakfast at home.

Are croûtons and croustades alike? Only in that they are both made of bread. Croûtons, the more usual name for croûtes, are diced bread, fried in butter until golden, served with soup; sometimes used as an ingredient (Knedliky—Czechoslovakian dumplings—for example); croustades, which can be made with pastry to receive fillings, are made by hollowing out the bread (sandwich loaves or crusted rolls), fried in deep fat until golden, then filled.

What is a cruller? A sweet, rich, egg batter, cut in strips or twists, then fried in deep fat, somewhat like a doughnut. *The Oxford Dic-*

tionary attributes it to: "U.S. 1818, apparently Dutch, from crullen, to curl." Such reliable books as *The Boston Cooking School Cook Book* and many others have cruller recipes mistakenly named "French crullers." The nearest thing to these so-called crullers are *beignets*, and it's not very near.

What are buttered crumbs?   Fine, dry bread crumbs sautéed in melted butter until saturated, buttery, and golden. Generally called for to top casseroles or to dress cooked vegetables.

Are farine and farina the same?   No. Farine is the French word for flour; farina properly means the flour of any grain or root, but in the U.S. it signifies either white cornmeal or a breakfast cereal.

What is French toast?   An old thrifty way of using up a stale loaf of bread practiced, apparently, by many nations other than the French. In Belgium, it's called "found bread," *pain trouvé.*

  To make French toast: For 12 slices of firm-textured bread, crusts trimmed, beat lightly 6 eggs and combine with ¾ cup of milk, 1½ teaspoons of salt in a shallow bowl. Dip bread slices into the egg mixture, one at a time, coating both sides. Fry on both sides in hot butter, then sprinkle with freshly ground nutmeg, and serve immediately.

What are gaufrettes?   Meaning "little waffles," they are charming, crisp, fan-shaped wafers, sometimes filled, often served with ice cream, tea, or wine. One of the large American manufacturers of crackers and cookies makes a version of the gaufrette in long oblongs. And out in St. Paul, Minnesota, there's a manufacturer who makes *oblaten,* the Czechoslovakian gaufrette, that originated in Carlsbad. My friend, Eric Schmidt, tells me it's the custom, in many parts of Central Europe, to serve oblaten with a glass of wine on the eve of feast days, such as Christmas and Easter, and to send little pieces by mail to absent friends. "Crumbs of love," as it were. His mother usually gets a bit of oblaten from the other side of the world at Christmas and/or Easter.

What is a rissole?   A sort of fritter. Pastry of one kind or another, filled with a forcemeat, fried in deep fat, served with fried parsley, fresh lemon, or a sauce, as a hot appetizer or a light entrée.

What are rusks? A sort of dried bread, browned, cut into slices. Used in many ways as an ingredient in cooking, it is most popular in Holland and Belgium. Available packaged.

What is Scotch woodcock? Buttered, toasted bread, made into sandwiches with a filling of chopped anchovy fillets, served with a hot sauce made of egg yolks, cream, and seasonings.

What is sour dough? A fermented dough used as a leaven in making bread. It became so necessary a part of the old Alaskan prospector's grubstake, that he became to be identified as a "sourdough." The mixture dates back at least 6,000 years and its discovery is generally believed to have been the happy accident of an Egyptian cook. Although sour dough bread is commonly known, the "starter," as the fermented dough is called, is also used to make hotcakes, cornbread, biscuits, waffles, rolls, even cookies and cakes. The older a starter, according to the knowledgable, the better.

What is stollen? A German yeast bread made with almonds, currants, and candied peels.

What are tortillas? As Helen Evans Brown wrote in her superb *West Coast Cook Book*, "The staff of life to Mexicans and to Californians with a Mexican heritage." There are two kinds: those made with masa, and those made with flour. Commercial tortillas are heated on a hot griddle until they "freckle" on both sides. *Tostadas* are tortillas fried crisp in hot lard; *tacos* are a Mexican's idea of a sandwich, a rolled tortilla filled with meat.

What does bake "blind" mean? This is an old cooking term seldom found in modern cook books. It simply means baking unfilled pie shells or tarts which are to be filled later with an ingredient that does not require further cooking. In *The Art of Baking*, Paula Peck, an extremely talented pastry cook, says, "Place chilled pastry shell in the oven, taking it directly from the freezer or refrigerator so it is as cold as possible. Prick bottom all over with a fork, prickling 3 or 4 times during the first 10 minutes of baking to prevent bottom of pastry from puffing up. If sides of pastry should sink down during the first 10 minutes of baking, simply press them back with a fork."

How does a cook determine when a cake is baked to a turn?   There
are several ways: (1) it begins to shrink away from the sides of the
pan slightly; (2) the cake springs back when touched lightly on the
top with your finger; (3) a cake tester, toothpick, or straw plunged
into the center comes out dry—that is, without any batter clinging
to it.

Do frosting and icing mean the same thing?   The terms are used interchangeably in this country but in England you "ice," not frost, a cake.

What is an "air" cake?   Any cake that depends entirely on eggs (whole
or the whites) to make it rise. In short, cakes that do not call for a
leavening agent such as baking powder or soda. Typical examples
are angel cake, sponge cake, and the famous *génoise* of France.

How do you cut air cakes?   Cut you do not! You pull them apart with
two silver forks.

Why do baked cakes sometimes have "air holes"?   It's because the
batter hasn't been evenly distributed and there are, quite literally,
pockets of air. This usually only happens in rich, butter cakes such
as pound cake. Once the batter is in the pan, run a spatula through
it, then give the pan a good bang on a table. Don't, however, be
tempted to do any banging with an air cake, or you'll bang out the
air that makes it light.

Why is it necessary to "hang" angel cakes until cold?   The American
Institute of Baking tells us, "Delicate air cakes such as the angel,
sponge, and chiffon must hang until cool to allow the cake structure
to become firm so the cake won't collapse." They also say that "the
varied instructions for the removal of cakes from pans are based on
the time it takes the cake to firm up during the cooling process." Some
angel cake pans are made with "legs" and need only to be turned
over; those without can be suspended by fitting the tube over a funnel
or bottle.

Is a baba the same thing as a savarin?   Not exactly. They are both
made of sweet, leavened dough and both are steeped in kirsch or rum
after cooking. The baba was adapted from the gugelhuph, a Polish
cake made with raisins—now usually cooked in individual molds. It

was the inspiration of King Stanislas Leczinski, who conceived the idea of sprinkling the cake with rum and flaming it. He then named it Ali Baba after one of the heroes in his favorite book, *The Thousand and One Nights*. The creators of the savarin (named in memory of Brillat-Savarin, the great French gastronome), made a baba dough without raisins, baked it in a ring mold, then soaked the baked ring in a sweet syrup perfumed with rum, filling the center with *crème pâtissière* (soft custard), *crème chantilly* (sweetened whipped cream) or fruits. Today, the savarin ring is painted with an apricot glaze and decorated with almonds and glacéed fruits or fresh strawberries or raspberries.

Is there such a thing as a quick baba? Yes. Here it is.

INSTANT BABA
Take a yellow cake mix, prepare according to package directions; fill a well-greased 9-inch ring mold ¾ full with the batter (bake remainder into cupcakes or something). Bake according to the manufacturer's instructions.

While baba is baking, make up a simple syrup (heat 1 cup of water and ½ cup of sugar until sugar has dissolved. Take off the heat and stir in 1 cup dark rum). Turn the baba out on a serving plate, and pour ¾ of the rum syrup over the entire surface. Just before serving, pour remaining syrup over the baba, and fill the center with whipped cream.

What is baked Alaska? Once known as Alaska-Florida, it is a piece of cake, sponge or pound, topped with very firm ice cream, thickly and completely covered with meringue; then baked in a very hot oven until the meringue is flecked with gold. Served immediately. A lot of work for something that doesn't amount to much.

What are cat's tongues? *Langues de chat*, in French. Little tea cookies —actually dried petits fours. Someone once suggested the name refers to "tea gossips."

What is a génoise? The basic cake of the French cuisine. Made without liquid or a leavening agent, it is the most delicate of all cakes. The classic recipe is the base for many great French pastries.

What is a gugelhupf? It has been described as a volcano-shaped cake, of middle European origin, made of a sweet yeast dough, with almonds and raisins, then baked and glazed. Although it is sometimes spelled without the "e" (*guglhupf*) the correct spelling is with an "e." The classic gugelhupf mold, similar to a Turk's mold, is cone-shaped, fluted, with a hole in the center.

How can you prevent a jelly roll from cracking when rolled? Any rolled cake should be rolled the minute it comes from the oven, while still warm and flexible. Invert the cake on a towel, lift off pan, peel off the paper carefully, then trim the crisp edges with a sharp knife. Roll up in the towel and cool 10 minutes. Unroll so the cake will be on the towel, then spread with filling. And reroll.

What is a Lady Baltimore cake? An original recipe created by Mrs. Alicia Rhett Mayberry, of Charleston, who became the central character in Owen Wister's early 19th-century novel, *Lady Baltimore*. Described in detail by Wister in the book, it became one of the most popular American cakes. Many-layered, filled with a mixture of frosting, nuts, figs, and raisins, it is finished with White Mountain frosting.

What is a lebkuchen? From Old German, *lebe* meaning life, and *kuoche*, meaning cake. (A "lively cake" because of spices.) Originally a spiced nut and honey cake, baked in different shapes and molds, depending on the occasion for which it was to be used. Today, most European countries have a version of the lebkuchen which can be a loaf or flat cake, even a cookie.

What are madeleines? A *génoise* batter baked in small, oval, fluted madeleine molds.

What is panettone? An Italian fruit cake made with yeast, originally baked only for the Christmas holidays. Really, more bread than cake, it is made with candied peel and raisins. Every town in Italy, it seems, has its own pet panettone recipe.

What is zuppa inglese? Not, as you might think, an English soup, but a very fine Italian dessert cake flavored with rum, garnished with whipped cream and candied fruits.

What makes the cookies on the edges of a cookie sheet brown more than those in the center? They are nearer the walls of the oven and get more of the reflected heat. When baking cookies on a sheet, do not place them near the edges, do not crowd them, and place the cookie sheet in the center of the oven.

Why are some cookies removed immediately from the baking pan, and others not? It depends on the nature of the cookies. Cookies high in sugar and fat, which are crisp when baked and cooked, are removed from the cookie sheet immediately after being taken from the oven to avoid their sticking to the pan and to lower the temperature of the cookies quickly, so they will crisp up. Cookies that are allowed to cool on the baking sheet are those that need a longer cooling time and also time to develop a firmer texture.

What are drop cookies? Some have a cake-like texture, others are crisp or even brittle. One characteristic that is common to all of them is a soft dough that is dropped in mounds on a cookie sheet, then baked. Consequently, the shapes are more or less irregular.

What are refrigerator cookies? A rather soft cookie dough that is shaped into long rolls, wrapped in foil, and chilled. Then they are sliced and baked. One great advantage is that the dough can be frozen, then sliced and baked as needed.

What are shaped cookies? Cookies made of a fairly stiff dough, chilled, then molded by hand or a cookie press into balls, wreaths, crescents, oblongs, or stars, etc.

What are eccles cakes? An English cookie made with currants.

What is pfeffernuesse? A spicy German cookie, traditional at Christmas, the secret ingredient being black pepper, undoubtedly the reason for its name, which means "pepper nut."

If it's a pie, is it a tart? Yes and no. Pie means a dish of meat, fish, fowl, fruit or vegetables in a pastry shell, covered completely with pastry, or finished with a lattice or some comparable topping. It also means a deep dish pie without a bottom crust, covered completely with a top crust. Such as deep dish apple pie, chicken pie, etc. Tart, from the French *tarte*, is a pastry shell, individual (example, Barquette) or large. Today, it is always made with fruits or sweet fillings and it can be, or not, finished with a lattice or some other design conceived by the cook, or a glaze. It is never completely enclosed. Pies are served hot, lukewarm, or cold, depending on the filling; tarts are served cold. *See* flan.

My friend, Sylvia Vaughn Thompson, author of *Economy Gastronomy,* an excellent cook book, currently working on a book about Catherine de Medici and her role in bringing *haute cuisine* to France, has explored the subject of tarts so well that I now quote from her *The Tart Cook Book:* " 'Tart' comes, according to the Oxford English Dictionary, from the Latin *'torta panis,'* and rather meant a kind of loaf or bread. *'Torta panis'* became, in old French, *'torte'* or *'tourte,'* and meant a disk-shaped cake or loaf, also a pastry. *'Torte'* then turned into *'tarte'* in thirteenth century French, and was by then an open pastry (although *'torte'* stayed *'torte'* to describe the superb family of flat sweet cakes the French create). The English, after a time, dropped the final 'e' and it was, at last, 'tart,' a flat piece of pastry, with no crust on the top."

A tart, then, is simply any pastry shell with a dinner plate air about it. And a pie is a tart with a lid on.

As for other names by which a tart is known, they are many, mainly variations born of local dialects and cooking customs. Whether the word has conformed in the manner of *torte* to suit Italian mouths, or *taart* which is how the Dutch say it, or *torth* as in Wales or a Breton's *tors,* they all describe the same thing. But the French, having developed the art of tartery to its fullest extent, have defined the matter further.

There is *tourte,* which is a round tart, large, and generally of a savory nature rather than sweet; *flan,* used interchangeably with *tarte; tartlettes,* of course, are our tartlets, little tarts usually of a sweet nature—but can, when filled with something like glazed baby carrots, be a beautiful fancy garnish to meat. *Croustades* have survived from the Middle Ages as cases made of pastry (or sometimes whipped potatoes, semolina, rice, or hollowed-out loaves of bread)— either small hot hors d'oeuvres or savory main courses. *Bouchees* are little cases made only of puff paste, baked blind, usually filled with something savory, and *vol-au-vents* (flight-in-the-wind, and your puff paste might take one, were it not filled full!) are entree-size *bouchees.* *Barquettes* are little boats, shallow oblong tartlets (first launched by a chef as he daydreamed out his quay-side window at a barge floating by?). And then there are the very specialized local names of tarts, foremost of which are the *quiches* originating in the province of Lorraine, savory custard tarts usually served as an hors d'oeuvre; and the Ligurian and Neopolitan *pizzas*, Nicoise *pissaladieres*, and Marseillaise *pissaladinas*, great flat tarts made, in the manner of the original tarts, of bread dough, triumphant of black olives, sardine or anchovy fillets, tomatoes, onions, sausages, whatever fragrant the larder has to offer."

What is pastry? It covers a multitude of sins. It is, first, a dough made with flour, fat (butter, lard, vegetable shortening or oil, egg yolks, or suet) with or without the addition of sugar, and a small amount of liquid. However, we use the word "pastry" generically to include many kinds of sweets, regardless of whether they are made with pastry or not: for example, cream puffs, elaborate cakes (large and small), meringues, etc.

Are there many types of pastry? Innumerable. Some of the more familiar ones are:
   Ordinary pastry. This is nothing more than flour, a dash of salt, and fat, with a little ice water for mixing.
   Rich, short pastry. This is similar to, but richer than, ordinary pastry, with the addition of egg yolks.
   Puff paste (pâte feuilletté). One of the great achievements of the French cuisine. Not difficult if you know how, but time-consuming to make. Always made with fine butter, no other shortening. Broadly speaking, it belongs in the professional kitchen, but many fine, home cooks make it successfully. The English make a version called Rough Puff Paste, which calls for somewhat less butter and less time.
   Pâte sucrée. Very rich, very short, it is made with butter, sugar, salt, egg yolks, and ice water.
   Pâte brisée. Similar to pâte sucrée except for the sugar which, in this case, is a mere pinch.
   Pâte à chou. This is the dough used to make cream puffs, also *profiteroles* (*éclairs* is another name). Chou, by the way, means puff, as well as cabbage. This same pastry is also used in other cookery. *Gnocchi à la Parisienne,* for example, *pommes de terre à la dauphine,* and, unfortunately, by some restaurants, to make phony soufflés.

Strudel. Tissue-thin pastry used to make the famous Hungarian apple-cheese strudel. It can sometimes be bought, already to use, in certain foreign markets.

Phylo. Pronounced fee-low (sometimes spelled fillo), is not unlike strudel. Tissue-thin, it is the base for the sweet, rich honey dessert, baklava. Some cooks use strudel dough in place of phylo. Phylo can be bought, fresh or frozen, in stores specializing in Greek foods.

How do you fit pastry in the pan? It should be fitted in loosely without stretching, otherwise it will shrink during baking. For single-crust pies, trim off the pastry leaving about an inch and a half extending over the edge of the pan. Trimming can be done with a knife or scissors.

How do you crimp the edge of pastry on a pie? Fold the pastry that extends over the edge under to form a high standing rim all around the pan. Then, with your right index finger on the inside of the rim, left index finger and thumb on the outside, press pastry with right index finger and pinch the dough with left thumb and index finger to form a V. Repeat all around the rim. Then do it a second time so the design will be very precise. There are many ways to finish a pie, but this is the simplest.

Why is pastry sometimes brushed with egg yolks? The yolk, usually whipped up with 1 or 2 tablespoons of water or milk, gives a glaze and better color to the pastry. Egg wash, as it is often called, is also sometimes used on freshly baked bread.

How do you finish a two-crust pie? With a sharp knife, trim the bottom pastry even with the rim of the pie pan. Fill the pie with your mixture, roll the remaining pastry up on the rolling pin, then unroll it over the mixture, leaving a good 1½ inches over the edge, all around. Trim to 1 inch, then crimp. Slash the top pastry in several places to allow steam to escape. If it's a juicy pie, berries, for example, better put a pan on the rack below to catch any overflow.

Why do you prick the bottom crust of an unbaked pie shell? To keep the pastry from buckling and shrinking from the pan while baking.

Why do recipes recommend slashing the crusts of unbaked pie? To allow the steam to escape, forestalling a soggy crust.

Is there an easy way to make a lattice top for a pie? Make it off of
the pie. Cut a circle of wax paper slightly larger than the pan and
weave the lattice on the paper. Place the whole business in the
refrigerator or freezer, on a flat surface, and chill until the dough is
very firm. Then, slide the lattice onto the pie, trim off the ends, and
secure the strips to the edge of the pastry with dabs of cold water.

*If an apple pie turns out dry, when cooked, how can I make it juicy
and edible?* Cook up a little simple syrup, add a dash of rum or
cognac, and pour it through the slashes on top of the crust.

What is black-bottom pie? It's a rich filling composed of eggs, chocolate, milk, rum, cream, and gelatin in a baked crust. Chill before
serving.

What is a barquette? Barquette means small boat. So, it's a tiny oval-
shaped pastry shell filled with fruit, served as a dessert; or filled with
a savory such as lobsters in a sauce, mussels, shrimp, oysters, cheese
custard, etc., and served as an hors d'oeuvre.

What is a gâteau St. Honoré? Classically, it is a *galette* (shell) of
pâte brisée, with a crown of glazed, filled cream puffs (*choux
paste*), sometimes alternating with candied fruits, the center filled
with a *crème pâtissière*.

Is a linzertorte like a Sacher torte? No, although they are both famous
Austrian confections. A linzertorte is a tart shell made with ground
almonds, filled with raspberry jam, finished with a lattice pastry.
The Sacher torte, which originated at the Hotel Sacher in Vienna,
where it is made and served to this day, is a rich egg and chocolate
cake, coated with apricot purée and chocolate frosting. It is always
served on its home ground, we are told, with whipped cream. Dobos
torte, also Austrian, is a seven-layer cake, with a chocolate butter-
cream filling and a caramelized sugar frosting.

What is mille-feuille? Meaning a "thousand leaves," the confection
familiar to all of us as the Napoleon—layers of puff paste sandwiched
with a rich cream filling, then glazed. *Feuilletage*, the French word
for the pastry, is used in innumerable ways by imaginative French
chefs.

What are pasties? Essentially, little pies with a meat, fish, chicken, herbs, bacon, vegetable, egg, or fruit filling. Made in Cornwall, England, for centuries, it is customary there for each pastie to have the initial of each member of the family cut into the pastry.

What are petits fours? Tiny pastries. In other words, small sweet cakes such as *tuiles* and macaroons, squares, triangles, or fingers of a *génoise,* frosted and ornamented.

What's a vol-au-vent? A large patty shell from which several can be served. Like patty shells, it is made of puff paste.

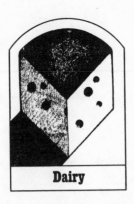

Dairy

What are the various types of milk and how are they used? For drinking, cooking, baking, we have: whole milk; homogenized milk; buttermilk (good for reducing, too); evaporated milk; dry milk, which must be reconstituted. In addition, we have skim milk with most of the butterfat removed, with half the energy value of whole milk, generally used in reducing and low-fat diets; and condensed milk, whole milk to which sugar is added, half the water removed, and canned. This last is rarely used in conjunction with sugar.

What is homogenized milk? Milk that has had, by a mechanical process, the fat broken up into small particles and distributed throughout the milk. Cream does not form on homogenized milk because the fat particles do not rise to the top of the milk.

What does au lait mean? Lait is French for milk. Therefore, *au lait* means with milk: for example, café au lait (coffee with milk).

What is Devonshire cream? The cream, skimmed from fresh, unskimmed milk, that has been allowed to stand over warm water, over low heat, for several hours. The thick, delicious "clots" are marvelous with fresh fruit, but a Jersey cow in your meadow is almost a prerequisite.

How long will sour cream keep in the refrigerator? The National Dairy Council says, "a week to ten days." What happens is the cream "wheys off" (that's the clear fluid that rises to the surface), which makes it less desirable for eating, but it can be used in cooking. If there isn't too much whey, just stir it in. You, actually, will have to judge for yourself when the cream is no longer usable.

Why does sour cream curdle when combined with a hot liquid? It's the nature of the beast, really, and there isn't much you can do about it. Grin and bear it—it doesn't affect the flavor a bit.

Can sour cream replace crème fraîche? No. In *Mastering the Art of French Cooking,* the authors say, "Commercially made sour cream with a butterfat content of only 18 to 20 percent is no substitute; furthermore, it cannot be boiled without curdling. French cream has a butterfat content of at least 30 percent." They add, however, "American whipping cream (heavy) with its comparable butterfat content may be used in any French recipe calling for crème fraîche. If it is allowed to thicken with a little buttermilk, it will taste quite a bit like French cream, can be boiled without curdling, and will keep 10 days or more under refrigeration; use it on fruits, or desserts, or in cooking." The proportions are 1 teaspoon commercial buttermilk to 1 cup whipping cream. Stir the buttermilk into the cream and heat to lukewarm (not over 85° F.). Pour the mixture into a loosely covered jar and let it stand at a temperature not over 85° or under 60° until it has thickened. This will take 5 to 8 hours on a hot day, 1½ days at a low temperature. Stir, cover, and refrigerate.

Just for the record, crème fraîche or *crème double,* its other name, is matured cream. That is, lactic acids and natural ferments have been allowed to work in it until the cream has thickened and taken on a nutty flavor. It is not sour.

Is there any way to whip cream without splashing it all over the place? Not entirely. But try placing the bowl of cream (or whatever) in the sink. Then beat, holding the beater straight up in the center of the bowl, until the cream begins to thicken. Or, try this device suggested by a professional home economist: Make a little tent of foil over the top of the bowl with the beater breaking through it. It's said to work fine. A third possibility, and the best, is the new, straight-sided, deep Pyrex mixing bowls. Because the sides are straight, mixtures that in other bowls would climb up the sides, now slide down, thus eliminating spatter. These bowls have the additional virtue of being oven-proof.

Why is it frequently difficult to whip heavy cream so that it has real body and will stand up for awhile? The cream should, of course, be heavy, but chefs will tell you it should also be at least two days old. Fresh cream, whipped, will not give you the same volume and thickness.

What exactly is yoghurt? Also spelled yogurt, it is a fermented milk food extremely popular in Europe, Asia, and Africa, and becoming increasingly so in this country. The standard yoghurt is plain without salt (aficionados, especially Europeans, often sweeten it with sugar), but flavored yoghurts are also available, including vanilla, strawberry, coffee, apricot, pineapple-orange, prune whip, fruit cup, red raspberry, and blueberry. Will keep for 2 weeks, refrigerated.

How do you care for cheese in the home? All natural cheeses must be kept under refrigeration, covered. The soft cheeses (such as Camembert), quite perishable, should be used within a few days of purchase. Ripened or cured cheeses (such as Gouda), if protected, will keep well refrigerated, preferably in the original wrapper. Failing that, the cut surface should be tightly covered with foil or plastic wrap to keep it from drying out, the whole then enclosed in more foil or a polyethylene bag. If mold develops, scrape it off or cut it out of the cheese. This is not true of the blue cheeses (Roquefort, Stilton, Gorgonzola), because their particular molds are an integral part of the cheese. Strong cheeses (Limburger, for example), should be stored in a tightly covered jar or container so as not to impose their flavor on neighbors in the refrigerator.

Can cheese be frozen? It is not recommended. Nevertheless, small pieces (1 pound or less), not over 1 inch thick, can be frozen up to 6 months (no longer) if the freezer compartment maintains zero temperature and the cheese is tightly and securely wrapped, all air squeezed out, in moisture-proof wrapping. According to the Department of Agriculture, the cheeses which can be successfully frozen include: brick, Cheddar, Edam, Gouda, Muenster, Port-du-Salut, Swiss, Provolone, Mozzarella, and Camembert (in their original package). Thaw in the refrigerator, bring to room temperature, and use immediately.

What is the difference between unripened and ripened (cured) cheese? The first point to remember is they are both natural cheeses. Unripened are soft cheeses such as cottage, cream, etc., which should be consumed while fresh. However, there are firm unripened cheeses (Norwegian Gjetost and Mysost are examples) which, because of their low moisture content, can be kept for several weeks, or even months. Ripened, or cured, cheeses are divided into four groups: soft, semi-soft, hard, and very hard. Soft ripened types (this includes Brie, Camembert, Limburger) ripen from the outside in, and usually contain more moisture than the semi-soft; semi-soft ripened (Bel Paese, Port-du-Salut, brick, etc.) ripen from the interior as well as from the surface. They, in turn, contain more moisture than the firm ripened; firm ripened cheeses (Cheddar, Edam, Provolone, Swiss, etc.) ripen throughout the entire cheese, usually have a long curing period, and are lower in moisture than the semi-soft; very hard ripened cheeses (Parmesan, Romano, etc.) cured very slowly, very low in moisture, have a higher salt content than other ripened cheeses; with blue-vein mold ripened cheeses (Roquefort, Stilton, etc.), the curing is accomplished by mold along with the aid of bacteria to produce the characteristic flavor and appearance.

At what temperature should cheeses be served? At room temperature, if you would savor them at their best. Room temperature can, of course, be anything—a hot kitchen or a cool pantry. For best flavor, we suggest the coolest room you have. In general, allow a couple of hours out of the refrigerator before serving for cheeses on the firm side and somewhat less for soft cheeses.

Is the rind on soft cheeses left on when served? Not only left on, but eaten. Any Freshman would tell you it's the best part. Typical cheeses with a rind are Brie and Camembert.

Is it all right to grate hard cheeses, such as Parmesan, before storing in the refrigerator? You can, of course, but it is not recommended if you want to savor the full flavor of the cheese. The most practical approach is to buy only as much cheese as you think you will use up in a relatively short time and grate as it is needed. Hard cheeses can be grated in an electric blender, cheese grater, or on a hand grater. Each gives a somewhat different texture.

Is there any way to use up a piece of dried-out cheese? It can be grated and used in cooking. For example, stirred into scrambled eggs, sprinkled over vegetables, incorporated into a soufflé or scalloped potatoes, etc. It's an easy way to flavor innumerable dishes.

Can a Bel Paese be compared to a Taleggio? They are both Italian, both creamy, with somewhat the same texture, but the Taleggio has a slightly more definite, attractively aromatic flavor. The imported, gentle Bel Paese (meaning beautiful country) is a thoroughly dependable cheese that keeps well. But there is an American adaptation, made in Wisconsin, which is very good, indeed, although it is not an exact reproduction of the original, and we should not expect it to be. The packaging of the domestic is such a "steal" on the imported, keep your eyes wide open to see which one you are paying for. Both are excellent table cheeses that can also be used in cooking.

What are blue cheeses? Cheeses with the characteristic blue veining. The most famous are Roquefort, Stilton, and Gorgonzola. Although the "blue" family is rather large, the others available in the United States include the imported Danish blues, the pale Norwegian blue, and the American blues.

How can you use a piece of left-over blue cheese? If you are faced with not being able to finish off a piece of blue, combine it with the same amount (by weight) of sweet, softened butter, mix in a good dollop of cognac, place in a jar, cover securely, and refrigerate. Serve on crackers as an hors d'oeuvre.

What is a Brie? A French cheese considered by many "the queen of all cheeses." The authors of that brilliant work, *The Cheese Book*, describe it thus: "Brie is often likened to the moon because it is so white, so large and round, and as thin as men in bygone ages imagined the moon to be." Adding, ". . . the taste of this cheese is like no other. It is a mixture: part mushrooms, part cream, part cognac, part earth—as earth smells upon the roots of leeks, with a shade of truffle, and with something of the scent of ripe Anjou pears, perhaps." What more can one add except the prosaic facts? A perfect Brie should be soft, glistening yellow from the top to the bottom rind. If it is caked in layers, it is too young; if it is over runny, it is too old. Like all ripened cheeses, it should be served at room temperature and, the uninitiated should know, the white, powdery crust is always served.

Available wherever fine cheeses are sold in 8-ounce packages to 4-pound wheels as well as in 4½-ounce tins.

French Brie should be bought between October and April, the best months being December through March. American Bries, the best of which can be extremely good, are packed in 2-, 4-, and 6-pound wheels.

How does American Camembert compare with French? It compares extremely well unless you are so fortunate as to be in France and able to get the real thing right from Normandy. Camembert is made from unpasteurized cow's milk, which gives it its special flavor. A good French Camembert is best when it is pale yellow, soft to the touch, and has the same consistency throughout. The mold on a French Camembert gives it a golden crust, whereas the American is crusted in shades of white and off-white. Reportedly, French Camemberts are at their best only from October to June, the best months being January to April (but Dr. Frank Kosikowski tells me he has had splendid Camemberts in Paris in the middle of summer). American Camemberts, because they are made differently, are more dependable than French in warm weather. Whichever country you patronize, remember the Camembert should be plump, soft to the touch, and unshrunken. Imported Camembert comes in 4-ounce half wheels or portions, packed in boxes; 8-ounce whole wheels or portions, packed in boxes; 4½-ounce wheels in tins. American Camembert comes in 8-ounce whole cakes; 1⅓-ounce portions. All Camemberts should be brought to room temperature before serving. An excellent dessert cheese, it also graces the cocktail table.

Is Cheddar an English or American cheese? Of English origin, the Cheddar made in England cannot be imported into the United States (because of fixed quotas set by our government). So, the Cheddar available in this country (variously known as "American," "factory," and "store") is made in America. The best Cheddars are those of New York State and the best of New York State are the "June" Cheddars (inclined to be more yellow than those made at any other time of the year, they sell at a premium), because they are made in May and June when the cows first go out to pasture. Scientists attribute the unique flavor and delightful bouquet to some component of the early grass. Like fine wine, it ages beautifully. To judge a Cheddar, any Cheddar, it should have a good bouquet, smooth texture, in other words, "life," and it should have aged a minimum of 5 months but, better, from 2 to 2½ years for peak quality. If aged longer, it will over-ripen. Fine Cheddars have a minimum of holes or "eyes." If small, circular, and uniform, it indicates poor flavor; if small to large and triangular, it means a mechanical failure which in no way affects the flavor. If possible, rub a bit of the cheese you are buying between your fingers. If it is well aged, it will be waxy, not rubbery or pasty.

Cheddar has some English cousins we are allowed to import which include Cheshire, Gloucester, Leicester, Caerphilly, Scotch Dunlop, and white Wensleydale. Usually only available in stores specializing in cheeses.

What is Coon cheese?   A cheese that starts out as a Cheddar in a wheel, is bandaged, then placed in a warm, high-humidity room to form mold or a "green mat." Following this aging period, it is dipped in a paraffin bath which turns the surface black under high heat. The result is an interesting bright yellow cheese with a unique flavor in a stylish black coat. Use as you would Cheddar.

Are cottage cheese and pot cheese the same thing?   They're similar, as are Dutch (Schmierkase) and Bakers'. They are all soft, uncured cheeses made from skim milk. In buying cottage cheese, it is advisable to read the label carefully in order to determine what it offers in the way of curd size and salt and fat content, for manufacturers do not follow the same pattern. Pot cheese is not salted and Bakers' is not usually salted. Today, however, most cottage cheese sold is creamed. In other words, mixed with cream to add flavor and give the cheese a smoother texture. Federal standards require that creamed cottage cheese contain at least 4% butterfat.

It is generally found in two curd sizes: large-curd cottage cheese, sometimes called "country" or "California style" (package will usually say large curd) is especially good combined with other foods; small-curd cottage cheese, frequently referred to as "old-fashioned" cottage cheese, has small, firm, but tender curds, and holds its shape well. It is good in salads or any cooked dishes calling for a fine curd. If the package does not indicate the curd size, it is probably a small curd since this type originally dominated the market.

Cottage cheese is quite perishable, should always be refrigerated, and *always* bought out of the refrigerated cabinet of your market. To store at home, keep in a tightly covered container in the refrigerator and use as soon as possible after purchase—preferably within a week. Whipped cottage cheese, rather new on the market, is in limited distribution.

Are cream cheese and Neufchâtel alike?   They both belong to a family of fresh, soft cheeses which include the imported Gervais and Petit Suisse. They are all white, soft, uncured cheeses made from whole milk, cream, and other milk products. Neufchâtel, which takes its name from the town in northern France, is spelled without the "f" when it originates in Switzerland. Domestic Neufchâtel differs from American cream cheese only in its fat content, which is somewhat less. Petit Suisse, imported under the name of Demi Suisse, frozen (because it is so perishable) changes its texture somewhat on thawing, which does not affect its flavor. All these cheeses should be kept refrigerated and used within a week after buying—at the most. Can be used both for the table or in cooking.

TRACY'S LITTLE DESSERT

Choose any one of these soft cheeses and serve with marmalade (ginger or orange), or Chinese preserved fruits, with saltines. A charming end to a good meal with a minimum of pressure on the cook.

Is Crèma Danica cheese like Brie?   Creamy, soft, rich, it has been compared to both Brie and Camembert, but it is more delicate than either, although its texture is somewhat like a Brie at its best. It is a great, original cheese, invented by a Dane, and first introduced to this country in 1957 or thereabouts. One superb feature of Crèma Danica is that it ripens perfectly and uniformly which means that, all things being equal, every Crèma Danica you buy is a perfect Crèma Danica. It comes packed, two to a little square box, each weighing 6 ounces. Stores will usually sell it singly, if a customer wishes it. Serve at room temperature and allow longer than the usual hour to bring it to room temperature.

How does Edam cheese differ from Gouda?   Originally Dutch cheeses, the Edam came from northern Holland, the Gouda, from southern. Today, the two types are also available domestically. The basic difference in the imported lies in the butterfat content. Edams are made from partly skim milk, and Goudas from whole. Edams and Goudas are never good unless well aged. The imported, familiar, red-coated Edams are made in a perfect ball shape; the domestic, either ball or loaf. The imported Goudas come in wheels, with a yellow rind; the domestic, ball-shaped and red-coated with flattened tops and bottoms.

What is farmers' cheese? Reminiscent of cottage, with a somewhat higher fat content, and a subtle flavor, it differs in that the curd is pressed into a flat package so the cheese can be sliced. Like all un-cured cheeses, it should be refrigerated and used as soon after pur-chase as possible. Used primarily in cooking.

What exactly is feta? A Greek cheese, made of goat's milk, soft and blinding white, cured in brine, it is somewhat sharp and slightly salted. Aphrodite Lianaides, a marvelous cook, uses it to fill her *bourekia* (charming pastries made with strudel dough), also as an appetizer with fresh fruit, especially melon and grapes, and she adds some to shrimp and chicken casseroles just before serving which, she says, gives a delicious fillip.

How great is Italy's Fontina cheese? Turophiles say it's one of the great cheeses made today, adding it should be addressed by its proper name, Fontina d'Aosta, and for a good reason. A number of other lesser cheeses trade on the good Fontina name. The imported, made from ewe's milk, has been described as combining "the sweet butternut flavor of a fine Emmenthal, with the special tang of Gruyère, and a hint of Port-Salut." At room temperature it becomes creamy, but still retains its shape. Although it is, essentially, a table cheese, it is used in cooking and, if it becomes hard, can be grated.

What is a fondue? A famous Swiss dish composed of grated natural Swiss cheese (either Gruyère or Emmenthal or a combination of both), a whisper of garlic, pepper, dry white wine, and kirsch. The fondue is cooked in an earthenware or glazed iron casserole, then set on the table over a heating element. Hard-crust French or Italian bread, cut in bite-size cubes, is speared on a fork (preferably long), then dipped into the bubbling mixture. Kirsch always accompanies a fondue in a Swiss home. The American version of this great, classic dish is an uninspired casserole consisting of milk, bread crumbs, grated cheese, whole eggs, and seasonings, baked in the oven. By what legedermain beef fondue, sometimes called fondue bourguignonne, got into the picture remains a mystery, since fondue, from *fondre*, means "to melt." The one common denominator is that you eat it as you do fondue. Thus, spear cubes of raw beef on long forks and cook at the table, to your taste, in bubbling oil. Serve with condiments such as chili sauce, mayonnaise, mustard, etc.

What is fromage de chèvre?   The generic name for any type of goat cheese produced in various regions of France, of which there are many. The better known, imported into this country, include: Banon, Cabecou, Chabichou, St. Marcellin, Valençay. These are young cheeses, relatively fresh, semi-soft to firm, with a most distinctive flavor. Available in 4- to 8-ounce tins, boxes, or attractively wrapped in grape leaves. Delicious with French bread, unseasoned crackers, or brown bread.

Gjetost, the other goat cheese you may come across, is from Norway. It's sweetish, and naturally brown because the lactose (milk sugar) and proteins combine to form a brown cheese. Although highly nutritious and very popular in Norway, many people unfamiliar with the flavor think it leaves a great deal to be desired. When made with cow's milk, rather than goat's, the name changes to Mysost.

Is Gorgonzola a blue cheese?   It is classified with the blues by cheese experts, although the characteristic veining is pale green rather than blue. A most seductive, soft-ripening cheese, it is very rich and creamy with a flavor distinctly its own. One of the great cheeses made anywhere in the world, it is Italy's answer to France's Roquefort and England's Stilton. The American Gorgonzola, good as it is, has not captured the special qualities that distinguish the imported. Gorgonzola, like the other "blues," is a fine dessert cheese, excellent in salad dressings and, naturally, makes a delicious addition to the cheese tray.

What is grape cheese?   Known in France as *tomme au marc* or *fondue aux raisins*, the crust is made of grape pulp, the "marc" that remains after grapes are pressed for wine. Whether to eat the crust or not is up to you. Some do, some don't. It has a delicate, distinctive flavor and a smooth, creamy texture. Serve as you would Brie and Camembert with a dry white wine.

What is head cheese? An old-fashioned dish, once made with cheese, hence the name, that calls for a calf's head or feet, seasonings, and herbs. Cooked, then molded, it is served cold, sliced with Sauce Ravigotte (a vinaigrette to which capers, fresh herbs, and minced onion have been added). Also known as brawn.

Are Limburger and Liederkranz alike? To some extent. Made of whole milk, they are both vivid aromatic cheeses, Limburger being somewhat heavier and stronger than Liederkranz. Although we usually associate Limburger with Germany, it actually originated in Belgium. Liederkranz (meaning "wreath of songs") is one of five cheeses still on the market that originated in the United States. (The others are cream cheese, Coon, brick, and Monterey [or Monterey Jack].)

Liederkranz is generally considered superior to Limburger, but neither cheese is for the uninitiated. Creamy and soft, Liederkranz is distinguished by a russet surface; Limburger, semi-soft, more robust, has a yellowish surface. Both should be served fully ripe. The adventurous might try some Liederkranz with a slice of onion, some good pumpernickel or sour rye bread, and a glass of cold beer. (They, along with brick cheese, have been aptly described as the "beer cheeses.") Liederkranz is only available in 4-ounce packages; Limburger in 8-ounce, 1 pound, and 2 pounds, and processed in jars. The domestic Limburger is considered more reliable than the imported.

Is Muenster like brick cheese? Somewhat, except that it's milder. Although neither is as authoritative as a Limburger, they are both reminiscent of it. You might describe them as midway between a typical Cheddar and a Limburger. Muensters are both imported and domestic, but the brick is a native American. Muenster, both a cooking and table cheese, can be bought in cakes, blocks, wedges, slices, or segments; the brick (brick-shaped, hence the name), a table cheese only, is available in various shapes, but usually rectangular, by the pound, sliced, or cut portions. Store as you would any ripened cheeses.

Is Monterey (or Monterey Jack) like Cheddar cheese?   Often called Cheddar in California where it's made, one taste would quickly show you it does not merit the comparison. A semi-soft, rather bland cheese, with a high moisture content, it is a good, everyday cheese. Actually there are two types of Jack or Monterey cheese: the whole-milk cheese, which is best for table use, and the partly skimmed or skim-milk cheese, called "dry Monterey" or "dry Jack," best for grating. If anything, the Montereys lean toward the American Muensters in flavor. The imported Welsh Caerphilly is similar to Jack cheese.

What is Mozzarella?   An unripened cheese that originated in Italy and was made from buffalo milk. Today, even in Italy, with fewer buffalos, there is less of the true Mozzarella. The domestic version, made from whole or partly skimmed cow's milk, is soft, white, with a slightly acid, walnutty flavor. At its best, it is juicy when sliced. A good table cheese that is used extensively by the Italian community in cooking. It is usually round or pear-shaped.

Are Parmesan cheese and Romano alike?   No, but of the same family. Italy produces a whole group of finely and closely grained hard cheeses. From this graining comes the name, *grana*, which is used generically to describe all these cheeses. A good Parmesan, considered the greatest, made in Parma, and called there Parmigiana, should be at least two years old, pale yellow and honeycombed with pinpoint holes. (Dr. Frank Kosikowski of Cornell University thinks the word Parmesan was invented by an American for Parmigiana-type cheeses made in the U.S.) Although fresh Parmesan is eaten in Italy, it is not imported into the U.S. An Italian Parmesan is mild, but piquant, not too salty, with a sweet, somewhat bitter aftertaste. Romanos, as hard as Parmesans, have the same characteristic graining, with a much stronger flavor. Sardo, often mistaken for Romano, and used interchangeably in the U.S., is similar but with an entirely different flavor. The domestic granas do not rank with the imported, although we understand there is a superior Parmesan made in Fond du Lac, Wisconsin.

Classically, Parmesan is used, grated, with pastas, in soups, in certain meat dishes, casseroles, soufflés, sauces, etc.

What is pont l'évêque?   Meaning "bishop's bridge," it is a French cheese produced in Normandy for centuries. Made of cow's milk, pale yellow with miniature holes, it has a hearty, rich flavor. Shaped into small, square loaves with a washed crust, it comes packed in wooden boxes. You can further identify it by the cross-hatch markings on the crust, formed by the straw mats on which it has lain. An excellent dessert cheese to serve with a full-bodied red wine—both at room temperature.

Is there more than one type of Port-du-Salut cheese? Yes. Oka, a great Canadian cheese, currently not in production but, hopefully, will be soon again; Danish, American, and a Tilsit (also called Tilsiter Kase and Ragnit), that is made in Germany, Switzerland, and the United States. The French Port-du-Salut (also spelled Port-Salut), is a mild, creamy, semi-soft cheese with a little bite; the Danish is much stronger, with an earthy quality; while the American falls between these stools. It's less unctuous than the Danish, but closer in flavor to it than to the French; Tilsit, the American copy, milder than the original, is a typical Port-du-Salut type, on the sharp side, firmer than either the French or Danish. If you are familiar with a Muenster, brick, or mild Limburger, you will have a good notion of the flavor that identifies Port-du-Salut cheeses. The tiny holes that puncture all these cheeses are one of their identifying characteristics. Used generally as table cheeses exclusively.

What is processed cheese? A pasteurized cheese made by mixing and heating several lots of natural cheeses with emulsifying agents into a homogeneous plastic mass, followed by air cooling. Obviously, it lacks the flavor of natural, aged cheeses, which are biologically alive.

Are Provolone cheese and Cacciacavallo alike? To some extent. In *Italian Food,* Elizabeth David describes them as the same kind of cheese. Both are salty, made of cow's milk and, as they age, resemble sheep's milk cheeses. Provolone is usually smoked but not always; and Cacciacavallo, less likely to be smoked. Smooth, pale yellow, and firm, it looks like a big fat tube, bound with cord; Provolone, yellowish, hard, in salami-shaped links, is also bound and hung with cords; the small Provolone, called Provolette, is packaged in the same way. Good table cheeses, they also cook well. Both domestic and imported are available.

What is ricotta cheese?   A soft, nutty-flavored, uncured cheese, made from whole milk, in the eastern United States, but in other parts of the world, including Wisconsin, from whey. If made from whey, it is used as a table cheese but, also, grated for cooking. Obviously, the ricotta made from whey is not as appetizing or desirable as that from whole milk. Used extensively in Italian cooking, very particularly lasagna and ravioli.

What is Roquefort?   The king of cheeses, it has been called, made of ewe's milk, cured in the caves of Roquefort, it is blue-veined, with a rich, heady flavor. Unlike other "blues," Roquefort remains chalky white after aging. Only Roquefort is identified by the red sheep emblem. Available in ¾-ounce, 1¼-ounces and 3-ounce portions wrapped in foil, and 6-pound, foil-wrapped wheels. One of the most versatile of cheeses, it is used in salad dressings, as an ingredient in cooked dishes, with fruit, and, of course, served *au naturel* at room temperature with French bread.

What is Stilton cheese like?   A "blue," as they say, that ranks as one of the great cheeses of the world. It is to England what the Roquefort is to France. Made of the richest milk, with the cream of other milk added, Stiltons are quite different from all other blues with, quoting *The Cheese Book*, "a distinctive flavor which is a blend of the characteristic blue-veined taste and the clear undertone of Cheddar. Whereas some blue can be almost shrilly pungent, Stilton is mellow." The rind is dark, crusty, and wrinkled, the cheese itself off-white. It should be served at room temperature with unseasoned biscuits (and port, if you are English) but it can also play the same role as Cheddar with a good, tart apple pie. Stiltons should never be cut with a knife, English authorities say, but, rather, with a wire to prevent crumbling. This would seem to indicate you don't spoon it out as is often recommended.

Are Swiss and Gruyère cheese comparable?   Yes. But let's discuss the Swiss first. Known in Switzerland as Emmenthal (or Emmenthaler), it has, like Cheddar, been copied by virtually every country that makes cheese. Easily identifiable by the holes or "eyes," a good imported Swiss cheese is pale yellow, with round or oval, evenly distributed, large, shiny eyes, and a sweet, mellow, hazelnut flavor. Gruyères (they are manufactured by both the Swiss and the French, on each side of the Jura Mountains), also have eyes, but much smaller than the Emmenthal. The pale ivory to yellow color is much the same, but the rind of a Gruyère is brown and wrinkled, unlike the smooth, amber color of the Emmenthal. The flavor of a Gruyère is slightly sharper than an Emmenthal. Broadly speaking, the two cheeses can be used interchangeably. The famous Swiss fondue is made with Swiss Gruyère only or combined with Emmenthal.

Although these cheeses make splendid table cheeses, they cook beautifully in sauces, casseroles, soufflés, quiches, cheese pies, with vegetables, etc. Imported and domestic Swiss and imported Gruyère are available by the pound, in slices, or pieces. Domestic Gruyère, a processed cheese, is available, by the piece, foil-wrapped.

Is Welsh rabbit, or rarebit, correct?   Both *Webster's* and *The Oxford Dictionary* prefer Welsh rabbit, although Welsh rarebit is often mistakenly used in some modern cook books. The *Oxford* dates rabbit 1725 and rarebit 1785, which indicates it is a corruption of the former. The likelihood is that cooks began calling it "rarebit" because it sounded more refined. Actually, the name rabbit is a culinary joke perpetuated by Welsh housewives who, when the hunter's bag was poor, cooked cheese instead of rabbit. The true Welsh rabbit, which is the English version of the Swiss fondue, is a combination of good Cheddar cheese, beer or ale, and seasonings.

Desserts

What is ambrosia? A popular Southern dessert, served traditionally, in some areas, at Christmas. It is composed of sectioned oranges and coconut, although sometimes, other fruit, such as bananas, pineapple, grapes, and berries are added.

What is angelica? According to André Simon's *Encyclopedia of Gastronomy*, it is "an Alpine plant that grows all the way from Lapland to Spain that is cultivated in France for making liqueurs and for flavoring as well as for decorating sweets and confectionary." Candied angelica is generally available in stores in the U.S. that specialize in candied fruits and is especially attractive for decorating cakes, especially Christmas cakes and cookies because of its beautiful green color. Wrapped securely, it keeps almost indefinitely and a little goes a very long way, since it is cut or sliced very thin.

What is apple pandowdy? A Pennsylvania Dutch dessert consisting of apples, flavorings, sugar, butter, molasses, etc., baked in a deep dish, lined and covered with pastry. Before it is finished baking, you "dowdy" the dish by cutting the crust into the apples. Interesting?

What is Shoo-fly Pie? Right out of the Pennsylvania Dutch country, with molasses the major flavor ingredient. In *The American Heritage Cookbook*, it says, "There are many types of Pennsylvania Dutch Shoo-fly Pie. Those who dunk prefer a dry version. . . . Others prefer what is called wet-bottom Shoo-fly. . . . The presence of molasses is responsible for one widely held theory about the way Shoo-fly pie was named—that flies are partial to molasses and have to be chased away while the cook is making the pie." Obviously, some time before screens and DDT.

The dry version is a one-crust pie with a regular pastry. Part of the crumb mixture (flour, brown sugar, butter and spices) is combined with molasses to make the filling, and part sprinkled over the top. It seems to me, Shoo-fly Pie is one of the less appealing "creations" of American pioneer women.

What is bombe glacée? Originally, a sort of ice cream made in a spherical mold (hence the name), it is now made in other shapes. The mold is coated with a plain ice cream and the center filled with a rich, perfumed cream, to which fruit is sometimes added. It is then frozen.

What are bonbons? *Bon*, in French means good, so *bonbons* might be translated into "good goodies." It means, of course, confections.

What is a bûche de Noël? The traditional French yule log, sold by all confectioners in France at Christmastime. Usually made of a *génoise*, rolled, filled with butter cream, decorated, and finished to look like a log. Another symbolic Christmas cake in France is shaped to look like a shoe.

What are candied violets? Real violets dipped in a syrup, coated with sugar, then dried. Used to decorate cakes and other confections. In addition, there are candied roses or rose leaves, mint leaves, sometimes yellow carnations, lilacs, and mimosa, all edible and all imported from France where they are used extensively. Usually available in stores specializing in fine imported foods. Expensive, but they go a long way.

What is a charlotte? An *entremets*, probably created during the reign of Charlotte, wife of George III of England. The oldest recipe is apple charlotte. Charlotte russe resembles its ancestor only in appearance. The apple charlotte is made with bread and a purée of apples; the russe with lady fingers and a *bavarois*.

What are cherries jubilee? Dark, sweet cherries, poached, then flamed with kirsch. Said to have been created by Escoffier on the occasion of his fiftieth anniversary. My friend Jacques Pépin tells me they are practically unknown in France.

Should chocolate dishes be refrigerated?   Unless the recipe specifically calls for it or the weather is catastrophic, it is better not to. If necessary, cover securely with plastic wrap or foil. In general, chocolate dishes taste better if served at room temperature.

Why do recipes specify "melt chocolate over hot, not boiling, water?" Water and fat (which chocolate is) do not mix. If chocolate is melted over boiling water, there is a chance that steam will rise, condense, and drop into the melting chocolate. Even a minuscule amount of water can tighten the chocolate and make it impossible to use, hence this caution that you find in recipes calling for melted chocolate. However, help is at hand. If this should happen to you, add 1 to 2 tablespoons vegetable shortening, not butter (butter also contains moisture). This will re-liquefy the chocolate.

Is chocolate that has turned "gray" usable?   Yes, if it is melted. The "bloom," as it's known professionally, does not affect the cooking quality of the chocolate. In high temperatures (around 90°), the cocoa butter rises to the surface and, on cooling, remains on the surface, making the chocolate "crumbly."

How do you grate chocolate?   To grate, you must have a firm, sizable piece. There are three ways: (1) with a mouli grater; (2) with a hand grater; (3) in the electric blender. Chocolate "bits" can also be done in the electric blender.

How do you shave chocolate?   Take firm chocolate, in one piece, and shave with a potato peeler.

How do you make chocolate curls?   Soften a square (1-ounce size) slightly by allowing it to stand in a warm place for about 15 minutes. For large curls, draw vegetable peeler across the broad, flat side of the square carefully; for smaller curls, draw peeler across the side of the square. To avoid breaking, lift curls with a wooden pick.

Can the various chocolates be used interchangeably?   Yes. One square (1-ounce size) of unsweetened chocolate is the equivalent of one envelope (1-ounce size) of no-melt chocolate; 1 ounce of semisweet chocolate pieces is the equivalent of 1 ounce of any sweet cooking chocolate or one square (1-ounce size) semi-sweet chocolate.

Can you substitute cocoa for chocolate? Yes. If you find yourself without any unsweetened chocolate, 3 tablespoons of cocoa plus 1 tablespoon of shortening will equal 1 ounce (one square) of unsweetened chocolate; and the same proportions plus 1 to 2 teaspoons of sugar for 1 ounce (one square) of sweet or semisweet chocolate.

Can you combine spirits with melted chocolate? Yes, but you must add at least 2 tablespoons of the liquid (water, spirits, coffee, juices, etc.), otherwise it will tighten up—the case with a few drops.

This interesting chocolate recipe from Helen Britt, of The Nestlé Company, can be frozen and stored weeks ahead. A new twist to me.

ALL-PURPOSE FILLING, FROSTING, DESSERT

1 6-ounce package (1 cup) semi-sweet chocolate morsels
⅔ cup brown sugar, firmly packed
1 3-ounce package cream cheese, softened
½ teaspoon vanilla
Dash salt
1 egg yolk
1 cup heavy cream, whipped

Melt the chocolate over hot, not boiling, water. Meanwhile, beat the sugar, cream cheese, vanilla, and salt together until creamy; beat in the egg yolk; next, stir in the melted chocolate; finally, fold in the heavy cream. Cover and refrigerate until thick. About an hour and a half.

This rich chocolate mixture can be used as a filling in cakes, in cream puffs, in sponge and angel cakes (the centers hollowed out and filled), as a frosting, or frozen as a dessert. When she serves it as a dessert, Mrs. Britt pours a soupçon of Grand Marnier or cognac in the bottom of the dish, then turns the dessert out on top of the liqueur.

To freeze, place in a suitable container, securely covered, in the freezing compartment of the refrigerator; to thaw, leave at room temperature until soft—10 minutes or so should do it.

How do you flame a Christmas pudding? Turn the hot steamed pudding out on your handsomest platter, spoon warmed brandy or cognac (2 tablespoons or so) over the pudding and light with a match. Place a sprig of fresh holly on top and proudly carry it flaming to the dinner table.

What is coeur à la crème? Despite diligent research, no reference to this recipe could be found in any dictionary of French foods, including *Dictionnaire de l'Académie des Gastronomes, Larousse Gastronomique, Le Répertoire de la Cuisine.* However, the recipe is in many American cook books and, specifically, in Joseph Donon's *The Classic French Cuisine.* The recipe varies from book to book but, essentially, it is a mixture of cream and cottage cheese, in equal parts, mixed with heavy cream, molded in a cheese-lined, heart-shaped basket, then allowed to drain. It is served unmolded, usually accompanied by sweetened strawberries, as a dessert. It's my assumption that it was adapted by some unknown cook from the *fromage blanc à la crème* made by housewives, from cow's or goat's milk, all over France. In Lyons, Jacques Pépin tells me, they serve it fresh with cream and sugar, sometimes berries, and often with salt, pepper, garlic, and/or chives.

What is meant by coupe? It's the French for wine cup or champagne glass, but it also means a dessert served in such a glass. Ice cream, for example, or fresh fruits. If a parfait were not served in the traditional tall parfait glass, but in such a glass, it would then be called a coupe.

Is crème brûlée French or English? English. It means, of course, "burnt cream," and it is a specialty of Trinity College, Cambridge. It is also sometimes known as Cambridge cream. Thomas Jefferson's cook, James, served it at the White House, which is possibly the reason it has been credited to the U.S., specifically to New Orleans. Many old cook books have recipes for burnt cream. Crème brûlée is essentially a rich custard which, once cooked and cooled, is covered with an even layer of sugar (the English use white; Americans, brown), then placed in the broiler until the sugar has melted and formed a brittle crust. It is served cold.

What is crème Chantilly? Whipped cream sweetened with confectioners' sugar, and perfumed with brandy, rum, or a sweet liqueur, or vanilla. To 2 cups heavy cream, add 2 tablespoons sifted confectioners' sugar and flavoring to taste.

Are crème pâtissière and crème Anglaise alike? Crème pâtissière is a cream filling, thickened with flour, and used in cream puffs, etc.

Unlike crème Anglaise, which is a light custard made of egg yolks, sugar, and milk (very ticklish to make, but worth the effort). Crème à l'Anglaise is crème Anglaise to which butter is added and such perfumes as kirsch, rum, orange liqueur, coffee or chocolate.

Does refrigerating baked custards cause the liquid in the bottom of the dish? No. If custards "weep," as the saying goes, there is some imbalance in the recipe or they have been baked incorrectly. Restaurants bake and refrigerate custards days in advance without any such dire results. We can only answer you by saying, "Find a good recipe and follow it exactly."

How can you tell when a soft custard is properly cooked? Egg cookery is always touch and go and calls for not only a sharp eye but a knowing hand. As you begin to stir the custard, you'll notice large, gossamer bubbles, not unlike soap bubbles. While you continue to stir and the custard begins to cook and thicken, the bubbles become smaller and heavier and finally disappear. At this point, the custard has probably reached the maximum thickness and will, if left on the heat longer, probably curdle.

Is it possible to uncurdle a curdled soft custard? Yes. Take 1 teaspoon of any liquid that is compatible with the custard, such as milk or a liqueur, and beat into it briskly, with a wire whip, 1 tablespoon of the curdled custard until mixture is creamy. Add remaining custard very gradually—no more than 1 tablespoon at a time—beating in each addition until it, too, is creamy. When all the curdled custard has been combined, follow original recipe instructions.

What are entremets? Desserts. Precisely, desserts of this type: charlottes, *crêpes flambées*, ice cream, soufflés, meringues, etc.

What is a flan? Literally, a custard. In Spain, a baked custard is called a flan. However, *Dictionnaire de l'Académie des Gastronomes* defines it as a "kind of tart." Often, today, it's a pastry shell with a sweet or savory filling. The ring in which the pastry is baked is also called a flan, which means a metal disk.

What is fondant? A type of French confection. Fondant comes from the French, *fondre*, "to melt"—and they do, literally, melt in your mouth. The same word is used for frostings used to coat cakes, *petits fours*, etc.

What is a fool? In cookery, it is an old English sweet originally made with whipped cream folded into cooked, sweetened, puréed gooseberries: hence, gooseberry fool. Today, it is usually made with custard. Either way, you combine equal quantities of the two ingredients. Actually, it can be made with any puréed fruit, cooked or fresh, even though this is not traditional.

What is frangipane? A rich vanilla custard, said to have been the invention of an Italian, le marquis Frangipani, finished with crushed macaroons. Used as a filling for cakes, tarts, crepes, etc. But a *panade a la frangipane* is a mixture not unlike choux paste used as an ingredient in stuffings.

What is Indian pudding? An old dessert, from pioneer days, consisting of cornmeal, milk, spices, and molasses. Extremely good served warm, with heavy cream, although there are many who like it with ice cream.

What is meringue? Stiffly beaten egg whites with sugar added (proportions vary according to the recipe), used to top pies (lemon meringue, for example); to make meringue shells, the famous vacherin, or kisses (miniature shells with nuts added), etc.

How can you keep meringue on a pie from shrinking? By following these basic rules: use correct amount of sugar to egg whites (the usual proportion is 2 tablespoons sugar to 1 egg white); make sure meringue touches all sides of the pastry; use correct oven temperature (350° F., or slow, is recommended in good, standard cook books).

How does Italian meringue differ from other meringues? In this respect: a sugar syrup is cooked to the "thread" stage, then, while still hot, poured slowly onto the stiffly beaten egg whites, beating constantly. It's really the same thing as our good old American boiled frosting.

What is Nesselrode? Classically, it is a consommé, a thick soup (*potage*), a fish soup, or a *bombe glacée*. The latter we know as Nesselrode pudding, which is a custard combined with cream, chestnuts, candied fruits, flavorings, and then frozen. The Nesselrode pie, an American innovation, adapted from the pudding, is made with gelatin and served in a pie shell.

What are oeufs à la neige? Oeufs à la neige, as they are called in France, or "snow eggs," as they were referred to in Jefferson's day, are known in the U.S. as "floating island." Actually, floating island is even more descriptive than the original name, since the dessert is a rich custard with poached, egg-shaped meringues "floating" on top. *Île flottante*, the floating island dessert of France, is an extraordinarily rich *entremet*, reminiscent of English trifle.

What is orange-flower water? A flavoring agent made by distilling orange blossom petals. Used in cakes, cookies, etc.

What is a parfait? It's the French for "perfect" and, originally, meant a coffee ice cream frozen in a plain, unlined mold. Today, it means a mixture of eggs, sugar syrup, with one flavoring, such as cognac, or rum, and whipped cream, frozen in a parfait glass. The American adaptation, a poor imitation, is nothing more than layers of ice cream, interspersed with nuts and/or sauces. Traditional parfait glasses are available at modest prices in most stores selling glass and china.

What is pearl tapioca? One of several foods derived from the manioc, a tropical plant. Widely available, it is used primarily in making desserts—tapioca pudding, for example. There is a quick-cooking tapioca that can be used for desserts, but is also used as a thickening agent. Recipes will indicate its use.

Why is plum pudding called plum pudding, since it's made without plums? It was once. Originally called "plum porridge," it stems from a dish known as frumenty (there are many spellings) which, at one time, was Christmas fare in many parts of England—a rather uninspired concoction composed of boiled wheat, milk, and eggs and served with venison or mutton. Later, spices and prunes or plums were added, the latter eventually being supplanted by raisins. By the end of the 17th century, it had become a proper steamed pudding, with fruits and spices, but the name "plum" stuck, and has to this day.

What does poires Hélène mean? Pears poached in a vanilla-flavored syrup, served on vanilla ice cream, with hot chocolate sauce; apples are also presented in this manner.

Poires Condé are poached pears arranged on a savarin, served with apricot syrup, perfumed with kirsch.

Poires cardinal, poached pears coated with kirsch flavor are sweetened with raspberry sauce and garnished with chopped almonds.

Poires Melba, inspired by *Pêches Melba,* which were first created by Escoffier, in London, for the great opera star. To make pêches or poires melba, place a thick layer of fine vanilla ice cream in a dish, add peeled peaches or pears, previously poached in a syrup, cover with raspberry purée, slivered, toasted almonds and whipped cream.

What are pots de crème? Little pots of a rich cream, such as vanilla, coffee, chocolate, etc., served cold, with or without whipped cream.

What is rose water? A flavoring made with rose petals used in pound cakes, puddings, custards, sweet jellies, etc. Beloved by the English, Egyptians, Turks, and Lebanese.

What is rote grütze? A German fruit dessert usually made with raspberries and red currants, although other berries can be used, sweetened and cooked until somewhat thick. Served cold with cream, vanilla sauce, or whipped cream. Perfectly delicious.

Ellen-Ann Dunham, a vice president of General Foods, makes it often when the berries are in season. Here is her well-tested, good recipe.

2 pint boxes fresh, ripe raspberries	⅞ cup quick-cooking tapioca
4 pint (or 2 quart) boxes ripe red currants	Pinch of salt
	2 scant cups sugar

Cook the washed, drained fruits (stems off the currants) together with 4 cups of water in a heavy pan for about 10 minutes. Push through a sieve.

To the purée, add the tapioca, salt, and sugar, stirring until sugar is dissolved. Allow to stand until cold.

Serve with or without cream. Makes a little over 2 quarts. Keeps well refrigerated.

Is sabayon the same thing as zabaglione? Yes. Sabayon is the French corruption of the Italian, zabaglione. A creamy mixture composed of the yolks of eggs, sugar, wine (in Italy, marsala), and flavoring, it is cooked over hot water, beaten constantly until it thickens. Usually served in individual glasses or cups as a dessert but, also, sometimes as a sauce.

What is a sherbet? A water ice, made with fruit juice, lemon-flavored syrup, sometimes fortified with wine or a liqueur, frozen, then mixed with Italian meringue or whipped cream. It is served in chilled glasses because it is inclined to melt rather quickly. The *sorbet* (very fashionable in the 19th century in the U.S.), similar to the sherbet, is sometimes served in France between the main courses at a large banquet to refresh the guests' taste buds. More often, sherbets—the variety and methods of preparation are almost endless—are served as a light, cool dessert.

Are tortoni and spumoni similar? Both are Italian-type ice creams. Tortoni, as we know it in this country (it is considerably more complicated when made in Italy), is essentially an almond ice cream, frozen in a cup, the top sprinkled with finely ground almonds; spumoni is a rich ice cream combined with fruits and nuts.

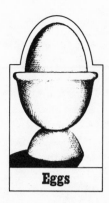

Eggs

What sizes do eggs come in? Extra large, large, medium, and small. All sizes are available in all grades. Weight for weight, small eggs are the equal of large eggs of the same quality. If a recipe calls for one large egg, you can always substitute two small ones.

Will you explain the difference between the various grades of eggs? There are three grades. Fancy fresh or Grade AA and Grade A are top quality eggs with a higher proportion of thick white and a firm yolk. They are most desirable for eating purposes—cooked in the shell, poached, fried, or baked. The other two grades, B and C, have thinner whites and flatter yolks which break easily. For these reasons they are less expensive, although the nutritive quality remains the same. It is best to use them for cooking.

N O T E : Many fine eggs are sold under a brand name or trademark without a "letter" grade.

Should eggs always be refrigerated? Yes. But they should be brought to room temperature before using, unless you want to separate them. This can be done more easily if they are cold.

Is there any difference between brown and white eggs? None whatsoever, except in the color of the shell. Nutritionally, they are of equal value; the reason for the difference in the color of the shell is due to the pigment produced by the hen. But certain regions have decided preferences. In New England, for example, housewives swear brown eggs taste richer. On the other hand, some cooks insist on brown eggs for cooking, white for eating. There is no advantage in paying more for either brown or white eggs of the same quality and size.

How do you separate eggs? Have two bowls ready, a large one for the whites, a smaller one for the yolks. Crack the egg sharply on the edge of the bowl, mid-center, to break the shell. Pull the two halves apart, holding them upright, over the egg-white bowl. The yolk, because it's heavier, will automatically remain in one shell, with the white running out. Work the yolk back and forth between the two shells until all the white has disengaged itself and dropped into the bowl. If, by mischance, you should break the yolk and some gets into the white, lift it out with the shell or, failing that, with a piece of paper toweling. The white will not beat up properly if there is even so much as a drop of yolk.

How do you fold one ingredient into another? Folding is one of the most important techniques in cookery because you are combining a fragile mixture, such as beaten egg whites, with a heavier one, such as a soufflé base or cake batter. The objective is to retain the air incorporated into the whites. The usual technique is to beat about one-third of the whites into the base mixture, whipping vigorously with a whisk. This lightens the base so the remainder of the beaten whites can be folded in, without sacrificing any of that all-important air.

To fold, using a rubber spatula, scoop the remaining whites on top of the mixture. Cut the spatula down from the center to the bottom of the bowl, then run it along the bottom toward you and against the edge of the bowl, rotating the bowl as you work. Make sure the spatula reaches the very bottom and sides each time and brings the mixture up over the top. Keep repeating the process until all the whites have been folded in. Work speedily, but carefully.

What size bowl should be used in beating eggs? If properly beaten, whole eggs will double in volume; egg whites will triple in volume; and egg yolks will about double. But you must think how the eggs are going to be used. If ingredients are to be added to the beaten eggs, you must take that into consideration in choosing the bowl. If

beating 1 whole egg, 1 egg white, or 1 yolk, use the smallest bowl
that will accommodate the beater.

Can you explain why egg whites sometimes refuse to beat up properly?
Egg whites will not beat up stiffly if there is even a particle of egg
yolk in the whites, if the beater is not absolutely clean and perfectly
dry, or if there is any moisture or grease in the bowl.

How do you whip egg whites "stiff but not dry"? The whites are
beaten to the point where they stand in glossy peaks, look "wet" and
shiny, and cling tightly to the whip or beater when it is held straight
up. This is the correct stage for all beaten whites, for all recipes,
unless the recipe specifies otherwise. If whipped to the dry stage,
which is definitely incorrect, the whites become granular and will
break up when folded into the main mixture. A soufflé, for example,
would not rise and would be grainy in the center if the whites were
dry. This is one of the most important cooking techniques, and
any person interested in doing fine cooking should learn it thoroughly.

How long will egg whites stand, once beaten? No time at all, and
once they begin to thin out, it is impossible to bring them back to
the required stiffness. If sugar is added, often called for in recipes,
the whites will remain firm much longer.

Can egg whites be frozen successfully? Indeed, they can. Since one
egg white fits neatly into an individual plastic ice-cube container, it
is the ideal way to freeze them. It also makes it easy for you to tell
at a glance how many whites you have on hand. Use a polyethylene
bag to protect the frozen whites in the freezer. Thaw and use exactly
as you would fresh egg whites.

How can you use up left-over yolks and whites? In innumerable ways:
in custards, in sauces (Hollandaise, mayonnaise); in gold cakes; in
rich pastry, etc. Whites, which freeze so successfully, can be kept
until you have some free time for cooking. One obvious use, when
you have 10 or so, is in angel cake; 3 or 4 are good for meringues; and
you always need 2 or 3 extra whites for soufflés.

How long do you beat egg yolks to achieve "lemon color"? This is an old-fashioned cooking term that has really no meaning whatsoever, because the color of the yolks depends on what the hens have been fed. Sometimes they are deep orange, sometimes pale yellow. In the old days the term meant to beat the yolks until they were very thick and lightened in color. Today, we usually say as thick as mayonnaise.

How can you store egg yolks?   Unlike egg whites, yolks will not freeze successfully. They can be preserved for several days if placed intact in a container and covered with cold water; if placed in individual plastic ice-cube containers with a seal of plastic wrap right on top of the yolk, then, refrigerated, of course. With either method, they should be used as soon as possible. Yolks can be hard-cooked immediately and used in many ways.

How do you combine egg yolks with a hot mixture?   Beat the yolks until thick. Then add a small quantity of the hot liquid to the beaten yolks, stirring vigorously. Then gradually add to the hot mixture, whipping constantly. Another way is to beat the yolks with a small amount of a cold liquid (if it is an ingredient in the recipe), then add this mixture very carefully, very slowly to the hot mixture, whipping constantly.

Why do egg yolks stick like glue to pots, pans, dishes, egg beaters?   Chances are you wash them in hot water, which makes the remnants of the egg stick harder. Cold water is the answer. Allow equipment or implements to stand in or run under cold water as soon after use as possible, then wash in hot suds.

How do you soft-cook eggs?

Cold-water method: Place the egg or eggs, straight from the refrigerator, in a deep saucepan—deep enough to accommodate the eggs without crowding. Add 5 to 6 cups of cold tap water, regardless of the number of eggs, making sure all the eggs are covered by at least a generous inch of water. Bring up to a boil, 220° F. on the thermometer, uncovered, over high heat. This will take about 10 minutes or a little more. Take off the heat, cover, and allow to stand from 1 to 3 minutes. Timing depends on how firm you like the whites and yolks; it can best be determined by testing. Plunge the cooked eggs under cold water to prevent any further cooking and to make them easier to handle.

Boiling-water method: Bring 5 to 6 cups of water to a high boil, slip each egg into the water with a spoon, take off the heat, cover, and allow to stand 6 to 8 minutes. Cool as above.

How do you hard-cook eggs?

Cold-water method: Follow same instructions for soft-cooked eggs to the point where the water begins to show signs of reaching a rolling boil 220° F. on the thermometer). Reduce heat to simmer (180 to 200° F.) and hold this temperature for 12 minutes. Plunge eggs into cool water at once to stop the cooking. Another way is to remove pan from heat, when water reaches a rolling boil, cover, and allow eggs to stand for 15 minutes. Cool immediately as above.

Boiling-water method: Follow same instructions for soft-cooked eggs, reducing heat to keep water simmering, and cook for 20 minutes. Cool immediately as above for cold-water method.

Is hard-cooking eggs the same thing as hard-boiling?   No. The term "hard boil" in relation to eggs, whether soft or hard-cooked, has long since been abandoned because it implies high, fast heat which can only lead to rubbery whites, discolored yolks, cracked and leaking shells, waterlogged and lopsided eggs. With one or two exceptions (omelets, for example, which are cooked quickly), eggs should always be cooked slowly over low heat.

How long can hard-cooked eggs be refrigerated?   No more than a couple of days. Make sure you mark the shell so you won't get them mixed up with raw eggs.

Can you cook a cracked egg?   Yes. Just add a few drops of vinegar or lemon juice to the water, and the egg will stay intact while it simmers.

What is the easiest way to shell an egg?   Tap the shell all over with the back of a knife until it is "mapped" with cracks. Then, holding the egg in the palm of your hand, peel off the shell and inner skin.

If any small particles of shell cling to the egg, dip the egg briefly in cold water rather than attempt to pick them off by hand.

Do you serve egg dishes on hot or warm plates?   Warm. If served on hot plates, the eggs would go right on cooking.

Is it eggs Bénédict or Bénédictine?   *Hering's Dictionary of Classical and Modern Cookery* describes Bénédict as poached eggs, toast, fried ham, Hollandaise sauce, and truffles; Bénédictine as tartlets, poached eggs, puree of salt cod, truffles, cream sauce. *Le Répertoire de la Cuisine* uses Bénédictine for both the codfish dish (above) and poached eggs, tongue, toast, and Hollandaise. *Dictionnaire de l'académie des Gastronomes* says Bénédictine is cod and potatoes, gratinéed. Whatever the name, today it is usually sautéed ham on English muffins (or *brioches*), poached eggs, and Hollandaise. Bénédictine, a French liqueur, was created by monks (17th century).

What is meant by coddled?   This applies exclusively to eggs and simply means to lay eggs in cold water and bring slowly to a boil, then take off the heat and "coddle" for 8 to 10 minutes. "Coddle," an old English word from which we get "cuddle," really means "to boil gently." Also, "to treat as an invalid," which is, perhaps, the reason coddled eggs are thought of as especially desirable for invalids. Actually, it's nothing more than another way to boil eggs.

How do you fry eggs perfectly?   Philip S. Brown, one of the best cooks I know, and with his late wife, Helen Evans Brown, author-editor of the recent *Shrimp and Other Shellfish Recipes*, fries them like this. In his own words, "For one 2-egg pan, add 1 tablespoon of fat (butter, oil, or bacon fat). Heat until hot but not sizzling. Break the eggs into the pan (if you're unsure of yourself, break them into a cup first, then slip them into the pan). Reduce heat to low, cover the pan, and cook slowly until done the way you like them. Turn with a pancake turner if you like them cooked on both sides. Season with salt and freshly ground pepper. Serve at once."

What are oeufs mollet?   They have been described as eggs "betwixt and between" because they are simmered longer than soft-cooked eggs, but not as long as hard-cooked.

Oeufs mollet are served cold, glazed in a clear aspic, on a bed of greens with vinaigrette sauce, or hot, on puréed spinach. They can also be served in the same ways you serve poached eggs.

How do you poach eggs?   Fill a frying pan or shallow skillet ¾ full of water, add white vinegar (1 tablespoon to 1 quart of water), and bring to a boil. Reduce heat to simmer (the water should be shivering only—a simmering temperature), the heat at which the egg should cook throughout. Break each egg separately into a cup or saucer and slip it into the water, holding the dish as close to the water's surface as is comfortably possible. Poach 3 to 5 minutes, depending on how firm you like it or until the white solidifies sufficiently to enclose the yolk and permits handling the egg. Lift out of the water with a slotted spoon and drain on paper towels. The French always use vinegar, claiming it "firms" the whites. If it proves necessary to keep the egg, place it in a pan of ice cold water to cover. Reheat by putting it in a pan of warm water (not too hot or it will cook further) until it is warm through.

To trim a poached egg: Cover your left hand with a clean, dry cloth. Then lift the poached egg into the palm of this hand, with a slotted spoon, and trim with a sharp knife or a pair of scissors.

What is a quiche Lorraine?   An open-faced tart, with a rich crust, that is usually composed of a custard, with or without Swiss cheese, and bacon. Tomatoes or crabmeat can also be used—in fact, almost anything that combines well with eggs. It is a perfect luncheon or supper dish, with a green salad, and a bottle of cold white wine. Tiny, bite-size quiches can be served as hors d'oeuvres.

What is the best way to scramble eggs?   There are as many methods as there are cooks. My way is like this:

SCRAMBLED EGGS

Melt a good lump of butter in a heavy saucepan, add the well-mixed, seasoned eggs (no liquid)—2 eggs per person—and stir with a wooden spatula over a very low fire until they just start to thicken. Stir in another lump of butter, take the pan off the fire, and continue to stir (the heat from the saucepan continues to cook the eggs) until you have a smooth, creamy mixture. If the eggs must stand for any length of time, stir in a whole, raw egg just before spooning them onto a warm platter. This little trick helps to keep scrambled eggs moist and soft. You can vary scrambled eggs with either fresh, minced herbs (chives, tarragon, parsley, chervil, etc.) or thinly sliced truffles before putting the eggs in the skillet.

Is a shirred egg cooked on top of the stove or in the oven? Shirred eggs, as the French do them, are started on top of the stove and finished in the oven. They are known in France as *oeufs sur le plat* or *oeufs miroir* ("looking-glass eggs"). Baked eggs, as we call them, are cooked entirely in the oven.

SHIRRED EGGS

Butter a small, round or oval baking dish, season with salt and freshly ground pepper. When butter is hot, break two eggs into the dish and cook slowly on top of the stove. For *oeufs miroir*, place in a preheated hot oven for 4 to 5 seconds after the eggs are cooked to glaze the top of the yolks.
To cook in the oven, prepare as above and place in a preheated 350° F. oven for 8 to 10 minutes.

What is a soufflé? Nothing more than a Béchamel sauce (in the U.S., we call it white or cream sauce) combined with a flavoring, a purée, or other ingredients into which stiffly beaten egg whites have been folded. The success of the dish depends almost entirely on perfectly beaten egg whites; enough whites (a ratio of 6 to 7 whites to 4 yolks); the right beating equipment; the proper preparation of the mold; the proper folding of the whites into the base ingredients; and the correct baking temperature.

What's a cold soufflé? Somewhat like a *mousse*, less rich, and made with gelatin. It's really a misnomer, since soufflé means "puffed," and in a hot soufflé, the puffing is due to the egg whites. Cold soufflés are made to look high and puffy by tying a band of oiled paper around the top of the soufflé dish to allow the mixture to come above the rim. This is removed before the soufflé is served.

What is a soufflé omelet? Also called a puffy or fluffy omelet, unlike the more traditional omelet, the eggs are separated and stiffly beaten, the whites are folded into the seasoned, beaten yolks, as in soufflés. It is cooked on top of the stove, then finished in the oven.

What are "thousand-year" eggs used in Chinese cookery?   These are eggs that have been cured in lime for about six weeks, which gives them a grayish color, suggesting antiquity. They are available, imported or domestic, in Chinese food stores. Usually shelled and cut up, combined with fresh eggs, and steamed, the dish is served cold.

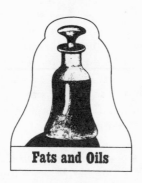

Fats and Oils

How can you soften butter quickly? You can place it in a dish on top of a gas stove; the heat from the pilot light will help to soften it. Lacking that, heat a bowl with hot water, dry, place over the butter, which should be in a dish. This helps to speed the process. Other than that, you'll probably just have to sit it out.

What is clarified butter? Butter that has been heated until it liquefies and the milky residue sinks to the bottom of the pan. The clear, yellow liquid on top is clarified butter. To clarify, cut butter into pieces and place in a saucepan over moderate heat. When butter has melted, skim off the foam, and strain through several layers of cheese cloth into a bowl. Use the milky residue in soups or sauces if you're of a thrifty turn of mind. Clarified butter does not burn as readily as ordinary butter when heated to high temperature.

To freeze the butter, pour into plastic ice-cube containers and place in the freezer. Thaw at room temperature. You will notice the clarified butter becomes cloudy on freezing but clears when thawed.

Can butter be frozen? Most successfully. Wrap it properly, however.

What is the difference between "unsalted" and "sweet" butter? None whatsoever. Any butter made from sweet cream is sweet butter, salted or not. But here in America we have come to call unsalted butter "sweet" butter.

NOTE: Some recipes definitely call for unsalted ("sweet") butter.

What is whipped butter? Butter into which air or some inert gas has has been whipped, thereby increasing the volume and making it

115

easier to spread. Much of the whipped butter sold in this country is unsalted. It is usually sold in 8- and 12-ounce paper containers.

What does butter score mean?   The score depends on the grade. The U.S. grades and score relationship are as follows: AA or 93 score, A or 92 score, B or 90 score, and C or 89 score.

How can you tell when butter has reached the right temperature for browning meats and vegetables?   As butter begins to get hot, it foams up; the foam diminishes when the butter is properly hot. The food should be browned at this point before the butter begins to brown.

Can you always substitute margarine for butter?   Yes. The modern margarines, a far cry from the product that first turned up on the market (fifty or so years ago), can be used interchangeably with butter. But you should remember one thing, butter adds flavor, which margarine does not.

Without a thermometer, how can you tell when fat is hot enough for deep frying?   Drop a 1-inch cube of bread into the hot fat. If it turns a golden brown in 1 minute, the temperature is approximately 350° F.; if it browns in 40 seconds, the temperature is about 375° F.; and when it browns in 20 seconds the temperature is approximately 385° F. Still, you'd be better off with a thermometer.

Can any fat be used for sautéeing?   Yes. But if butter, it is safer to combine it with oil, since butter cannot be heated to the necessary high temperature without burning. Allow approximately 1 tablespoon oil to 2 tablespoons butter. Or you can use clarified butter, which does not readily burn at high temperatures. Recipes usually specify the type of fat to use.

Can I reuse fat that has been used for deep-fat frying?   Yes, but you have to use your head. It should be cooled, strained, and refrigerated. It can always be reused if it doesn't carry any odor from the previous frying—fish, for example. However, fat can be clarified by adding a few slices of potato, and reheated slowly, stirring occasionally. Then strain and store. Of course, there comes a point when it should be discarded and you should start with *fresh* fat.

What is lard?   The fat rendered from the fatty tissue of pork. Usually found in meat markets, it is used as cooking fat and, sometimes, as shortening in pie pastry. The two types on the market of interest, are: refined, steam-rendered lard which makes up the bulk of the available lard; and leaf lard, produced in limited amounts, made from "leaf" fat (the name comes from the leaf-veined look of the fat before rendering). The two can be used interchangeably in cooking.

What are lardons?   Small, regular, thick strips of bacon cut from a piece (not a strip) inserted in, or cooked with, a meat.

What is fat back?   Fat from the back of the pig, *lard gras* in French. It is preferred when a recipe calls for fresh pork fat because it is firm and does not disintegrate as easily as fat from other parts of the animal. But it is not always readily available. The alternative is fat salt pork, which must be blanched in simmering water for 10 minutes or so to remove the salt. Fat bacon is another alternative, but it, too, must be blanched as above.

What is the difference between beef fat and suet?   Beef fat comes from the flank of the animal and is generally used for rendering. (Rendered fat is nothing more than solid fat cooked slowly on top of the stove or in the oven until it melts.) Suet, a hard, crumbly fat from around the kidneys and loins, is used in making steamed puddings such as plum, and mincemeat.

What is shortening?   Fat, such as the solidified vegetable oils (cottonseed and soybean oil), lard, butter, margarine, rendered poultry or beef fat, drippings from bacon fat, salt pork, ham, beef, or lamb. Generally applied to fats used in making breads, cakes, pastries.

Should vegetable shortening be refrigerated?   No, the manufacturers tell us.

Is it necessary to refrigerate vegetable oils?   No. If refrigerated, they often turn cloudy and, in some instances, solidify, which makes it a problem when you want to use them, since they must be brought back to room temperature.

Are vegetable and salad oil the same thing?   Yes. The *Handbook of*

Food Preparation, published by the American Home Economics Association, says: "All edible oils commonly used in the American home are of vegetable origin. The most frequently used oils are: corn, cottonseed, soybean, safflower, olive, and peanut." The last two are both imported and domestic. Walnut oil, imported from France, is now available in the U.S. in stores specializing in fine foods. Like peanut oil, it is used in France to make salad dressings. However, it has a distinct flavor that is, more often than not, a cultivated taste.

Fish and Seafood

A Bouquet to Some Fish Men

I COULD almost say I grew up on fish because it played such an important role in our diet. Kippers, smelts, mackerel, finnan haddie, halibut, an occasional mess of fresh water trout and, in season, oysters and lobsters, and clams we dug ourselves. And through those long Nova Scotia winters we looked forward to the first run of shad from the St. John River and fresh salmon, in July, with peas and potatoes from Mother's garden. But, curiously, I can't remember ever putting a foot in a fish market until I came to New York. Inevitably, by osmosis perhaps, I picked up a certain amount of information by just eating a lot of fish, but what I know now I learned from John von Glahn of the Fishery Council, and the three men who serve me at the Tudor Fish Market where I shop: Joe Lagattuta, Al Pappalardo and Jerry Scancarelle—anyone of whom will drop whatever he is doing to answer my questions, and will even clean my mussels for me. Could a cook ask for more?

How much fish should you buy?   Generally, you should figure on ⅓ to ½ pound of cooked fish per person, on the assumption there will be more to eat at the meal than just the fish. Fish fillets are all edible, steaks about 85%, and dressed fish, 45%. Your best buy is fillets, even though you may pay more per pound. Obviously, fish in season is always the cheapest.

How do you judge fresh fish?   Assuming you are dealing with the whole fish, the eyes should be bright, full, clear; the flesh so firm, im-

119

pressions made by your fingers do not remain; scales of a high sheen and bright color. But if you are buying a piece, you must depend on the integrity of the fishmonger. Your nose can help you here. Fresh fish has no odor whatsoever, and the flesh has a translucent, lifelike quality.

How long can you keep fresh fish? You should be guided by that old maxim "Fish and guests turn sour after two days!" Actually, fresh fish should be cooked and eaten as soon as possible after it comes from the market. Even if it hasn't deteriorated, it will decrease in flavor after storage.

How do you scale a fish? Here's some practical advice straight from New York's famous Fulton fish market. Place the fish on a board, tail to your left (if you're right-handed), and drive a nail through the tail to hold the fish securely. Then, make your own scaler with a couple of bottle caps, nailed to a board. Scrape off the scales beginning at the tail end, working against the grain, toward the head. You can buy professional scaling knives, but the real fish men say there is no equivalent for this homely tool because it scrapes efficiently without damaging the flesh.

How do you defrost frozen fish? What is true of frozen meat or fowl is true of fish. It is best to defrost it in the refrigerator until it is pliable enough to handle. For a 1-pound frozen fillet, allow about 8 to 10 hours. If time is short, the fish, in its original wrapper, or a polyethylene bag, securely tied, can be defrosted under cold running water—how long depends on the size of the fish. Frozen fish sticks and steaks should be thawed exactly as you would any frozen fish.

How do you pan-fry fish? Probably the easiest way of all to cook small, whole fish, fish fillets, or steak. Dip the fish in flour, next in an egg beaten up with milk (⅓ cup milk to 1 egg), then in dry bread crumbs or cornmeal. Heat enough butter or oil in a heavy skillet to make a film over the pan. Sauté the fish in the hot fat until nicely brown on one side, then turn and brown the second side. Test with a fork to see if it flakes easily. Salt and pepper to taste. Serve with lemon butter.

How do you broil fish steaks? To prepare steaks for broiling, dust lightly with flour, dot generously with butter or sprinkle with oil. Preheat the oven for 10 minutes at full heat. To prevent fish from sticking, place on a well-oiled broiler pan or a well-oiled or foil-lined pan. Season fish after it comes from the broiler with salt, freshly ground pepper, etc. The time and temperature charts that follow for steaks, whole dressed fish, split fish, fillets and baked fish are those recommended by the Fishery Council.

NOTE: The broiler tray should be 2 inches from the source of heat and steaks are broiled longer on the second side, so they have a nice, rich color when presented.

Type of Steak	Thickness (in inches)	First Side (in minutes)	Second Side (in minutes)	Basting Time, Each Side
Halibut	1	4	5	2
Salmon	1	3	5	1
Striped bass	1	4	5	2
Swordfish	1	3	5	2

How do you broil whole, dressed fish? Preheat the broiler at full heat for 10 minutes. Like fish steaks, whole, dressed fish must be broiled on both sides (with one notable exception, flounder, which should not be turned, but go into the broiler, white side up, and stay that way throughout the cooking period).

Dust the fish lightly with flour and dot the top side generously with butter or sprinkle with oil. Place, buttered side up, on a well-oiled broiling pan, in the broiler. Season after the fish comes from the broiler.

NOTE: Remember to baste often.

Type of Fish	Distance from Source of Heat (in inches)	First Side (in minutes)	Second Side (in minutes)
Bluefish	3	4	5
Butterfish	3	4	5
Carp (up to 3 pounds)	6	12	14
Croaker	6	5	8
Flounder	3	10, in all	Don't Turn
Mullet	6	5	9
Pike	6	5	8
Porgy	3	3	6

How do you broil split fish?   Any fish weighing less than 4 pounds can be split and broiled. If the backbone is left in, the fish is juicier and more flavorful. Do not turn split fish. Preheat broiler at full heat for 10 minutes. Place the fish, skin side down, on a well-oiled broiling pan or separate pan. Dust the flesh lightly with flour, dot generously with butter or sprinkle with oil. Season with salt and freshly ground pepper after it comes from the broiler.

Type of Fish	Distance from Source of heat (in inches)	Thickness (in inches)	Broiling Time (in minutes)	Bastings
Bluefish	3	¾	8	Often
Croaker	2	¾	8	Often
Hake	3	1	6 to 8	Often
Mackerel	2	¾ to 1	8 to 10	2
Mullet	3	¼ to 1	10 to 12	Often
Pike	3	¼ to 1¼	8 to 10	Often
Porgy	3	½ to 1	6 to 8	Often
Sea Bass	3	½ to 1	6 to 8	Often
Weakfish	2	½ to ¾	6 to 8	Often
Whitefish	3	½ to 1½	10 to 12	Often
Whiting	3	¼ to ½	6 to 8	Often

How do you broil fresh and frozen fish fillets?   If frozen, they should be thawed and brought to room temperature. Dry the fresh, or thawed, fillets with paper towels. Preheat the broiler at full heat for 10 minutes. Dust the fillets lightly all over with flour, cornmeal, or fine cracker crumbs. Place on a well-oiled broiling pan or in a well-oiled pan (foil-lined, if you like) under the broiler. Because fish fillets vary in thickness, the broiling chart is only an approximate guide. Always make the "flake" test for doneness. Fish fillets are not turned while broiling. Season after the fillets are cooked with salt and freshly ground pepper, and perhaps a bit of fresh lemon juice.

NOTE: Any fish that can be filleted can be broiled.

Type of fish	Thickness (in inches)	Broiling Time (in minutes)	Basting(s)
Cod	½ to 1	8 to 10	2
Flounder	¼ to ½	5 to 7	1
Fluke	¼ to ⅔	5 to 8	2
Sole, gray	¼ (most usual)	3 to 4	1
Whitefish	¼ to ¾	6 to 8	1

How do you bake fish? Baked fish takes less time to cook, so it is of the utmost importance to know the exact weight in order to gauge the cooking time on the nose. All baked fish, except salmon, should be cooked with the head on, to seal in the flavor, those good juices, and to shorten the cooking time. The head can, obviously, be cut off before the fish is served, but it won't look as impressive.

First douse the fish in cold, salted water quickly, then dry thoroughly with paper toweling. Preheat the oven at 400° F. for 10 minutes. Place the fish in a foil-lined pan, shaping the foil around it into a little boat to hold the juices. (Foil is also useful in removing the baked fish from the pan without breaking it.) Sprinkle the top side lightly with flour and spread generously with softened butter. Do *not* slash the fish (some novices are prone to do this) to hasten the cooking, which does nothing more than release the juices. Fatal to a good fish.

N O T E : Baste often and well with butter or a mixture of butter and wine. Use the following chart as a guide, remembering the best test is the "flake" test.

Type of Fish	Thickness (in inches)	Baking Time (in minutes)
Croaker	1½	1½ per ounce
Flounder	1	2 per ounce
Haddock	3¼	10 per pound
Mackerel	2½	2 per ounce
Mullet	2	1½ per ounce
Pike	2¼	1¼ per ounce
Porgy	2	1 per ounce
Salmon (head off)	2¼	11 per pound
Sea bass	1½	1⅔ per ounce
Striped bass	2½	12 per pound
Weakfish	1½	1⅔ per ounce
Whitefish	1½	15 per pound
Whiting	2	1¼ per ounce

How do you poach fish? Whether cooked in a court bouillon or salted water, tie the fish up, whole or the piece, in cheesecloth, leaving long ends so that it can be lifted from the hot liquid easily. If you are using a court bouillon, cook it for 20 to 30 minutes before adding the fish; if boiling, salted water, just bring to a rolling boil. Once the fish has been added to the hot liquid and it comes to a boil the second time, reduce heat to simmer (it should shimmer, just barely move), and cook 6 to 8 minutes per pound. Another way to judge cooking time, recommended by the Canadian Department of Fisheries: measure the fish at the thickest point (don't guess, use a ruler) and allow 10 minutes per inch. If, for example, the fish, or piece, measures 2 inches in depth, over-all, simmer it, after it comes to a boil the second time, a total of 20 minutes. Take from the broth immediately once it's cooked.

How long should fish be cooked?   All fish should be at room temperature before cooking. That means frozen fish must be thawed in the refrigerator, then brought to room temperature. As The Fishery Council emphasizes and I underscore, fish is cooked to develop flavor, not, like meat, to tenderize it. Fish do nothing but swim, splendid exercise which keeps them in such flawless condition they never develop muscles such as you find in meat animals. Remember, in cooking fish, that butter helps to bring out all its good flavor. Not true, generally, of other fats.

The three methods for cooking fish for which it is absolutely essential to know the exact weight are: poaching, baking, and braising. The latter method, very popular in France, is rarely done in this country.

Why and how do you flake fish?   To test for doneness. Properly, it is done with a fork and you should always test the thickest part. Probe it gently to see if the flesh separates and falls easily into its natural divisions. Cooked *à point*, fish becomes opaque, but is still moist. If it looks dry or has begun to shrink, it is overcooked.

To flake fish done up in cheesecloth: You have no choice, if you're nervous about your timing, but to lift the fish (a large, whole fish or piece), out of the liquid, untie the cloth, and flake. If it isn't cooked sufficiently, rewrap and return to the broth. Although this is troublesome, it won't hurt the fish.

Specifically, what sauces should be served with broiled fish?   The majority of fish are lean so, on the whole, they can take some pretty fancy companions. For example, Hollandaise, béarnaise, mousseline, (also called Chantilly), Aurore, Mornay, tarragon, or a light curry sauce. But they are equally delicious served with the simple sauces like lemon, parsley butter, or maître d'hotel. Butterfish, salmon, whitefish, mackerel, and shad are all fat fish. So, broadly speaking, should be accompanied by less unctuous sauces.

Can you fry fish without smelling the house up? Yes, if you take care not to allow the fat (whatever you use) to reach the smoking point.

What are anchovies? A nice, little member of the herring family, about 5 inches long, that's been around since the old Roman days and the best of which are still caught in the Mediterranean. Those available to us are always preserved in one way or another: salted, pickled, or packed in oil. The fillets come either flat or rolled around a caper. Anchovy paste, and extract, are also available. It's good housekeeping to keep a can or so on your shelves for unexpected company at cocktail time. And the paste, used with a wise hand, can work small wonders with dull left-overs.

What is caviar? The roe (eggs) of sturgeon, imported from Russia and Iran. Black caviar is the most famous and the finest. The Beluga is the largest grain; the next size, not as large, is simply known as sturgeon caviar; and the smallest is the Sevruga. In addition, there is a caviar, called Amour, from Siberia, also sturgeon roe, that is of a much lesser quality. We have as well the Canadian caviar, also sturgeon roe, which is smaller and generally lighter. (Neither of these even approach the Russian and Iranian.) Red caviar, of course, is the roe from salmon. Good in itself, but not, in any way, comparable to the "black" caviars.

If you buy fine black caviar on the basis of price, you would choose the Beluga (it retails around $70 for 14 ounces); but if you buy "by taste," you would choose the Sevruga which, although from the same sturgeon family, is a smaller grain and much less expensive. These are both whole-grain caviars. There is a third type, Osetrouva, with, we are told, a very good taste, which, because it is preserved in boric acid, cannot be imported into the U.S.

The color of whole-grain caviar varies from light to dark gray to charcoal. Some is even greenish, but color has nothing to do with the quality. Occasionally some blond caviar (a sport) turns up. This tastes exactly the same as the true colors, but most people eschew it, undoubtedly because of lack of familiarity.

What is pressed caviar? It is roe from sturgeon, which may be too mature or not mature enough, so that the grains don't separate as they do when the roe is *à point*. It is from the same type of fish and, except for this idiosyncrasy, the same caviar. Salt is added to it, then the caviar is pressed to get rid of any excess liquid. Dyed-in-the-wool caviar aficionados prefer the pressed to the whole grain, and Russians won't eat anything else. On a price basis, it costs about one-third of the great Beluga.

How do you eat caviar? "With a spoon," says Mr. M. N. Cherneff, New York importer of Continental specialities. Not only a spoon, but "a big spoon." Correctly, Mr. Cherneff says caviar is eaten, chilled, on plain toast or even white bread, and never desecrated by hard-cooked egg, or even lemon garnishes. Egg garnishes, and such, are undoubtedly used to stretch this costly delicacy.

What is coulibiac? Essentially, a *pâté* of hot fish. In *Dictionnaire de l'Académie des Gastronomes*, it is spelled *koulibiak*, which Paul Steindler assures me is the preferred spelling. A Middle European himself, Paul also says that in Poland and the Ukraine, koulibiak is sold on the streets (like hotdogs in the U.S.) along with *piroshki, shashlik*, etc. The recipe as we know it, which has certainly moved up the culinary ladder, is made of salmon—although sturgeon, and even chicken and game are sometimes used—mushrooms, hard-cooked eggs, shallots, rice, or groats, etc., the whole enrobed in *brioche* and baked. Served with hot, melted butter. Chef Chenus of Le Pavillon, New York, frequently on Fridays serves a beautiful interpretation of the recipe, when fresh salmon is available.

What is finnan haddie? Smoked haddock. Named after the town of Findon, Scotland, finnan is Billingsgate for Findon. The dish is now known all over the world.

Are frogs' legs fish or meat? In zoological terms, frogs (the French is *grenouilles*) are amphibians. But because they are not, in the eyes of the Roman Catholic Church, "flesh meat," they are not prohibited on fast days. The bulk of the frogs' legs available in the market today are frozen—from Mexico, Japan, India, Pakistan, and Florida. The best of them are the Japanese. Fresh frogs' legs from Florida come into the big-city markets in very limited quantities. Here is the recipe for *grenouilles provençale* given to me by Chef Jean Nolle, one of the three brothers who own the La Croisette restaurant in New York.

LA CROISETTE'S FROGS' LEGS PROVENÇALE

Allow 7 pairs of baby frogs' legs per person. Cross the legs and soak 1 hour in milk, seasoned with salt and freshly ground pepper. Shake off any surplus milk and coat lightly with flour.

Combine butter and French peanut oil (half and half) in a heavy pan, enough to make a light film over the bottom, and heat over a moderate fire. Add a bit of finely minced garlic. Sauté the frogs' legs until lightly brown and crisp. Place on a warm serving dish. Pour the juice of half a lemon over the cooked legs.

Brown some butter in a heavy pan, add chopped parsley, a bit more minced garlic, and pour over the frogs' legs.

Serve with a generous spoonful of puréed plum tomatoes, boiled potato, and half a lemon.

To make puréed tomatoes: Strain the juice off canned plum tomatoes, then chop. Set aside. Chop enough onion to season the tomatoes nicely, sauté in hot olive oil with a little bit of minced garlic. Combine a bay leaf with the chopped tomatoes and cook over a low heat until all the liquid has evaporated. Season to taste with salt and freshly ground pepper.

What is gefüllte fish? A dish from the Jewish cuisine, usually made of whitefish and pike, sometimes with the addition of carp. The cooked, seasoned fish is made into balls and served hot or cold. If cold, the broth is jellied and the usual accompaniment is horseradish; if hot, the strained broth can be warm or cool. The variations on the recipe are almost endless.

What is kedgeree? An English dish, of Indian origin, made with smoked haddock (other fish can be used, although not traditional), rice, hard-cooked eggs, cream, butter, seasonings, and in most instances, either curry or turmeric.

What is lox? Lox is the Russian word for salmon, and lox—as we use the term today—means salmon that has been given a long, heavy cure in a salt brine, then soaked out and, finally, smoked. Lox (*lachs,* as it is called in Germany, and *lax* in Sweden) can be found pretty much all over Central Europe, the Scandinavian countries, and England, but because the Jewish people have more or less adopted it, we are apt to associate it exclusively with the Jewish cuisine. Lox is often served in Jewish homes at the beginning of a meal, and most especially for Sunday breakfast, with or without a variety of cheeses, such bread as pumpernickel, and bagels. Like other smoked salmon, it makes an excellent first course or an interesting addition to the cocktail table. You would serve it as you would Nova Scotia salmon (smoked in Brooklyn, by the way, and also available in a can), or the magnificent, imported Scotch salmon, well chilled, accompanied by lemon wedges, capers, buttered toast, and a pepper mill. The "Nova," more expensive than lox, which has a much shorter "cure" than lox and therefore has a milder, less salty flavor, currently seems to be giving lox a run for its money.

What does à la meunière mean? Meaning "miller's wife" or "mistress of the mill," hence, miller's style, it is a method of cooking fish. The fish, dipped in milk well seasoned with salt and freshly-ground pepper, rolled in flour, then sautéed in butter and oil (half and half), is served with freshly melted butter, a few drops of lemon juice and a sprinkling of parsley. Belle-meunière means the dish is garnished with sautéed mushrooms.

What is paella? An extremely involved Spanish dish that calls for chicken, lobster, shrimp, clams, mussels, seasonings, chorizo (hot Spanish sausage), vegetables, rice and, very particularly, saffron. It is not difficult to make but you have to be organized.

What is roe? The eggs of fish. Caviar is the eggs from sturgeon; red caviar, that of salmon; and eggs from shad are called shad roe. The roe of lobster is called "the coral" by food authorities, but fish men designate it as "the berry." It is coral red when cooked.

Are salmon in season the year round? Eastern salmon, all of which now come from Nova Scotia, New Brunswick, Quebec, and Newfoundland, is a summer fish, available from late June through August. This is the "true salmon of Shakespeare," identical with the salmon caught off the coasts of Scotland, England, and Scandinavia. Pacific Coast salmon, the big King or Chinook, caught the year round, are regularly flown to the East, fresh, at fancy prices. The West Coast Silver salmon, smaller, less desirable, is available in August only.

It's amusing to note that Kennebec salmon, touted by some restaurants, hasn't been available for years.

Although West Coasters would disagree, epicures generally find the East Coast salmon more delicate than the King. They differ in color, that of the East Coast being a pale pink and, of the West Coast, a red-orange. Scientists once thought salmon found their way back to their home rivers, after their flight to the sea, by the taste of the water at the river's mouth. That theory, however, has now been exploded. Robert Ardrey in his remarkable book, *The Territorial Imperative*, writes, "The navigation of salmon remains as closed a secret as does the navigation of homing pigeons."

Salmon is always available frozen and canned.

What is seviche? An interesting Peruvian dish calling for raw, thinly sliced snapper, hot peppers (green and red), onions, and lime juice. The whole business is combined and allowed to stand overnight in the refrigerator, or longer, then served with toast.

Is shad indigenous to East Coast waters only? No. They are caught on the West Coast, in the North Sea, off France, and in the Mediterranean. Although today shad is the epicure's joy, in Colonial days it was considered so common, well-heeled people ate it on the sly, "lest they be suspected of not having a good supply of pork." When I was growing up in Nova Scotia, we served shad for lunch only and would never, under any circumstances, have served it for dinner or to guests. A marvelous fish, the only thing it can be reproached for is its numerous bones, which are formidable. Thanks to Mr. J. P. Morgan, who encouraged a skillful fishmonger at New York's Fulton fish market to learn the art of boning it, shad has, in a sense, come into its own. This is not to imply that a whole, stuffed shad is not one of the great dishes of all time but, rather, that the boned fillets are somewhat easier to cope with.

Shad roe, a fringe benefit, and one of our great treats, seems to be more prized in the United States than abroad. It is curious since the French, especially, have such respect for all fish and prepare it so beautifully. The two recipes that follow show off shad and shad roe at their best.

WARREN STOKES' OLD LYME BAKED SHAD

1 shad, about 4 pounds
Butter
Salt
White pepper, freshly ground
1 small onion, sliced very thin
2 or 3 small carrots, sliced very thin
1 small cucumber, sliced very thin

1 can (3¾-ounce size) grapes, drained, or 1 cup fresh, white seedless grapes
1 can (7½-ounce size) minced clams, drained, or 1 cup minced, fresh "little necks"
½ cup dry white wine or dry vermouth
Parsley

Have the shad split and boned. A 4-pound shad will net you 2 large fillets.

Pour 2 or 3 tablespoons melted butter into a large roasting pan—just enough to cover the entire bottom with a light film. Place the fillets, skin side down, in the pan. Sprinkle with salt and freshly ground pepper. Scatter the onion slices, in rings, over the fish, dot with butter, add the carrots, more butter, more salt and pepper, then the cucumbers. Dot these with bits of butter and another light sprinkling of salt and pepper. Top the cucumbers with the grapes and, last of all, add the clams.

Pour the wine or vermouth over all and place in a preheated 400° F. for 20 minutes or until the fish will flake with a fork. Lift the fillets, using the greatest care, with two large spatulas onto a warm serving platter and pour the sauce over them. Garnish with a bouquet of parsley.

Serve to 4 with a fresh green salad, crusty bread, and a bottle of chilled, dry white wine.

ANN SERANNE'S SHAD ROE BAKED IN FOIL

Allow 1 pair shad roe per person and prepare as follows: Cut a rectangle of foil large enough to encompass roe, envelope-fashion. Spread 3 tablespoons butter on center of foil, sprinkle with 3 tablespoons finely chopped parsley. Place roe on top, dot with 1 tablespoon butter, salt and pepper lightly. Pull foil up at sides, then add about 2 tablespoons dry white wine. Close foil and seal so that liquids won't escape. Bake in a preheated 350° F. oven for 20 to 25 minutes. Obviously, they should be taken out of the foil and served on hot plates with the juices.

Serve with garlic mashed potatoes and lemon wedges. A good bottle of dry white wine should accompany this dish.

Are lemon sole, gray sole, and English sole all the same thing? In this sense only—they are all members of the flounder family and all are legitimately classified as sole. The name derives from the Latin *solea,* meaning sole of the foot. Of the three, the most highly prized, from a gastronomical standpoint, is the European sole, popularly known as English, Channel, or Dover, which is caught in North Atlantic waters. It has a most distinctive, firm texture. This sets it apart completely from the lemon and gray sole which, unfortunately, some restaurants are inclined to pawn off on unsuspecting patrons as the "genuine" thing. "There should be a law," people say, to force restaurants to indicate clearly on menus what sole they are calling sole. English sole is imported to this country, frozen, and can be found in first-rate fish markets at rather stiff prices. A few deluxe restaurants fly it in fresh. Broadly speaking, the sole usually available is either lemon or gray, much softer-fleshed fish, which take their names from the colors they wear. Of these two, the gray is considered more desirable, especially by chefs, because of the rich gelatin yield— so important in preparing sauces and aspics.

What is truite au bleu? Trout poached in boiling water and vinegar. Called *au bleu* because the trout curls up and, literally, turns blue. Customarily served with plain boiled potatoes and Hollandaise sauce.

What are the different types of American tuna? American tuna comes in three different types of pack: solid (this is the white Albacore tuna); chunk style (the yellow-fin tuna that is somewhat more full-bodied in flavor than the white); and flaked (this is best for sandwiches). Vegetable oil is used to pack 85% of all American tuna; the remainder is in broth. The Japanese tuna imported into this country is not of the same quality as our own.

What are filets de thon? *Thon* is the French word for tuna. Unlike American tuna, imported French tuna is filleted into thin, narrow pieces, packed in olive oil or wine, sometimes with herbs and seeds. An elegant first course or hors d'oeuvre.

Are seafood and shellfish the same thing? Yes, the terms are interchangeable, although shellfish seems to us more descriptive since it refers specifically to mollusks and crustaceans: lobsters, shrimp, clams, crabs, oysters, mussels, scallops, crayfish, etc., whereas fish means any vertebrate "animal" with gills: salmon, trout, shad, flounder, etc.

How much shellfish should I buy? It depends, to a very large extent, on how it is going to be used, in or out of the shell; in a sauce; in a mixed dish; with or without accompaniments, etc. Further, appetites must be taken into consideration. For example, 1 pound of shrimp, with only a light sauce, will serve 2 sturdy appetites, but mixed with a large amount of sauce, it could be stretched to serve 4. One 1½-pound lobster in the shell is usually served to 1 person, but the same amount in a lobster Newburg, for example, would serve 2. Six oysters on the half-shell is par for a first course, but the same quantity would look pathetic in an oyster stew, which calls for 1½ pints of oysters to serve 4. Three soft-shelled crabs make a nice meal for 1, and 1 pound of cooked crabmeat will make enough crab cakes to serve 4 people. Four pounds of mussels, steamed, will serve 4 generously, and 6 dozen steamed clams will serve 6. As for scallops, 1½ pounds, sautéed, will serve 4, but in a *coquilles Saint Jacques,* the same amount, aided and abetted by mushrooms, cream, and cheese, will accommodate 6.

How can you tell if clams, oysters, or mussels are alive? The "mouths" should be clamped shut. If open, they should clamp shut when touched. Any that don't react like this should be discarded.

What are the different types of clams and how are they used? The two types found on the East Coast are: Soft clams or "steamers," distinguished by shells that are thinner, flatter, and less round (these are the fellows that spit at you when you go "clamming"); hard clams, referred to in New England by their Indian name, *quahog,* which come in three sizes: large chowder, used for chowders and soups; "cherrystones," and "little necks," served on the half-shell or as cocktails.

The Pacific Coast has many varieties, but the best known, and best, are the famous razor clams—the pismo from Pismo Beach, California, and the razor from Long Beach, Washington—considered by gourmets superior to East Coast clams.

How are clams bought? *In the shell,* sold by the dozen or by the pound. Make sure they are alive. Gaping shells indicate the clam is dead; *shucked,* by the pint or quart, with their liquor. Refrigerated or iced, shucked clams should be eaten promptly; *canned,* hard, soft, razor, and pismo clams, whole or minced, or as chowders, are all available canned only. *Clam juice* and broth are also available in bottles or cans. These are frequently used in cookery when fish broth is called for in a recipe.

How do you get the sand out of clams you have dug yourself?   Cover with fresh cold water, some salt, and a good handful of cornmeal for them to feed on. Allow the clams to stand overnight in a cool place. By this method, the clams actually de-sand themselves.

How can you preserve a partially used bottle of clam juice?   Cover securely and freeze. Of course, you know there should be some air space at the top to allow for expansion, otherwise the bottle will explode.

How can you tell if crabs and lobsters are alive?   They should be as lively as crickets and kicking. The legs should be moving, and the tail should curl up under the body when the lobster is picked up.

How do you cook live crabs you've caught yourself?   Boil them as you would lobster by plunging them head-first into fast-boiling sea or salted water or a mild court bouillon, allowing about 8 minutes for each pound of crab, after the water has come to a boil the second time. Take out of the liquid, cool, remove the back, the spongy parts under the shell, and pick out any solid meat. Crack the claws and remove the meat. After you've done this exercise a few times, you'll understand better why most people buy cooked crab by the pound— and why cooked crab is so expensive.

What are soft-shelled crabs?   They are not, as many people think, a species of crab but, rather, the blue-claw crabs found all along the Atlantic Coast. Crabs shed their shells many times before reaching maturity, and the soft-shelled crab is one caught just after it has emerged from its latest shell. The smaller the crab, the tenderer and more flavorful. In season from April or May to the middle of October. Hard-shell crabs and blue crabs are soft-shells that have hardened.

    To cook soft-shelled crabs: Dip the cleaned crabs, shell and all, in flour, sauté in hot butter, season with salt and pepper, and serve with the pan juices mixed with chopped parsley. Garnish with fresh lemon slices. Two, or possibly three crabs, makes an ample serving for 1 person.

    Cooked fresh crabmeat is available in many forms, but the most popular is the jumbo, lump meat packed in 8- and 16-ounce vacuum, pry-open cans. It must be refrigerated. Canned crabmeat is also available.

What are Dungeness crabs? A species of crab indigenous to the Pacific Coast. The meat from the body is white, and that from the leg, reddish.

Are King crabs and Alaska crabs the same animal? Yes. Once known as Japanese crabs, they are now a product of Alaska. The meat, taken from the legs, is available precooked, frozen; and the legs, intact, cooked and frozen, still in the shell. These last are currently only available in restaurants. Some King crabs, canned, are imported from Russia and Japan.

What are oyster crabs? Miniature crabs that, quite literally, "board with" oysters and for which there seems to be no explanation. Occasionally, in restaurants, you will find oyster crabs and white bait on the menu, but getting the oyster crabs is chancy, since all oysters do not accommodate boarders.

What are crayfish? A small (3 to 4 inches long), handsome, fresh-water shellfish that looks like a miniature lobster. The tail, the only edible part, is considered a great delicacy. Also known as crawfish, they are found in European waters as well as in our own. The season is from July through September. The French name is *écrevisse.*

What are escargots? Snails. An edible mollusk, both marine and terrestrial. Marine snails, otherwise known as periwinkles, much smaller than their land counterparts, are sometimes available in local fish markets. The best-known snail is the *Helix pomatia,* called in France the Burgundy. Consumed in enormous quantities by the French, they are gathered in vineyards, but also raised on snail farms. Their delicious, tender flesh is the result of a glorious diet of tender, young lettuce, fruits, and aromatic herbs.

Snails are imported from France in cans, accompanied by a bag of polished shells so they may be served in the approved way. Frozen, heat-and-serve snails are also available. Excellent, but expensive.

How do you eat snails? In a restaurant they are presented to you with a pair of snail tongs and a small fork. The tongs to hold the shell, the fork to extricate the meat. If you serve snails often at home, it is desirable to have the tongs and small forks (oyster can be used).

Are lobsters in season the year round? Yes. *Alive*, marketed in four sizes: *Chicken* (¾ to a pound); *quarters* (1¼ to 1½ pounds); *large* (1½ to 2 pounds); *jumbo* (over 2½ pounds); *freshly cooked in the shell*; *cooked lobster meat*, fresh or frozen, in pry-open, vacuum sealed containers; in summer only, hand picked *cooked fresh lobster meat, chilled*, is available in three forms: (1) meat from the whole lobster; (2) lobster claws and tails; (3) small, individual pieces—all are packed in pry-open, vacuum sealed containers (these types must all be kept under refrigeration); *canned*, vacuum packed. Although it is considerably more trouble, no lobster tastes as fresh, delicious, and succulent as that you cook yourself in a good, court bouillon.

How can you tell a "hen" lobster from a male? The question is academic, because you can't (fish men can) tell until you've cooked and opened the lobster. And then, only if "she" has eggs, the roe.

Will live lobsters drown in fresh water? Yes. Restaurants are able to keep lobsters alive and kicking because they hold them in tanks to which salt and other elements found in sea water have been added—miniature, ersatz oceans, as it were. Fresh lobsters should be cooked as soon after purchase as possible. But if there is, of necessity, a short time lag, place the lobsters on a tray, cover with sacking (an old bag is fine) that has been wrung out in cold water, and scatter some ice over the top. Take care, however, to see that no water drips on the lobsters' heads, because even a small amount of fresh water can drown them.

Will you explain the difference between langouste, langoustine, and langostina? Langouste is the French name for rock or spiny lobster; langoustine, *nephrops norvegicus*, the French for Norwegian or deep-sea lobster; and langostina, the Spanish and Chilean name for a double-clawed crustacean that looks more like a long-clawed crab than lobster. Both South African rock lobster tails and langostina are available frozen. The former must be cooked to eat, but the latter can be served either thawed or cooked. To cook, thaw completely and bring to room temperature. Wash under cold water, place in a heavy pan with the water that clings to the shells, cover, and cook over medium heat until the flesh becomes opaque—a minute or two.

How do you boil lobsters? Grab the lobster behind the head and plunge it, head-first, into fast boiling sea or salted fresh water. Allow 5 minutes for the first pound after the water comes to a boil the second time, and 3 minutes for each additional pound.

Mr. John von Glahn, head of the Fishery Council, cooks small lobsters, when he gets them straight from the ocean, 3 minutes all told, after the water has come to a boil for the second time; 5 minutes, for large ones.

To cook in court bouillon: Plunge the lobster into the boiling liquid, take off the heat, and allow it to cool in the bouillon. This is a matter of hours.

How do you extricate the meat from a boiled lobster? You go about it like this: Twist off the claws; crack each claw with a sturdy nutcracker or the back of a heavy knife (this is done in the kitchen in the home and in restaurants). Separate the tailpiece by bending it back until it cracks. Break the flippers (swimmerettes, in fishermen's parlance) off the tailpiece. Push the meat out of the body with a fork. Crack the knuckles of the claws and push the meat out with your little finger (far better than any implement). Unhinge the back, spread open the body, crack it, and extricate the little chunks of meat here, too (loads of people miss this good meat). Hook the meat out of the claws with the thin part of the upper claw. Don't miss the tomalley and the roe, if any, both considered great delicacies by epicures. Old lobster hands always suck the meat out of the small claws.

To enjoy lobster to the full, you have to forget all about etiquette. Tie a napkin around your neck and plunge right in.

How do you broil lobsters? To prepare: Lay the lobster on its back. Insert a sharp, heavy knife between the body and tail shell, to sever the spinal column and kill the animal; split in half, lengthwise; remove the stomach [the small sac between the eyes] carefully, and the intestinal vein which runs from the stomach to the tip of the tail; leave the green liver (tomalley) and the roe, if any; crack the claws.

To broil: Lay the lobsters as flat as possible, meat side up, on a

broiler pan, brush the meat generously with melted butter. Broil, in
a preheated broiler, about 4 inches from heat for 10 to 12 minutes,
basting frequently with melted butter. Salt and pepper to taste.
Serve on very hot plates with plenty of melted butter and lemon
wedges. Shoestring potatoes are the accepted accompaniment.

How do you eat a broiled lobster? The meat is removed from the
lobster much the way it is done for boiled, except for the body meat
which, because the lobster is split and exposed, is lifted out with a
fork. The remainder of the meat is in the shells. Although broiled
lobster is popular with Americans, dyed-in-the-wool aficionados consider it a desecration.

How do you steam lobsters? "Down Easters" think this is the only
civilized way to cook lobster, although many knowledgable people
prefer them boiled.
    To steam: Put an inch or so of water in a deep kettle, one with
a tight-fitting lid. Add a wire rack that will sit above the water. When
the water starts to throw up great gusts of steam, put the lobster on
the rack, cover, and steam for 20 minutes exactly. Take out of the
kettle. Allow to drain, then rinse off.

Is the homard of France like our North Atlantic lobster? Yes. They
are both salt-water crustaceans, characterized by two large, heavy
claws. The Latin name for the *homard* is *Homarus vulgaris* and for
our lobster, *Homarus americanus*. Both turn "lobster red" when
cooked.

Are South African rock lobster tails the same as the spiny rock? Yes.
The spiny rock lobster (indigenous to Atlantic, Pacific, and European waters) is a warm-water crustacean and the South African,
cold-water. Both are available frozen. The South African, which also
comes from New Zealand and Australia, has more fat and is, therefore, tenderer, with better texture, and infinitely more flavor. Fish
experts attribute these qualities to the fact that they live in the
coldest waters in which these lobsters can survive. Like our own
North Atlantic lobsters, South African rock lobster tails should be
boiled briefly.
    To cook: Drop the thawed tails into boiling, salted water (1 tea-
spoon to 1 quart)—enough to cover--or a court bouillon. When the

liquid comes to a boil again, simmer as many minutes as the tail weighs (your market should give you the weight of the tails when you buy them). A 4-ounce tail should be cooked 4 minutes after the water comes to a boil the second time. Overcooking, as with all fish, is disastrous to flavor and texture.

Is lobster à l'Américaine or à l'Armoricaine correct? Quoting that splendid authority, *Mastering the Art of French Cooking,* the authors say, "The origin of *homard à l'Américaine* is a subject for discussion. Some authorities call it *à l'Armoricaine,* after the ancient province of Armorique in Brittany where lobsters grow. Others say *Armoricaine* is nonsense because the tomato flavoring is quite untypical of Brittany and that the recipe is far more likely the product of a Paris chef with Provençal inclinations who titled his dish after an American client, or after the exotic origins of the tomato." Lobster à l'Américaine seems to be accepted by most knowledgable food experts.

What is lobster fra Diavolo? Italy's version of lobster à l'Américaine. The recipes are almost identical except that the lobster fra Diavolo is not flamed with cognac.

Are lobster thermidor and lobster Newburg alike? Both are prepared in a rich sauce (the thermidor is much the richer). With thermidors, the cooked lobster meat is served in the shell; with Newburgs, in croustades or patty shells or with rice.

What exactly is a mussel? A rock-clinging mollusk, adored by the French, with a rather thin, bluish-black shell. It is one of the most delicious and, in America, most neglected of our seafoods. It is commercially gathered all along both East and West Coasts.

To clean mussels takes muscle. They must be cleaned with the greatest possible care to remove all sand from their interior and to rid the shell of any slime or dirt. Scrub with a rough brush under running water and scrape off any incrustations with a small, sharp knife, leaving the shell absolutely clean. The "beard," which resembles old, dried grass, must be cut off. After the first cleaning, drop the mussels into a pail of fresh, cold water for a couple of hours so they will throw off any sand and lose a bit of their saltiness. When draining, always lift them from the water, otherwise they may collect the sand, if any, in the bottom of the pail. Following this interlude, they should be washed and drained again before cooking. Discard any that haven't their "mouths" pinched together. Mussels are available in fish markets the year round.

One of the most superb and delicate soups, Billi Bi, is made with mussels. Mussels can be served in many ways, but the most popular, in restaurants, is *marinière* (steamed in a rich broth). Lick up the good juices with French bread; serve with a bottle of wine. Two quarts of mussels marinière should serve about 4.

When are oysters in season?   In the "R" months, September through April. Actually, oysters are edible any time of the year, but they spawn in the summer, and are, therefore, thinner and less succulent. Further, by the very nature of things, if they were not allowed this spawning period (enforced by the government), there wouldn't be any oysters.

How do you buy oysters?   In the shell by the dozen, or out of the shell, shucked, by the pint. Some markets sell them out of the shell by count. If you want to serve oysters on the half-shell and don't want to open them yourself, the market will provide deep shells on which to serve them.

How long can you keep oysters once opened?   No longer than twenty-four hours, refrigerated.

How long do you cook oysters?   In a stew, just long enough for the edges to begin to curl. Really, no more than to heat through; about 1 minute. Fried, 1 minute exactly on each side.

What are angels on horseback?   An English dish consisting of nice, fat oysters, wrapped in bacon, threaded on skewers, broiled and served on hot buttered toast. Devils on horseback, another English savory, are stuffed prunes, wrapped in bacon, and baked in a hot oven. Also served on toast.

Are Olympia oysters like Blue Points?   No. The Olympia, the mutt of the oyster community, harvested only on the West Coast, is very tiny and, when occasionally shipped to the East, very costly. Blue Point, which formerly meant oysters that came from off Blue Point, Long Island, is now used generically for any 4-year old or, in fisher-

men's language, on-the-half-shell-size oysters caught off the East
Coast. The colder the water they come from, the better the oysters.

Are oysters Rockefeller and oysters casino alike?   There are a few
common denominators; both are served on the half-shell, both have
a rich garnish, and both have a brief interlude in a hot oven. Oysters
Rockefeller, invented at Antoine's, a famous New Orleans restaurant,
is more elaborate with Pernod or absinthe and fennel, the secret
flavor ingredients. Oysters casino are prepared with crisp bacon,
onions, green peppers, and seasonings. Clams can also be prepared
casino-style.

Are scallops a shellfish?   Yes. Also spelled scollops, bivalves of which,
in this country, only the sweet adductor muscles, firm-fleshed nuggets
of meat, called by scallopers, the "eye," are eaten. In contrast,
Europeans eat the entire body. We have two types of scallops in the
United States: bay scallops, very small, very sweet, very tender, considered by many epicures more delectable than the large, sea scallops.
The best bay scallops come from the cold waters off Long Island,
New England, and up into Canada, and are available from the
middle of September through March. There is also a bay scallop,
caught off the Carolinas, which is available in the summer, but it is
not of the same quality. Sea scallops, harvested in the cold Atlantic
waters, all the way from the New Jersey coast as far north as Newfoundland, are available the year round, fresh and frozen. There are
many who consider them superior to the bay because they are less
sweet and, if really fresh, have a delicious sea flavor.

In cookery "scallop" originally meant oysters with a rich sauce
baked in a scallop shell, but has come to mean a dish (scalloped potatoes, for example, or other vegetables, fish, or shellfish) in a sauce
baked in the oven.

My friend Eleanor Hempstead cooks scallops beautifully. But, as
you can see from her recipe, she takes great care and insists on
fresh scallops.

ELEANOR HEMPSTEAD'S BAY SCALLOPS

1 quart fresh bay scallops	¼ pound (1 stick) butter
Flour	2 cloves garlic (optional), minced
Salt	Finely chopped parsley
Freshly ground white pepper	Lemon wedges

An hour before you are going to cook the scallops, pick them over carefully, then wipe each one off. Place in a colander, and spray with cold water quickly, rubbing the scallops between your hands the way you do rice. Do not immerse them in water. Turn them out on a clean dish towel, cover with another, and pat dry. Set aside until dinnertime. Place some flour, seasoned generously with salt and pepper, in a paper bag, add the scallops, and shake the bag to coat them well. Return to the colander and give them a good shaking to get rid of any excess flour.

Heat a heavy iron or enameled iron pan until very hot. Add the butter and finely minced garlic. Turn heat to medium and add as many of the scallops as the pan will accommodate. They should lie flat on the bottom without crowding. (It may be necessary to use 2 pans.) Sauté quickly for 2 minutes.

Turn out of the pan onto a warm platter; shower with finely chopped parsley and garnish with lemon wedges. Serves 6.

Should frozen scallops be defrosted before cooking?   Yes. And they should not be refrozen, no matter how much you're tempted.

What are coquilles Saint-Jacques?   They are scallops in an egg, cream, and wine sauce baked in scallop shells (*coquille* means shell). Sometimes mushrooms are added, sometimes other shellfish. Before serving, they are dotted with butter, sprinkled with Parmesan cheese, and run under the broiler.

Is it possible to buy fresh shrimp?   Yes, but it is not always easy. A certain percentage of the catch is still coming in to the large cities, such as New York, Chicago, etc., but the quantity is decreasing every year. They are always available, apparently, in New Orleans—particularly if you are lucky enough to be sitting on the dock when the shrimp boats tie up.

Shrimp is generally available frozen, headless, with or without shells, in a solid pack; also frozen loose-packed, in 1½-pound bags; as fan-tailed breaded shrimp, ready to cook; and canned. Frozen, headless shrimp are sold according to size: small, medium, large, and jumbo. The price is determined by size.

Where do those very thin shrimp come from?   From all over the place. Those from Alaska (interestingly enough, called "titties"), Denmark, and Japan average about 40 to 50 to a pound, while those from Iceland, average about 300 to a pound. All are imported frozen.

Close to seventy countries export shrimp, of one size or another, to the United States making up about half the shrimp we consume annually.

What are green shrimp?   Raw, uncooked shrimp.

How do you shell and devein shrimp?   Simply pull off the shells with your hands, then make a shallow cut, lengthwise down the back of the shrimp and remove the intestinal vein with a toothpick or the tip of a paring knife. Sometimes there won't be any signs of an intestinal vein. Many cooks don't bother to remove the vein at all. Actually, it's more important, aesthetically, than anything else.

How do you cook shrimp?   Frozen shrimp in the shell should be thawed and washed under cold running water. Place in a heavy pan with the water that clings to them, cover and cook about 4 minutes or until the shrimp turn pink. Drain and shell.

Frozen, out of the shell, should be thawed and deveined. Drop into enough boiling, salted water to cover, or cook in a court bouillon. When the water comes to a rolling boil again, cover, reduce heat to simmer, and cook 2 minutes.

Shrimp that is to be added to a sauce should be thawed, shelled, deveined, and added directly to the sauce without prior cooking.

To deep-fat fry: shell, devein, or butterfly, and roll in a light batter. Fry in deep fat, 350° to 375° F. for 2 to 3 minutes or until golden. Drain on paper toweling.

Why does shrimp sometimes taste of iodine?   Not only shrimp, but sometimes flounder, at certain times of the year. It depends on where the fish are caught. Obviously, it's not harmful—probably good for you.

How do you butterfly shrimp?   Shell and devein shrimp, leaving tails on; split lengthwise down the back with a sharp knife, without cutting all the way through. Press the shrimp flat. Butterfly shrimp are usually deep-fat fried.

What is potted shrimp?   An English savory that is served at teatime with little triangles of soft toast or bread and butter. It makes a

delicious hors d'oeuvre to serve with cocktails. You will find it at
Fortnum & Mason, Harrod's and other fine shops in London.

CHARLOTTE ADAMS' POTTED SHRIMP

¼ pound green shrimp	Powdered mace
¼ pound fresh cod	Cayenne
12 tablespoons (1½ sticks) sweet butter	Anchovy paste

Wash the shrimp under cold running water. Place in a heavy pan with
only the water that clings to them. Cook over a moderate heat, covered,
for about 5 minutes or until the shrimp turn pink. Take off the heat, shell,
and toss the shells back in the pan with the remaining liquid. Add the
cod and cook for a few minutes or until the fish flakes easily with a fork.

Purée the drained fish in an electric blender or pound to a paste
in a mortar. Melt 1 stick of the butter and work into the cod purée
thoroughly. Season to taste with the mace and cayenne (be generous here),
and one good spot of the anchovy paste.

Cut the shrimp into rather small pieces and combine with the purée.
Place over the heat until hot, taking care not to let it brown. Press in a
1 cup (about) mold. Melt remaining butter and pour over the top.
Refrigerate. Serve with soft toast triangles.

Is a prawn a type of shrimp? No. It is an entirely different animal,
Nephrops norvegicus, of the same decapod crustacean family as the
langoustine and scampi. Although many people seem to be under
the impression that prawns are as large as our jumbo shrimp, this is
not true. The size varies greatly. The famous Dublin prawns are
imported, frozen, but are only available to the restaurant trade. In
the old days, Mr. John von Glahn, of the Fishery Council, tells us,
restaurants "merchandised" our large shrimp as "prawns."

Are scampi a type of shrimp? No. Scampi is the plural for *scampo,*
a decapod (meaning ten legs) crustacean, indigenous to the waters
off Italy. In *Italian Food,* Mrs. Elizabeth David writes, "Although the
scampi of the Adriatic are almost identical in appearance with the
Dublin Bay prawn (and the French *langoustine*) and are in fact, as
far as I can ascertain, precisely the same crustacean, there is a world
of difference in the flavor—those of the Adriatic being incomparably
superior. They are larger, their tails are fatter, and they are much
more meaty." "Imported scampi," often listed on restaurant menus, are

nothing more than big, American shrimp—which probably explains why many people think scampi means shrimp.

Shrimp are properly called in Italian, *gambero*, and the very small ones, *gamberetto*.

What is tempura?   A Japanese dish that we usually think of as made only with shrimp. Actually, it is also prepared with fish and vegetables, dipped first in a simple egg batter, then deep-fat fried. Various sauces are served with tempura, including soy sauce combined with slivered ginger.

What is tomalley?   The liver of the lobster, found in the body toward the head, which turns a soft reseda green when cooked. Unlike the liver of animals, it is an amorphous mass which is scooped out of the lobster with a spoon.

Fruit

How do you buy and store apples? If possible, you should buy the apples that are in season because they will be, as they should be, firm, crisp, bright, well-colored. Apples that were immature when picked will lack color and flavor. Apples love to be cold, so they should be refrigerated unless they are so firm some ripening seems called for.

What apples are best for cooking, best for eating? Some varieties are good for both. The following are only good for cooking: Gravenstein (July 15 to September 15), a great pie apple; Rhode Island Greening (October to February); Rome Beauty (October to April), the premier baker because it holds its shape (also good for sauce); Wealthy (August to October), good for apple pie when green; York (October to March).

The best all-purpose apples (they cook and eat well) are Golden Delicious (October to June); they do not tend to get brown when sliced; Grimes Golden (September to December); Jonathan (September to May); McIntosh (October to May) takes less cooking time than other varieties; Newton Pippin (October to June); Northern Spy (October to May); Stayman (October to April), good eating but a particularly fine baker; Winesap (November 15 to July).

The best eating apples are: Cortland (October to January), raw, slices do not brown when exposed to air; Delicious (September to May).

How do you keep apple slices from turning brown? Cover them with
145

acidulated water (water mixed with small amount of lemon or lime juice). Then drain and pat dry before using.

Are crab apples used in any way other than in jelly? Of course. They are absolutely delicious simmered in a simple syrup, stems on, until tender, then cooled, and served with heavy cream. Spiced crab apples served as a condiment are also delicious.

What is a lady apple? Known in France as *api* (from Apicius, a Roman who obtained this type of apple by grafting), it is a small, red, strikingly beautiful apple, suitable for decorative purposes or as a dessert apple. It is grown only in limited quantities, and usually only available in the holiday season at rather stiff prices.

When are apricots in season? In June and July only. Fragile and highly perishable, they must be stored in a cool dry place, out of the light. Refrigeration helps to inhibit aging. Select plump, firm, uniformly golden-yellow fruit; avoid those tinged with green and shriveled. Best to eat them as soon after purchase as possible.

Apricots are also available dried, in halves. Extremely attractive and delicious in this form, they are excellent eaten out of hand, in fruit compotes, or as an ingredient in steamed puddings. Australia sends us a most attractive candied apricot, which is sold by the pound, usually found only in stores specializing in deluxe foods. For eating only. Canned apricots—peeled or unpeeled halves or slices, whole pitted or unpitted—are in the market the year round, packed in water, apricot juice (nectar), or syrup; and also apricot preserves, which are frequently called for as a glaze in French cooking. Here is a recipe for Apricot Ice Cream, which is delicious.

APRICOT ICE CREAM

Mix 2 cups of heavy cream with 8 egg yolks in the top of a double boiler. Add 2 very thin slices of lemon rind and cook, stirring constantly, over simmering water, until mixture has thickened and coats a spoon. When the custard reaches the right consistency, stir in about 4 tablespoons of sugar, or to taste. Take off the heat, remove lemon rind, and cool.

Meanwhile, place a 12-ounce jar of apricot preserves in a saucepan with warm water, over low heat, until it has melted but is not actually hot. When custard is cold, stir in the apricot preserves very thoroughly. Pour into an ice-cube tray and place in the freezer. Takes about 4 hours to freeze, and should be stirred occasionally.

NOTE: This does not make a hard ice cream, but rather, a creamy one. Serves 4 to 6.

APRICOT SAUCE

Combine a 12-ounce jar of apricot jam with 6 tablespoons sugar and ½ cup water in a saucepan. Cook, stirring constantly, over moderate heat, for 5 minutes. Strain through a fine sieve. Then stir in a tablespoon of cognac, Grand Marnier, or kirsch. Serve hot or cold over ice cream.

Should bananas be refrigerated or not? Not until they are ripe. Bananas are one of the fruits which keep better and taste infinitely better if picked green, then ripened at a controlled temperature to the perfect-eating stage. When ripe, the skin is yellow. At this point, they should be eaten or refrigerated. Refrigeration inhibits further ripening—use within 2 or 3 days—and will turn the skins dark. Although less glamorous, this in no way affects the fruit.

Can bananas be cooked? Certainly, and they are extremely good. Here's one way: Take firm, ripe bananas, not green, 1 per person, peel, and place in a shallow baking dish. Sprinkle with fresh lemon juice, a whisper of sugar, and dot generously with butter. Bake in a preheated 350° F. oven until cooked but still firm. Or broil. Serve with steak and horseradish sauce. Bananas are also very good sautéed, served with fish, such as fillet of sole.

Are bananas and plantains the same thing? They are both members of the banana family, but there the resemblance ends. Bananas can be eaten out of hand or cooked. Plantains, which resemble the banana in shape, are considerably larger (up to a foot long). Sometimes called the "cooking banana," plantains are coarser, less sweet, and must be cooked to be eaten. In Sturtevant's *Notes on Edible Plants,* he says, "The plantain was probably cultivated in South America before Columbus." Like the banana, the plantain has three main stages of ripeness. First green, turning to yellow as it ripens, and deep black when fully ripe. It can be cooked in all three stages, but it is best when fully ripe. Plantains can be cooked in many ways, including baked, in or out of the peel; boiled; or peeled, sliced, and deep-fat fried.

Do berries come in quart boxes or pints?   Broadly speaking, all berries—strawberries, blackberries, red currants, blueberries, etc.—are sold in pints, the Fresh Fruit and Vegetable Association reports. However, raspberries are apt to be packed in half pints because they are so fragile. Local strawberries may be packed, in summer, in quart boxes. If there's any question in your mind as to the quantity, measure the berries in a measuring cup.

Are blackberries and boysenberries identical?   No, but so similar, they can, for all practical purposes, be considered as the same berry. Also, dewberries, the dark-red loganberries, and the wine-colored youngberries. Although some wild blackberries are marketed, the bulk of those available in the market are cultivated. The peak month is June, but they can usually be tracked down through August. There are few things more delicious than a bowl of fresh blackberries with sugar, and heavy cream.

In buying blackberries (or their running mates), choose large berries, rather than small, with bright color. Take a look at the box to see if there is any staining which indicates crushed, leaking fruit. If you can stand the cold eye of the grocer, turn the box out to see if there is mildew or other damning signs.

Are blueberries and huckleberries the same fruit?   Yes and no. The size of the seeds determines the difference. The U.S. Department of Agriculture says: "Berries with small seeds are blueberries; those with 10 rather large seeds per berry are huckleberries." Huckleberries, however, only grow wild; blueberries are both wild and cultivated. Those in the markets in June through August are big, blue, sweet, and beautiful. To buy, choose berries that are plump, fresh, uniform in size and clean (free of trash). Depending on variety, they may have a "bloom"—a natural, waxy protective coating. Avoid those that are dull, lifeless, and shriveled. Refrigerate and use quickly. Canned blueberries, packed in water or syrup, and frozen ones in syrup, are always available.

Is the cranberry indigenous to North America?   The cranberry in our markets is, but there is a type of cranberry, also known as mossberry, that grows in England, which is smaller and sweeter than our fruit. The Plymouth settlers called the cranberry *ibimi* (bitter berry), the name given the fruit by the local Indians. The origin of the word cranberry is obscure. There is some reason to believe they were first called "crane berries" because cranes living in the salt-marsh bogs ate them. Still another story says the bud and stem (not the fruit) of the cranberry resemble the head and neck of a crane. They were also once known as "bounce berries" because their ripeness was tested, and still is, by their ability to bounce. Whatever, these beautiful marsh "rubies" are in season in great abundance in October, November, and December. Fresh cranberries, which can be frozen by simply placing the package in your freezer, will keep fresh and firm for months. Remember, you should cook cranberries *only until they pop*. Cooked longer, they turn bitter.

FRESH CRANBERRIES AND ORANGE, À LA JAMES BEARD

2 pounds fresh cranberries   Sugar to taste
1 large navel orange   ⅓ cup bourbon or Grand Marnier

Put the cranberries and the whole orange through the meat grinder using the finest blade. Mix in enough sugar to sweeten to your taste, then stir in the bourbon or Grand Marnier.

Cranberries never looked so pretty and never tasted better.

What are Chinese gooseberries?   Also known as *kiwi* fruit, they are coming into our markets, from New Zealand, in increasing quantities. About the size of a lemon, oval-shaped, with a brown, hairy skin, lovely green flesh, and tiny black seeds (edible), they will keep in the refrigerator for weeks. They should be taken out for ripening a few days before they are to be eaten. When ripe, the skin is soft to the touch. The peeled fruit can be stewed, mashed, and sweetened to use as a cake filling; or diced and added to fruit salad; or halved and eaten fresh with a sprinkle of lemon or lime juice. The flavor will remind you of a very ripe melon with just a whisper of tartness. Very good.

How do you determine if raspberries are fresh?   They should be very bright in color, solid and plump; without caps and without any signs of moisture. Over-ripe berries are dull in color and sometimes "leaky." Watch out for mold, a sure sign of age. Use as soon after purchase as possible.

Should raspberries be washed before refrigerating? Definitely not. They are picked ripe, extremely perishable, and water tends to increase mildew. If necessary to refrigerate, cover so no air can reach them, and place in the coldest part of the refrigerator, short of freezing. Wash just before using, under tepid running water. Do not drain through a colander. Rather, lift the berries out of the water, and drain thoroughly on paper towels, patting them gently to absorb all the water. July is raspberry month, and remember, raspberries taste best when served at room temperature.

What are the marks of fresh strawberries? They should have a good, clear red color, with bright green caps attached, and be free of any moisture. Small, misshapen berries are usually of poor texture and frequently have small, hard, green spots. Watch out, too, for leaky berries. Stained containers are a sure sign of this. Ideally, you should turn out the box and see if there's mold underneath. Frozen strawberries, whole or sliced, are always in the market.

Should strawberries be hulled before or after washing? After, definitely. Otherwise they will absorb some of the water. Remember, they should be washed just before using, under tepid running water (if you have a spray, by all means, use that). After washing, lift the strawberries from the water with your hands onto paper towels to dry. Do not drain through a colander or the fruit may pick up some of the dirt you washed off. If you're in a hurry, pat dry with more paper towels. If strawberries are not to be used immediately after purchase (and they should be), refrigerate. Always serve strawberries at room temperature—never chilled—to enjoy the delicate bouquet to the full.

Nowadays strawberries are available pretty much the year round, but they are at their peak in May and June. Therefore, the least expensive. A good time to do any preserving you have in mind.

A MARVELOUS RECIPE FOR
FRESH STRAWBERRY SYRUP

Wash, drain, and hull 4 cups fresh, ripe strawberries. Place in a saucepan, add 1 cup water, and bring to the boiling point slowly. Reduce heat and cook very slowly for 10 minutes exactly, no more. The fresh flavor of this delicious syrup is dependent on minimal cooking.

Now comes the only tricky part. You need to strain off all the juice from the fruit through several layers of cheesecloth. So you will have to devise some way to hold the fruit in the cheesecloth above a large bowl so that it can drip—a little judicious squeezing is allowed to extract the maximum amount of juice. Once all the juice has been extracted, measure it into a saucepan (discard the pulp), and for each cup strawberry juice, add 1 cup sugar. Cook over a moderate heat, stirring until the sugar is dissolved and the syrup comes to a boil. Allow to boil 2 minutes exactly. Skim off all the froth. Pour the hot syrup into hot, sterilized jars or bottles. Seal securely.

This should make 1 pint of delicious syrup, but the amount will depend on the ripeness and juiciness of the fruit. Recipe can be doubled or tripled with equally good results.

Use as a sauce over ice cream, vanilla pudding, custards, rice pudding, bread pudding, or even cereals; as a flavoring for milk shakes and ice cream sodas, or just as a refreshing drink made with crushed ice and carbonated water.

Are black Bing and pie cherries interchangeable? No. The sweet, dark rich Bings, named after a Chinese worker who developed them in 1875 in Oregon, are best for eating; pie or sour cherries (and sour they are!) are used primarily for cooking. Both types are tree-ripened. The Washington State Fruit Commission says: "Fresh cherries will keep perfectly from 2 to 3 weeks in film bags, refrigerated." Other than the Bings, the sweet cherries include Tartarian, Lambert, Republican, and Sweets. It's not a bad idea if you intend to eat them, to make the "taste test." As is true of all fruits, look for cherries that are fresh, firm, and bright. On the market in May, June, and July.

Sweet and sour cherries are always available, frozen, and for non-pastry makers, there are frozen cherry pies. Cherries in cans or jars are chiefly light and dark sweet cherries, with or without pits; and the red, sour (tart) cherries, always pitted.

What are maraschino cherries? A sweet cherry, bleached, pitted, then steeped in a syrup of sugar, water, oil of bitter almond, and food coloring (either red or green). They are used in innumerable ways: in candies, cookies, cakes, sauces, fruit salads, as garnishes, with certain alcoholic drinks. Candied maraschino cherries, both red and green, are available around the holidays, especially Christmas, in shops that specialize in fine foods.

Maraschino is also the name of a liqueur distilled from cherries, often called for to perfume certain dishes.

Can I dry my own currants? No. Dried currants are made from a special type of currant, called Zante, raised just for this purpose. If currants dry out before use, cover with boiling water and allow them to stand until they plump up, about 3 minutes. Then drain.

What is a bar-le-duc? A red currant jam made in Bar-le-Duc, France.

How do you store citrus fruits? Naturally, they keep best refrigerated, but, like all fruit, they taste best when brought to room temperature before eating.

Do you grate or squeeze citrus fruit first? Grate, because you have the whole fruit to work with rather than a slithery piece. If, however, the recipe calls only for the rind and the fruit is intact, do remember to cover the "naked" fruit well in plastic wrap, a polyethylene bag, or foil so it won't dry out before you get around to using it.

What are candied peels? Citrus fruits (oranges, grapefruit, lemons) cooked in syrup, "candied" in granulated sugar, then dried. Served as candy or used to decorate cakes. Available commercially, or they can be made at home. Other candied peels include citron, pineapple, cherries, etc., used in cooking; primarily in fruit cakes.

What is citron? The only member of the orange tribe that was known to the ancient Romans. The fruit is grown for the peel which, after some prior preparations, is candied. A most important ingredient in fruit cakes, it is available by the piece, halved or diced, by the pound, or in jars.

How do you choose grapefruit in the market? Good grapefruits are firm, springy to the touch, well-shaped, and heavy for their size. Heavy fruits are usually thin-skinned and juicier than coarse-skinned, puffy fruit. A russet or bronze cast to the skin has nothing to do with quality. Seedless grapefruits are more expensive than those with seeds, which have a more intense flavor than seedless. Because of its inner color, pink grapefruit, with seeds, brings a higher price than white with seeds.

What grapefruit is best for squeezing? The Florida Duncan, both large and small, in the market from October through May. Loaded with juice, it is also loaded with seeds. However, people who like fresh grapefruit juice say it's worth the effort to extricate the seeds, because the juice is so rich and good. They can be, of course, halved and eaten with a spoon.

Are grapefruit good in the summertime? They are not at their best but there is a "summer" grapefruit from California available from June through September. It fills in, as it were, for the Desert grapefruit, a California-Arizona beauty, in the market from October into July. The Desert grapefruit sections perfectly.

Is it true the color is injected into pink grapefruit? Common sense should tell you the idea is too ridiculous for words. But it is true that the juice of the Marsh Seedless and Thompson or Pink Seedless (two types of Florida grapefruit in season November to June) does not remain pink once the fruit is squeezed. However, there is a comparatively new variety, the Florida Burgundy, that holds its color when squeezed.

How can lemons be kept from shrinking when refrigerated? Any citrus fruit will shrink and deteriorate if stored unprotected in the refrigerator, even in the hydrator, too long. However, if protected by a polyethylene bag, plastic wrap, or foil so that no air can reach the fruit, it will stay fresh a surprisingly long time.

Is a Key lime different from other limes? Yes. Actually, the name is a misnomer. It is really a Mexican or Tahitian-type lime which happened to be raised extensively on the Florida Keys. The delicious Key lime pie is a happy by-product. It is the only one of the "acid" group that is light yellow when fully ripe. Other yellow limes are insipid. With the exception of the Mexican (or Key lime), always buy limes by the "bright-green" rule. Limes can be used interchangeably with lemons in cooking and flavoring.

Do you strain fresh orange and grapefruit juice? It's best not to, if you want to benefit by all the vitamins and minerals in these delicious juices. But pick out the seeds, if any.

How do you choose oranges in the market? All oranges, as required by law, are picked mature. With that in mind, green fruit is as ripe as golden fruit. In fact, sometimes golden fruit picked all golden, turns green. Florida oranges may have color added. If so, the fruit is stamped "color added." Russeted oranges, like grapefruit, are just as good as the bright-colored fruit of the same variety.

Avoid, however, oranges that are light in weight, puffy, and spongy, because they will lack juice.

How do you section an orange? Holding the orange in your left hand, over a bowl to catch any juices, peel it with a small, sharp knife, round and round, right down to the flesh. Cut off any white skin you may have missed. Loosen the sections by cutting down as close to the membrane as possible, on both sides of each section. Drop the sections into the bowl as you cut them, and remove seeds, if any. Squeeze the membrane to extract all the juices. Grapefruits and lemons can be done in the same way.

What are blood oranges? A variety of orange that come mostly from Malta, Sicily, and Spain, noted for their blood-red or crimson-colored pulp and reddish rind.

What are kumquats? Also spelled cumquat, it is a sort of miniature orange, originally cultivated in China and Japan, as an ornamental tree. At one time, potted and dwarfed, they were presented at great banquets, so the guests could pluck the orange-gold fruit direct from the little trees. The rind is sweet and aromatic, the pulp acid, and most people eat the entire fruit, rind and all. Available fresh from November through February. Choose firm fruit, heavy for its size. Always refrigerate. Preserved kumquats are in the market the year round.

What are Mandarin oranges? In addition to many other things, the word mandarin means a loose-skinned orange. Botanically, the mandarin is a *citrus reticulata*, meaning thin, loose skin that separates readily from the pulp, and pulp that sections easily. The two principal types, known popularly as kid-glove or zipper oranges, are: tangerines, a dark orange flesh with a red peel; satsumas, pale with a light, yellow peel. These, rarely seen fresh in the market because they can be so easily ruined on the tree if not picked at the exactly right time, are the mandarins you meet in cans. The King tangerine or orange, a deep orange, larger than the familiar tangerine, has an irregular, bumpy surface and flattened ends. The flavor is very rich, but the fruit itself is not very attractive.

What is a tangelo? It looks like an orange but is actually a hybrid, a cross between the Dancy, the sweet, best known of the tangerines, and a tart grapefruit. A delicious eating fruit, tangelos run about the size of an orange, are dark orange in color, aromatic, juicy, and easily peeled. Reflecting their origins, the flavor is a combination of sweet and tart. In season from Florida, from late October through to February, with November the peak month. Tangelos can be used as you use tangerines.

How do you judge a good tangerine? They should be heavy for their size, which means lots of juice inside, with the characteristic deep orange, almost red, skin. A puffy appearance and feel is normal, but there should not be any soft, water-soaked areas, or mold. Like tangelos, they are an excellent eating fruit, and section as if by magic. The season is all too short: November to March.

What is the honey orange people are talking about? It's a fairly new variety, the Murcott Honey orange, with many characteristics of the tangerine and a quite apparent honey flavor. Very sweet, with few seeds, it's best eaten out of hand. In season from January to May.

What are juice oranges? Three varieties raised in Florida especially for juice are Hamlins, Parson Browns, and Pineapples. One or the other of these "raised-for-juice" oranges is in the market from October through February.

What are navel oranges? Seedless, extra-large, winter oranges that are very easy to peel and ideal for sectioning. The name comes from the small navel formation at the blossom end. California-Arizona navels come on the market in November and stay on through May; those from Florida, November through January.

What are temple oranges? A fine eating orange from Florida, easily identified by its "pebbly" skin. In season the beginning of December through March.

What are Valencia oranges?   This is the great summer juice orange (containing two to six seeds), equally good for sectioning. The California-Arizona crop comes into the market in April through October; the Florida, February to July.

What is ugli fruit?   A member of the citrus family, it's as unattractive looking as its name. However, inside that rough, puffy exterior, you'll find delicious flesh that tastes like a mixture of oranges, grapefruits, and tangerines. Imported from Jamaica in limited quantities.

Is a compote the same thing as a macédoine?   No. A compote is composed of fresh or dried fruit, or both, poached in hot syrup. (A *compotier* is a deep dish, on a raised base, in which compotes of cold fruit are served.) In some instances, boiling syrup is poured directly over the fruit. Compotes are always served cold. A macédoine is a mixture of seasonal, fresh fruits (essentially a fruit salad as we understand it in America), diced, macerated in kirsch and maraschino syrup, then chilled, sometimes covered with fresh cream.

There is also such a thing as a macédoine of vegetables. This can be a combination of vegetables, cooked separately, dressed with butter; cold, cooked vegetables, dressed with vinaigrette sauce or mayonnaise; hot, cooked vegetables dressed with cream; or cold, cooked vegetables in aspic dressed with mayonnaise.

What's an easy way to chop dried fruits?   Snip them up with kitchen scissors. Keep a damp cloth handy to wipe off the blades occasionally.

What exactly is a date?   The fruit of the date palm, originally imported from the Middle East and North Africa, are now grown extensively in California and Arizona. It's a delicious fruit that is good eaten out of hand but is used in cookery in such things as breads, pastries, fillings, etc. Good quality dates should be a rich brown, with a whitish membrane between the flesh and the pit, plump and soft, with a smooth, shiny skin. They are available by the pound, both pitted and unpitted. Store in the refrigerator, well covered.

When are fresh figs in season?   All varieties are in season from the end of August through September: Black Mission (purplish-black skin with brownish-amber flesh); Calimyrna (greenish-yellow skin, reddish-amber flesh); white Adriatic (yellow or greenish skin with red or white flesh); Kadota (yellowish-white skin, pale amber flesh); brown Turkey (purplish-brown skin, reddish flesh). All are sweet and all can be eaten out of hand, served sliced with sugar and cream (sweet or sour), or a sprinkling of lime or lemon juice; served with prosciutto ham in place of the ubiquitous melon. Fresh figs can be cooked in many ways: in pies, pickled, or baked with port and honey. Dried figs are with us all year round.

How can you buy figs? Fresh, of course. Dried, the most desirable fig is the Calimyrna or Smyrna-type. Because it is so large and tender, with such a rich flavor, it can be eaten out of hand or cooked; the other well-known dried fig is the Black Mission, which has the same uses as the Calimyrna. The Kadota is available canned, whole or split, packed in water, juice, or syrup.

How can you tell when grapes are fresh and ripe? Grapes, picked fully ripe and sweet, should be firmly attached to the stem (gentle shaking will tell the story), fresh, plump, smooth, well colored, with no stickiness. White or green grapes are at their flavorful best and sweetness when they are beginning to turn amber. Grapes should be refrigerated and used as soon as possible after purchase. When grapes are used as a garnish, they are more attractive in little clusters, on the stems.

Grapes are washed, if at all, just before using. In Europe, grapes are usually served with a crystal bowl filled with cool water and you dip the grapes into the water before eating. It's not only an attractive idea but a sensible one.

What are the varieties of grapes and how are they used? Almost all table grapes are grown in California, and the first to turn up in the summer, in June, are the Perlettes, similar to Thompson Seedless (probably the most useful, all-round, of any grape). The Cardinals come in mid-June and then the Thompsons. Ribiers start to market in August, Tokays in September, and Emperors in October (this is the grape available all winter into March). The Thompson Seedless are best in pies, tarts, and salads, particularly because they are very sweet and you don't have to extricate seeds. All grapes go well, eaten out of hand, with cheese.

The old familiar Concords are usually only available locally, in

September, but if you can get your hands on a basket, do try this wonderful kuchen.

CONCORD GRAPE KUCHEN

4 cups Concord grapes
2 cups sifted all-purpose flour plus 3 tablespoons
1 cup sugar plus 2 tablespoons
Juice ½ lemon
¼ teaspoon baking powder
½ teaspoon salt
1 stick (½ cup) butter
2 egg yolks
½ pint (1 cup) commercial sour cream

Wash the grapes, pull off the stems and measure 4 cups. Pinch each grape to squeeze out the pulp. Place the pulp in a saucepan; set the grape skins aside.

Cook the pulp over low heat, once it comes to a boil, for 7 minutes. Strain through a sieve into a bowl, pressing the pulp to separate the seeds. Mix the puréed pulp with the grape skins, 3 *tablespoons of flour*, *1 cup of the sugar*, and the lemon juice. Set aside.

Sift the remaining flour, baking powder, salt, and remaining sugar into a large bowl. Add the butter, and work it into the mixture with a pastry blender or your fingers until mealy. Dump into an 8-inch spring-form pan. Press the mixture all over the bottom and up the sides of the pan as far as you can—at least 1½ inches. You will be surprised how well it clings. Chill for 15 minutes or so. Pour the grape mixture into the prepared pan and place in a preheated 400° F. oven for 15 minutes. Meanwhile, mix the egg yolks and sour cream together, pour over the top of the filling carefully. Continue baking another 25 minutes. Serve at room temperature.

GREEN GRAPES IN COGNAC HONEY

Here's an interesting, easy recipe for Thompson grapes: Wash and stem enough grapes to make about 2½ cups. Mix 1 teaspoon lemon juice, ¼ cup honey, and 2 tablespoons of cognac together. Pour over the grapes and allow them to stand several hours (or overnight), giving them an occasional stir. To serve, spoon a little commercial sour cream over each serving.

What are lychees? Also spelled litchi and lichi, this fruit, very common in China, is about the size of a large cherry, with a large stone. The pulp is white, sweet, almost transparent, jelly-like, and deliciously refreshing. When fully ripe, the thin, hard, scaly shell is a beautiful bright red which peels off easily. They can sometimes be bought fresh, otherwise, they are dried and taste and look not unlike a raisin. They are always available, canned, out of the shell, and most Chinese restaurants present them in this form at the end of a meal for dessert.

When are mangoes in season? In April through August, with June the peak month. Native to tropical Asia, they are now grown in Florida and imported from Mexico, Puerto Rico, and the West Indies. A delicious fruit, the pale yellow pulp, delicate and juicy, tastes like a combination of apricot and pineapple. Mangoes have a smooth, outer skin, usually green with yellowish to red areas, the colors intensifying as the fruit ripens. Mangoes must be very soft before they are ready to eat. Once ripe, they should be refrigerated. To prepare, stand the mango on its end, pointed end up. Pierce with a sharp knife until you feel the long, flat seed. Then slice from top to bottom on both sides. Serve as you would an avocado half.

How do you cut a melon, saw-tooth style? Using a small, sharp, straight-edged knife, thrust knife into center of melon at an angle, then pull it out. Make the next cut at opposite angle. Repeat all around the melon. Remove seeds and serve with fresh lime or lemon juice, or fill with a mixture of fresh fruits perfumed with a little kirsch.

How do you choose a cantaloupe? The maturity and sweetness of a cantaloupe are determined by two things: (1) the netting or veining on the surface, which should be coarse, corky, of grayish color, standing out in bold relief against a grayish yellow background; (2) the condition of the stem end, known among growers as the "scar," mentioned by Pliny 1,900 years ago, which should be shallow and smooth, indicating the fruit separated from the stem readily. Cantaloupes should always be very firm when purchased, so don't be in a hurry to serve the cantaloupe you buy today. Better, when they are in season (June, July, Angust, and September), to keep a supply on hand at room temperature and eat them as they ripen—after two or three days. When perfectly ripe, the sides feel spongy to the touch, and the cantaloupes have a notable fragrance. This way you will have a delicious melon, with the flesh soft and juicy, and the sweetness more apparent than when the flesh is firmer. For best fragrance and flavor, cantaloupes should be served cool, but never chilled.

If it's a muskmelon, is it a cantaloupe?   Yes. Muskmelon is the old, original name (today used primarily by the growers) that encompassed the whole family of gourds, including watermelon. The muskmelon, introduced into Italy from Armenia, and first raised on a former country seat of the Pope, became *cantalupo*. The name cantaloupe (it can be spelled with or without an "e") is commonly used in the United States for the many varieties distinguished by a "netted" or "veined" surface and golden or salmon flesh.

Persian melons look like large cantaloupes, except they have flat ends, weigh as much as 10 pounds, and have a later season—July into November. They, too, have a heavily netted surface. When ripe, the rind is yellowish and the flesh pink.

Are Crenshaw, Casaba, and Honeydew melons alike?   No. The Crenshaws, in season from July to October, have a smooth rind, mottled with gold and green, a bright salmon-colored flesh. Very juicy and good when ripe (they will weigh up to 9 pounds); Casabas, in season about the same time, also very large, have a tough rind, profusely marked with deep long wrinkles. The two most common varieties are the Golden (orange-yellow to dark green, with golden flesh) and the Pineapple (green-white skin and light yellow flesh tinged with green), very sweet and juicy. Honeydews (or "Ostrich Egg") are in season most of the year—the peak being July through October—at an average weight of 6 pounds. The skin is creamy yellow (imported ones may be whiter), and the sweet flesh, green. Judge all for ripeness as you would cantaloupes. If ripe, refrigerate; if not, ripen at room temperature, then refrigerate. Ripe, whole (intact), they will keep about a week in the refrigerator; cut, from 2 to 4 days, if tightly wrapped.

How can you tell if a watermelon is ripe?   Color is the best sign. It should be a deep, rich color (this varies from green to gray) on top, with a yellowish underside. The old "thumping" test can only be practiced by experienced fruit vendors. Unlike other types of melons, often mistakenly served cold, watermelons are most refreshing when served chilled. They are in season in June, July, and August.

What are winter melons?   With the exception of the Christmas or Santa Claus melon, available in the dead of winter, most melons are in the markets the year round, although in a limited way at certain times. The Christmas melon looks like a small watermelon, with a hard, thick, slightly netted green rind, and the sweet flesh is light yellow to green. Judge as you would any melon.

What exactly is a nectarine? A "fuzzless" peach, with firmer flesh, greater aroma, and a distinct flavor. It is known among botanists as a "sport," or mutation. The trees, leaves, and seeds of both the peach and nectarine are indistinguishable, and either may produce a true peach. A fascinating, inexplicable horticultural phenomenon. Our native fruit is at its best in July through August. Imports from Chile come in in January and February. The delicate skin makes them unusually susceptible to damage, so when buying, take care to choose plump, firm, well-colored fruit. Once ripe and ready to eat, store, covered, in the refrigerator. Nectarines may be used in any recipe calling for peaches.

Are papaya and papaw (or pawpaw) the same thing? By a curious and inexplicable coincidence, there are two entirely different fruits that travel under the name "papaw." One, the wild fruit of a small tree of the middle United States; the other, the cultivated fruit of the American tropics. The North American papaw is shaped somewhat like a pear and although it is edible, a taste for it usually has to be cultivated. The tropical papaw or papaya is the fruit of a tropical tree, often called a tree melon, probably or perhaps because the flesh and flavor of the fruit is melon-like. When ripe, it can shade from pale yellow to a deep orange or even a rich red. Like a melon, it is eaten with a spoon and served with salt, lemon, or lime juice, and even à la mode. Available the year round, it is also used in making puddings, pies, jams, and pickles. Ripen at room temperature, then refrigerate. Should be eaten within a day or two, once ripe.

The papaw or papaya is the source of "papain," the enzyme used to make meat tenderizers.

How do you skin a peach? Cover with boiling water and allow to stand briefly, or drop the peaches into boiling water, one at a time, and boil for 10 seconds or so. If the skins don't peel off easily, put the peaches back into the boiling water.

What is a Cling peach? A type of peach grown almost exclusively for canning, which takes its name from the fact the pit clings tenaciously to the flesh. Available in halves or slices, packed in every type of liquid from extra heavy to light syrup, to water alone. The other canned peaches on the market are Freestone which, as you would assume, have a "free" pit or stone.

Can you cook white peaches? You can, but as the Fresh Fruit and Vegetable Association points out, "They are the most delicate of all peach varieties, with an exquisite flavor, and deserve to be eaten out of hand. Since the supply is limited, they are more costly than the yellow Freestones and Clings. The latter, because of their firmer texture, although excellent eating, are better for cooking." As a matter of interest, peaches are defuzzed mechanically these days, making them almost as smooth as nectarines. In buying peaches, choose those with a yellowish or creamy background (green indicates they were immature when picked) and firm to the touch. A "blush" may be present, but red color does not indicate the peach is edible. Avoid soft peaches unless they are to be eaten immediately. Peaches will ripen rapidly at room temperature, away from light, so if you want to slow down the process, refrigerate them, always remembering to serve them at room temperature to savor them at their best. June, July, and August are the peak months.

When are the different pears in season? The bell-shaped Bartletts (yellow or yellow with a red blush) start coming into the market in July and stay with us into November. Excellent eaten out of hand and good poached, they do not bake well. The little brown, wren-like Seckel comes along in September through December, giving you four good months to cook or pickle it. The winter pears come along in November and last into May: they are the chunky, Anjou, green or greenish-yellow; the Bosc, with a long, tapering neck, green or brown to golden russet; and the Comice, famous for its great size and beauty, greenish-yellow to yellow with red splashings. Unlike the Bartletts, these bake well, but they must be firm.

Pears are plucked before they reach full maturity, but they ripen perfectly at room temperature. When ripe, refrigerate. All varieties, when ripe, can be eaten out of hand, with or without cheese, sliced in salads or fruit cups.

In choosing pears, select those that are firm, plump, free from blemishes, with the stem attached. Canned pears can be purchased whole, quartered, or sliced, packed in water, syrup, or juice. They are also available in diet packs and baby food. Dried pears are available packaged in halves or mixed with other dried fruits.

What is pectin? The substance in fruit which, in the right proportion to sugar and acid, forms a jelly. Commercial liquid or bottled pectin is refined from apple pectin; powdered pectin is made from citrus or apple pectin, then dried and packaged. Commercial pectin should be used as directed in the recipe.

What are persimmons and how do you use them? An extraordinarily beautiful, and delicious fruit, in season for an all too-brief period: October, November (the peak month), and December. Persimmons have been grown in Japan and China for centuries, but there is a distinctly different wild variety that is native to the eastern part of the U.S. Those you are likely to meet in your market are the Hachiyas, the largest and handsomest of all the Oriental varieties—usually seedless, grown in California. The skin is glossy, a deep orange-red; the jelly-like flesh, when ripe, is sweet and rich. Persimmons are only edible when fully ripe (in their green state, there are few things more mouth-puckering because of the tannin—the same thing you find in over-brewed tea). When ripe, refrigerate and use as soon as possible.

Choose those that are very soft, with an unbroken skin, and the stem cap attached. Persimmons are eaten out of hand (have napkins ready), chilled, or peeled in a bowl with cream. They are also used in cooking such things as puddings, custards, and cakes.

How can you tell when a pineapple is ripe? Dr. Willis A. Gortner of the U.S.D.A. tells me it's a problem, but these are the points to look for: a bright, fresh appearance; at least a showing of some orange-yellow color starting at the base of the fruit; a fresh, green crown (top); and solid fruit. You can check this by thumping the fruit with the index finger. If it sounds similar to the thumping of your wrist, it is a solid fruit. These, Dr. Gortner emphasizes, are hints only and do not guarantee that the pineapple will be truly ripe. A final tip, do not store the pineapple at home to "let it ripen." The longer fruit is stored at home, the greater the chances of quality deterioration. Once picked, a change in the fruit color from green to yellow does not necessarily mean that the pineapple will be sweeter or better tasting. Avoid fruit with shriveled crowns; dull, brown color; bruised spots. And *don't* pull a crown leaf; this tells you absolutely nothing about the ripeness of the fruit. Slices, tidbits, and juice are also available in dietetic packs; there are frozen pineapple juice and chunks; and the slices and pieces are available candied and preserved.

How do you peel a fresh pineapple? The quickest way is to cut the whole fruit in four or six wedges (depending on the size) by slicing through from top to bottom, leaving the plume attached—just cut right through it. Then, take the meat off each wedge by running a sharp knife between rind and meat. Try not to come too close to the rind to avoid too many "eyes." Cut into chunks. To serve the pineapple in wedges, proceed exactly the same, leaving the meat on the rind, and the plume attached.

What are the guide lines in buying plums? Plums (and fresh prunes) are another fruit that must be ripe before picking. Choose fruit that is plump, fresh-looking, and soft enough to yield slightly when pressed. Softening at the tip is a good indication of ripeness. Some varieties are fully ripe when yellowish-green, others when red, still others when purplish-blue or black. Avoid fruit that is hard, shriveled, with poor color and no flavor. Plums can be ripened at room temperature but should be refrigerated once ripe. They will keep up to a week under refrigeration.

What is the difference between a plum and a prune? Botanically, both species belong to the Prunus group. In the fruit industry, however, plum means fresh fruit, and prune, dried. Actually, some types of prunes (the Freestone) are eaten fresh, having been given this name because they can also be dried.

Prune is, of course, the French word for fresh plums and, to further confuse the issue, fresh plums are sometimes called Italian prunes or Japanese plums. Although the growers prefer to call the lovely, purple plums—in season through August and September—Italian prunes, many housewives insist on calling them purple plums. Plums of the European type (of which the Italian is one) also include green, gold, and crimson. The most notable of which are the delicious, juicy-rich, heart-shaped crimson and gold. In good season in June, July, and into August.

Canned prunes are usually designated as purple plums on the can.

What are beach plums? A wild native plum that grows on our eastern beaches from Canada to Virginia. Not good raw, but they make a marvelous plum jam. Since they are not cultivated, you have to gather them yourself, or you can buy beach plum jam or jelly in the Cape Cod area, in season.

What are Damson plums? A cooking plum. Small, oval, firm, purple plums that grow wild, but are also cultivated. Good in pies, compotes, jams, preserves, etc. Pit after cooking. Available in stores specializing in fruits from May through September. Judge as you would other plums, use them within a week.

Can you suggest some ways to use prunes? They make a good breakfast fruit. If your energy is flagging, you can eat a few to pick you up; stuffed with nuts or fondant, they are charming confections. They also combine well with other fruits and they make interesting stuffings for meat or fowl. Of course, they are the *raison d'être* for prune whip, prune cakes, etc. Here is a most unusual and delicious recipe for . . .

PRUNES WITH CREAM

Soak 34 very fine, large prunes for 24 hours in 2 cups of the best red port. Then add 1 cup sugar, 2 more cups of port, and ½ vanilla bean. Cook, covered in an enamel saucepan over low heat until tender. Cool. Then refrigerate for 3 days. To serve, cover with whipped cream, sprinkle thickly with powdered macaroons, and garnish with candied violets.

Can prunes be eaten straight from the package? Yes. But since they are a dehydrated fruit, they should be "plumped" or softened in certain instances. The method recommended by the California Prune Advisory Board is as follows: "Cover prunes with water, bring to a boil, then simmer, covered, for 10 minutes. Take off the heat and allow to cool in the liquid. As a variation, prunes can be "plumped" in apple juice, orange juice, or other fruit juices. In which case, cover the prunes with the juice and allow to stand overnight."

What's a quick way to cook prunes? Place in a saucepan, cover with boiling water, then simmer for 10 minutes. Add a bit of orange or lemon peel, if you like.

Can you buy cooked prunes? Yes, cooked or stewed, in cans and jars.

Puréed prunes, in cans, usually associated with babies, and prune juice in bottles and cans are also available. In certain areas—particularly the West Coast—you may find fresh prune juice which is made from fresh prune plums.

Can you buy pitted prunes? Yes. In 12-ounce, clear plastic bags, in one size only. Prunes, with pits, come in various sizes: jumbo (20 to 35 to a pound); extra large (36 to 43 to a pound); large (43 to 53 to a pound); medium (53 to 67 to a pound); and breakfast (68 to 85 to a pound). With the exception of the jumbo, which is packaged in 1-pound boxes only, the others are available in 1- and 2-pound boxes or in transparent bags. Moist-packed prunes, a specialty, particularly good for eating out of hand, can, of course, be used in cooking, and are available in glass or cans.

What are pomegranates like and how are they used? They're about the size of a big apple or orange, with a thin, tough rind which should be pink or bright red, with crimson flesh. They have an enormous number of small seeds, each surrounded by a juicy pulp that has a spicy taste. In the Middle East the seeds are sprinkled over salads. If you want to try this, freeze the seeds to preserve them. Pomegranates are closely associated with grenadine since the syrup was originally made exclusively from this fruit (*grenade* is the French word for pomegranate, and *granada,* the Spanish). They can be halved and eaten with a spoon; or the pulp and juice can be made into a syrup, perfumed with rose water, and frozen into a sherbet as is done in the Levant.

In choosing pomegranates, they should feel heavy for their size, have a thin skin, bright and colorful. Available from the end of September to November. If fully ripe, refrigerate and use within 2 to 3 days.

To make pomegranate juice: Cut in half and squeeze the juice on a reamer as you would orange juice.

What is a raisin, what are the varieties, and how are they used? A raisin is a dried grape. (In France, *raisins* means fresh grapes, and *raisins sec,* dried.) The bulk of the raisins on the market are the sun-dried Thompson Seedless (those sweet, little green globes that turn up fresh the end of June). It takes 21 sunny California days for a grape to become a dark purple raisin. Golden Seedless, the same grape, is dried indoors, but does not turn dark, rather, a pale and lovely gold. These grapes can be used interchangeably in cooking, although in a light, or white, fruit cake, the golden is preferred. The third dried raisin is the rich, seeded Muscat (the seeds are removed mechanically), which come into their own during the Christmas holidays when all good housewives settle down to make their puddings, fruit cakes, and other traditional holiday delicacies. All these raisins are available in 15-ounce packages. The Muscat, seeds in, in bunches, on stems, are available in fancy packs only around the holidays. There are few things more nostalgic, on a winter's night, than to gossip around a big fire, cracking walnuts, and eating raisins.

How do you chop raisins?   If you have an electric blender, the California Raisin Advisory Board recommends this method: "Freeze the quantity of raisins called for in the recipe, drop the frozen raisins into the blender, turn the motor on and off three times for coarsely chopped raisins; for fine, turn motor to high speed for a couple of seconds." This works for both Seedless and the seeded Muscat raisins; but it does not work for other dried fruits. Lacking a blender, toss the raisins lightly in salad oil, then chop with a French knife. The oil helps to keep them from sticking to the knife.

Why do my raisins dry out?   You either didn't store them properly or you kept them on your pantry shelf much too long. The California Raisin Advisory Board says you should never buy more than a package or so at a time, taking into consideration how frequently you use them. If, however, they do dry out, they can be refreshed by covering with hot water and allowing them to stand for about 3 minutes.

WALNUT RAISIN SAUCE

Plump up a cup or so of raisins in boiling water. Drain thoroughly, cover, while still warm, with chocolate mint cordial and mix in a handful or so of coarsely-chopped walnuts. Allow to mellow for a day or so. Serve over ice cream.

Meat

Some Kind Words About Butchers

THE FIRST butcher I ever knew well, and he was only a good amateur, was Laurent Leblanc, the man who lived and worked on our place in Amherst, Nova Scotia, and who, every November, with my father masterminding the project, butchered the pigs we had fattened over the summer. It was an Italian butcher, so long ago I've even forgotten his name, who gave me, then a young and green Canadian, my first recipe for spaghetti sauce and I learned to prepare pastrami properly from the smiling butcher who now serves the James Beard Cooking Classes. More recently, through a wholesaler in the meat industry I found out how you pick a good goose in today's market. Currently, Mr. Fitz and the skillful butchers around him, David Adams and Frank Argiento, are an endless source of sound information and good meat.

It is predicted that in another 25 to 30 years, fresh meat will be a "delicious extravagance." It will be a sad day, indeed, when a woman can no longer go into her meat market and discuss, with her butcher, what she'll give her family for dinner that night.

What does "choice" stamped on a piece of meat mean? It indicates the quality of the meat and tells you it has been graded by the U.S. Department of Agriculture. The standards set up by the U.S.D.A. for beef, veal, and lamb (pork is federally inspected, but not graded) are as follows: Prime—the finest quality and most expensive. Prime beef, usually available only in markets specializing in quality beef, constitutes a very small percentage of all marketed beef. Choice—generally available in most retail markets, is considered the best buy on the basis of palatability and cost. Good—less desirable meat, is also considerably less expensive.

How do you gauge the quantity of meat to buy?   It's not easy, because one man's dinner is another man's snack. About ⅓ pound of lean, boneless meat makes a medium serving, and ½ pound is generous. If the meat has bone in it, allow at least ½ pound per serving, and if the bone is large, allow a good deal more.

Is it necessary to wash meat before cooking?   Many cook books suggest wiping (not washing) meat or fowl with a damp cloth before cooking. Unless you can actually see the need for it, which is extremely doubtful in this day and age, it seems to us a useless gesture.

How and how long can you store ready-to-serve meats?   They should be stored in the refrigerator but not in the freezer. Cured and smoked meats tend to lose flavor and change texture when frozen. If not vacuum-packed, they can be stored in the original wrapper about a week; if vacuum-packed, they will keep for several weeks, but once the package is opened, they, too, should be consumed within a week.

How long can frozen meats be stored?   Ground beef and sausage, 1 to 3 months; fresh pork, 3 to 6 months; veal and lamb, 6 to 9 months; beef, 6 to 12 months. Smoked meats should never be frozen.
    N O T E : This freezing-time guide should only be followed if you have a separate freezer or your refrigerator freezing compartment maintains zero temperature.

Can frozen meats be roasted without thawing?   Yes, but you must allow 10 to 15 minutes extra roasting time per pound for roasts under 5 pounds; 15 to 25 minutes more per pound for larger roasts. Unless you're a naturally good "timer," we think it's much better to thaw the roast.

Can frozen meats be broiled?   Yes. But as is true of roasts, you have to allow more time. Increase the broiling time ⅓ to ½. We would not recommend it unless you're in a real jam.

Should all broiling be done at the high broil point?   No. Broiling is fastest at that position, but unless the meat is all of the same thickness, there is a very real possibility of over-cooking the thin part and under-cooking the thick (chicken is good example). Also, the surface can cook so quickly, the inside of the meat can be quite raw (steak, for example). With gas, the broiling is done with the oven door closed, and in modern stoves there is a range of temperatures which the cook should learn to use as she uses the oven. The best guide is, obviously, the use and care book that comes with the stove, but common sense can play an important role, too. With electric stoves, the broiling is done with the door ajar. Here, the broiling pan must be moved up and down, as the case may be, to arrive at different temperatures. The manufacturers of electric ranges suggest 1 to 3 inches from the heating unit for rare meat, 3 to 5 for medium rare, and 6 inches for well-done. All foods, with the exception of flank steak (London broil), to be broiled should be brought to room temperature before broiling.

Can meat ever be broiled on both sides at the same time?   Yes. In certain extremely modern electric ranges.

Why do you slash the fat on beef and ham steaks?   Because the fat shrinks and curls up, and the meat won't lie flat when cooked.

Should meat be pierced before marinating it?   No. A French chef would be horror-stricken at the very idea of making holes in the meat and allowing all the natural juices to escape. With meat tenderizers, you are instructed to pierce the meat in order to help the tenderizer penetrate the flesh. But that's a long way from a marinade.

How long can ground meat be kept after purchase?   Ground meat is very perishable and should be used within 24 hours. Always refrigerate, loosely wrapped, in the coldest section.

Should you season meats before or after cooking?   Opinions differ. French chefs salt and pepper before, in the belief the meat is then only properly seasoned; others claim the salt tends to draw moisture to the cut surface and delays browning.

Should you sear meats before roasting?   There are two schools: the sear and non-sear. The National Live Stock and Meat Board is "non-sear," but many fine cooks and chefs always sear. The theory behind searing is that it seals in the juices, although the Meat Board says, "Seared meat looses fat rather than juices."

To cook roasts by the searing method: Place the roast, fat side up, in an open roasting pan, in a preheated 450° F. oven, for 20 to 25 minutes, then reduce heat to 300° F. (open the oven door for a few minutes to cool it off) and continue roasting for the required length of time. Do not cover; do not add water.

To cook roasts without searing: Place roast, fat side up, in an open roasting pan, in a preheated 325° F. oven. Do not add water; do not cover. Roast for the required length of time.

What are silver sides?   A term used by butchers for pieces of meat they want to get rid of. For example, short cut sirloin steaks, rump, top sirloin, etc.

At what temperatures should meats be roasted?   This is not an easy question to answer because there are so many variables. As James Beard says, "Although roasting is the earliest known method for cooking meat, it is by no means the easiest. Variations in cuts, grades, and sizes of roasts can all affect the end result, and the charts that time a roast by weight are not only fallible, but practically useless. A really fine roasting cook must still be blessed with, or acquire, the practiced eye, sensitive finger, and the uncanny intuition of the exact moment to take the roast from the oven." We recommend, with Mr. Beard, roasting by a meat thermometer, using the weight of the meat as an approximate measure only of the time the roast will take in the oven. One factor that is of major importance is the internal temperature of the roast before it goes in the oven. Obviously, a roast frigid from the refrigerator will take longer to reach the correct cooked temperature than one that has been brought to room temperature, prior to being put in the oven. Despite the professionals in the meat industry who frown on this procedure, we recommend bringing meat to room temperature before roasting.

All roasts (any kind of meat) should be placed on a rack, in a shallow pan. In short, above the drippings. Otherwise, the meat stews in the fat and juices, while the top of the meat browns. Lacking a proper rack, use the broiler pan.

Roasting beef: Beef may be roasted at temperatures as low as 180°

to 200° F., but will require much time. As always, gauge doneness on your meat thermometer.

Rare beef, the most desirable way to enjoy it, is pink from the outer fat to the bone or center—not *bleu*—but juicy and pink (or red, according to your definition of color). With that in mind, here are my recommendations for the preparation of beef and the cooking time. Score the fat, rub it and the flesh on the bone side well with freshly ground pepper. Place on rack, rib side down. Salt the meat during the last 15 minutes of cooking and after testing the temperature the final time. To roast a 2-rib roast (about 6 pounds) in a 325° oven, use a 0° to 220° meat thermometer and follow this chart.

	Approximate Time	*Thermometer Reading*
Rare	2¼ hrs. to 2½ hrs.	110° to 115°
Medium rare	2½ hrs. to 2¾ hrs.	115° to 120°
Medium	3 hrs. 25 min. to 3 hrs. 40 min.	130° to 135°

What are the various roasts and how are they prepared?

Rib roast: If from quality beef, this is the finest of beef roasts, but there is a good deal of waste because of the bones and fat. The first 3 ribs are the best. If you are going to roast it "standing," have the butcher remove the chine (back) bone and cut the rib bones short to facilitate carving. Never buy less than 2, better, 3 ribs. It's the handsomest way to present a roast and the easiest to carve. However, many people prefer it rolled. In which case, the butcher simply removes the bones, rolls and ties the meat.

Sirloin roast: This is the classic English roast of beef. American butchers much prefer to sell sirloin steaks, but if you can prevail on yours to produce a prime roast, you may agree with the English that it's better than a rib roast, even if it costs you more money. The bone and fillet should be left in. Traditionally served with Yorkshire pudding.

Rump roast: Rolled or standing, this can be extremely good roasted, if from prime meat. Otherwise it should be braised.

POT ROASTS AND BRAISED DISHES: All the less tender cuts —rump, chuck, eye of round, bottom or heel of the round, brisket, sirloin tip, English or Boston pot roast—call for long, slow cooking, by braising or simmering in liquid. The meat should always be well-done.

BOILED BEEF: Brisket is a very fat piece of meat, some of which should be removed before cooking and used to brown the meat.

Braised, in a good broth, seasonings, and vegetables, it makes a superb family meal. The French use this cut to make *pot-au-feu*. Corned beef is cured brisket, the cut used to make New England boiled dinner, America's pot-au-feu.

BEEF STEWS: For stews and other dishes that call for meat cut into pieces, round steak or top grade chuck are less wasteful. Meat should be cut into good, big cubes—1½ to 2 inches.

Can you roast meat in a covered pan?   You can, but you shouldn't, because the net result is steaming, not roasting.

Why are all roasted meats supposed to "rest" after coming from the oven?   This applies not only to meat but to fowl, too. The meat (or bird) goes on cooking for quite a few minutes once it's taken from the oven. A "rest" period of about 20 minutes allows the juices to settle and makes the meat (bird) much easier to carve.

Should you remove the strings on a roast before taking it to the table?   Yes, for plain rolled, stuffed roasts and crowns. If the meat was roasted properly, allowed to rest, and is carved well, it should keep its shape. A rolled roast of beef, cooked to death, might fall apart without the strings to keep it together, but then, it shouldn't be cooked to death. Stuffed roasts are roasted with the fold under, which is additional security. In removing the strings in the kitchen, it should be done with great care so as not to disturb the meat. (Incidentally, if you have any dogs or cats around, the strings, tasty to animals but disastrous if they eat them, should be immediately put out of harm's way.)

How do you carve a rolled roast of beef?   Place the roast on its side, not standing up, on a warm platter. Beginning at the right end, steadying it with a fork, slice down vertically in even slices, with a good, sharp knife, removing the string as you go along. When you have sliced as much as you need, turn the roast, cut side up, so the meat won't "bleed" and lose its juices.

How do you carve a standing rib roast?   Place the roast on a generous, warm, serving platter, the ribs facing the carver, with the largest end down. Steady the roast with a fork or your hand (experienced carvers are inclined to use their hand, holding the tip of the bone). Using a short-bladed knife, cut along the ribs to loosen the meat. Then, with a long, thin, sharp knife, cut off a fairly thick slice and set aside (old hands usually save the delectable outside cut for themselves). Now, slice across the grain from the outside edge toward the ribs. In England, it is customary to slice the beef very thin—a mark of elegance—known as the English cut. Lift the carved slices to one side of the platter or to the dinner plate.

Should you stand or sit while carving? In general, it is more comfortable to stand, although it was once considered bad form. Unless the carver is a natural contortionist, it is quite a feat to carve well, seated.

What cuts of meat should be braised? The National Live Stock and Meat Board recommends: Veal steaks and chops (on top of the stove or in the oven), thick pork chops, pot roasts, Swiss steaks, corned beef. Although some cooks broil pork chops, it has been our experience they turn out tough and stringy.

What is clod? It is a cut of beef off the shoulder. Quite an interesting piece of meat that should be braised.

Does reheating cooked meat toughen it? It's inclined to, unless care is taken. The point to remember is not to cook the meat further. If just heated up in a compatible liquid, it will keep the meat moist and heat through without cooking it. Chicken pie, for example, is made with cooked chicken. Meat pie, for example, is often made with cooked, left-over beef or steak, but the pie is only in the oven long enough to bake the crust.

How do you reheat a roast? Generally, it is not recommended because the time needed to heat it through (if it is of any size at all) means more cooking, and more cooking means drying out. All roasts are good cold and, if initially cooked properly, taste better than reheated. Sliced meat can be heated in a sauce or gravy just to the boiling point. No longer.

What is a côtelette? *Côte* means rib and côtelette means little rib or, more precisely, chop. *Côtelette d'agneau* is lamb chop; *Côte de boeuf* is a rib of beef; *côtes de porc*, pork chops.

What is beef Stroganoff?   Although attributed to the Russians, there are those who disagree. It has been bastardized to such an extent here that its own "father" would disclaim it. The pure Stroganoff, if there is such a thing, is made with fillet of beef, cut in strips, sautéed quickly in butter, then combined with sautéed shallots, a dash of Worcestershire, and sour cream.

What is beef Wellington?   Roasted fillet of beef, coated with *foie gras* or *duxelles*, wrapped in pastry, then baked. Customarily, served with *sauce Périgueux* (Madeira and truffles).

What is boeuf bourguignonne?   A really great French stew made with beef, red wine (in France, Burgundy), mushrooms, bacon, and onions.

What is a carbonade of beef?   Also spelled carbonnade, meaning "braised beef," it is really a stew made with lean beef (usually chuck) cut in thin slices, sautéed, combined with a *bouquet garni*, and stock, then braised in the oven. In the Midi, onions and garlic are an important addition; and in Belgium, the famous *carbonades de boeuf à la flamande* is made with the same ingredients, more or less, plus beer.

Are dried and chipped beef identical?   Yes. Made from beef round, it is cured, smoked, dehydrated, and chip-sliced. Available from some butchers sliced to order or in cans, jars, and transparent vacuum packages. Refrigerate after the container has been opened, but if bought out of the meat case, it should be kept refrigerated. Ready to serve.

Are flank and flanken the same cut of meat?   No. You are not even close. Flank, called London broil in restaurants, is cut off the belly of the steer. Flanken is the first four ribs of 'the rib section. It can be braised, roasted, substituted for short ribs or turned into a stew. An excellent, flavorful cut.

What is goulash?   A sturdy meat stew, of Hungarian origin, cooked with plenty of onions and paprika.

What's the difference between red flannel hash and corned beef hash?   Red flannel hash is the aftermath of a boiled dinner served *with* sliced corned beef and a mixture of vegetables, particularly beets. Corned beef hash is a blend of cooked corned beef and boiled potatoes. If the beef gave out, a poached or fried egg was served in its place.

What is a miroton? A sort of stew made with cooked, left-over beef, sliced, and onions, with a trace of vinegar.

What is pastrami? A Rumanian spiced beef made from flat pieces of lean meat, dry cured, rubbed with spices, coated with cracked pepper, smoked, and cooked. Ready to serve.

What is a pot-au-feu? Ever since the Middle Ages, the pot-au-feu (pot on the fire) has been the stand-by in the French peasant's home—family-style boiled beef with vegetables. *Poule-au-pot* is also pot-au-feu, except that it's made with chicken rather than beef. It was Henry IV of France, it was said, who wished for his subjects, "A chicken in every pot."

What is a ragoût? The French word for stew.

What are empanadas? A South American version of meat turnovers, made with beef, chopped black olives, hard-cooked eggs, and raisins.

What is piroshki? Russian meat turnovers made with a yeast pastry. Often served with borsht.

What are the various cuts of steak and how are they prepared?
   Porterhouse: The choicest, and most expensive cut, because it includes the tenderloin (or fillet), which comes from the large end of the short loin. It should be cut at least 2 inches thick, better 3 to 4. Broil or sauté.
   T-bone: Also includes the tenderloin but, since it is from the opposite end of the short loin from the porterhouse, it is a smaller steak with less of the tenderloin. Broil or sauté. It's practical and good eating to have the butcher grind the tail and tie into the center of the steak.
   Shell: Cut from the short loin, is like a T-bone, with the tenderloin removed. Sauté or broil.
   Delmonico: The smallest steak from the short loin, has very little

or no tenderloin at all. Cut rather thin, it makes a superb steak *à la minute,* sautéed quickly over a good heat.

Tenderloin: The fillet from the loin, is the tenderest but not necessarily the most flavorful cut. Individual steaks from the tenderloin are known as *chateaubriand, petite filet, tournedo,* and *filet mignon.* The *chateaubriand,* from the butt end, is the largest, the *filet mignon,* from the tip, the smallest. Other than the *chateaubriand,* which is cut 2 inches thick, they are all cut about 1 inch thick and all are cooked the same way—either sautéed or broiled.

The whole tenderloin, wrapped or barded with fat, can be roasted in one piece at a high temperature. Although very costly, because it contains no fat or bones, it averages out, by weight, about the same as a fine porterhouse.

Sirloin: This steak comes from the high or broad end of the loin. Many people prefer it to even the expensive porterhouse but, because of the high percentage of bone, there is a good deal of waste. A whole sirloin, cut thick, makes a splendid meal for a big party. Because of the size, it can be handled more easily in a broiler or over charcoal.

Strip: Or boneless loin (also known as New York cut in the West, but not in New York) has very little fat, is a porterhouse steak without the tenderloin. Sauté or broil.

Rib: Cut from the first few ribs, is better with the bone left in. Excellent, if not too fat. Sauté or pan-fry.

Rump: Normally used for roasting or braising, this makes a good boneless steak, if cut from prime beef. Should be about 3 inches thick. Sauté or broil. Slice "on the bias."

Chuck (or Blade): This, too, is a piece that is usually preferred for braising but, as with rump, if cut from prime beef makes a flavorful, inexpensive steak. If not from prime meat, it should be marinated to tenderize before sautéeing or broiling.

Round: Three steaks are cut from the round—round, top (the most tender), and bottom (this is preferred for Swiss steak). Cuts from the round are generally braised but, like rump and chuck, can be sautéed or broiled, if from prime meat. It's of mild interest to note that the terms "top" and "bottom" round relate to the position of the meat on the butcher's table. The top means the inside of the leg or the top half of the round as it rests on the meat block; the bottom, the part of t! e leg that rests against the wood of the cutting table.

Flank: Known in restaurants as London broil, it's the triangular piece on the underside of the loin. Free of bones, fat, and cartilage, it is all good, edible meat. It's an excellent cut for outdoor cooking, should always be broiled, cold from the refrigerator, and served rare. Before broiling, be sure to remove the tough membrane on the outside. Flank can also be rolled, in which case it should be braised.

Skirt: Similar to flank, except that it's thinner. Juicy, with excellent flavor, but not very tender. Should be pan-fried.

How can you test steaks or chops for doneness?   Cut a small gash close to the bone toward the end of the cooking time. The color of the meat will tell you if it's cooked to your taste.

Why do my pan-fried steaks and chops often look anemic?   Chances are, they were damp when they went in the pan and as a result would not brown.

How do you carve a steak?   Steadying the steak with a two-pronged fork, cut down and around the bone with a small, sharp, boning knife. Remove and discard it. With the bone out of the way, begin to carve the steak, across the meat, on the diagonal, in fairly thick slices.

What is Salisbury steak?   Raw beef, either scraped or chopped, mixed with eggs, seasonings, bread crumbs, and capers. Then broiled.   -

What is steak Diane?   Individual steaks, pounded, cooked quickly in butter, in a chafing dish, flamed with cognac, the sauce flavored with sherry and chives.

What is steak au poivre?   The secret of this fascinating dish is coarsely ground pepper in generous quantity. Each side of the individual steaks is covered with freshly, but coarsely, ground pepper, then pressed into the steaks by the heel of the hand. The steaks are sautéed, seasonings added and, sometimes, they are blazed with cognac.

What is Swiss steak?   Beef, preferably round steak, braised on top of the stove or in the oven.

Why are my hamburgers often dry and tasteless?   There could be any number of reasons. The quality of the meat is one factor. But, no matter what you do, you can't get a good hamburger from poor meat. Nor if it's cooked too much, handled too much, or mixed up with a lot of extraneous ingredients. Hamburger should be handled like a baby—very gently. The quickest way to murder hamburger is to squeeze it together and pound it into shape.

Hildegarde Popper prepares hamburgers beautifully, and here's how: Buy 1 pound of sirloin, ground, without any fat, shape into 3 patties. Pan-fry 3 minutes on each side in hot, melted butter. Place on a warm platter, sprinkle lightly with salt and pepper. Wipe out the pan, add more fresh butter. When melted, add about 3 tablespoons of finely chopped fresh parsley and 4 tablespoons of dry vermouth. Stir to mix, pour over hamburgers and serve at once.

What are the various cuts of lamb and how are they prepared? In "How to Identify and Prepare Cuts of Lamb," a handy, informative little booklet, the American Lamb Council shows thirty cuts. The lamb's configuration is the same, more or less, as that of other meat animals, so the cuts, to a large extent, are similar.

For years lamb was the most unpopular meat in the country. Perhaps because of lack of familiarity but, more probably, because it was mostly roasted until it was gray-brown, stringy, and of poor flavor. In short, cooked to death. Currently, we seem to be joining hands with the French who have always served lamb rare or, at least "pink," when it is at its most succulent. The more luxurious cuts, baby lamb, saddle, leg, and the rack are usually roasted; chops, broiled or pan-fried; lesser cuts are more often cooked by either braising or simmering. One point to remember about lamb, regardless of the cut or method of cooking, is that it should be served piping hot, on hot plates, since it is inclined to cool more quickly than other meats.

N O T E : Leg of lamb is carved the same way ham is.

THE DELUXE CUTS OF LAMB Baby lamb: the leg, available at very fancy butchers at premium prices; baron: both loins or the saddle together with the legs; saddle, both loins; leg: bone in or boneless (rolled and tied); rack; crown roast: two or more ribs (the rack), shaped into a crown; loin roast and boneless loin roast (rolled and tied); sirloin roast: bone in or boneless (rolled and tied); loin chops: French lamb chops or English lamb chops; sirloin steaks: top sirloin cut into steaks.

SOME OF THE LESSER CUTS OF LAMB Boneless rolled

shoulder: roast or braise; boneless stew: usually from the forequarters, lean, with most of the fat cut out; lamb kebabs: cubes of boneless meat, sometimes available pre-threaded (on wooden skewers), broil; breast of lamb, inclined to be fat: braise, barbecue, or broil; riblets: from the breast, best braised.

Cut of Lamb	Oven Temperature	Approximate Minutes per Pound	Thermometer Reading
Baby lamb	450° F.	10	130° to 135° F.
Roast leg		"pink," 12 to 15	115° to 120° F.
of lamb	325° F.	well-done, 30 to 35	130° to 135° F.
Crown roast	325° F.	"pink," 12 to 15	115° to 120° F.
		well-done, 30 to 35	130° to 135° F.
Loin of lamb	325° F.	"pink," 13 to 15	115° to 120° F.
		well-done, 30 to 35	130° to 135° F.
Rack of lamb	375° F.	"pink," 13 to 15	115° to 120° F.
		well-done, 30 to 35	130° to 135° F.
Saddle of lamb	325° F.	"pink," 12	115° to 120° F.
		well-done, 20 to 25	130° to 135° F.
Boneless roast	325° F.	"pink," 10	115° to 120° F.
		well-done, 30 to 35	130° to 135° F.

Lamb chops   Place chops on broiling pan in a preheated oven 4 inches from heat. Season after you take them from the broiler. The time given is for total broiling time. Turn the chops at half-time.

Thickness	Total Broiling Time (in minutes)
1½ inches	rare, 6 to 8
	medium-rare, 8 to 10
	well-done, 10 to 13
2 inches	rare, 9 to 12
	medium-rare, 12 to 14
	well-done, 16 to 20
3 inches	rare, 12 to 15
	medium-rare, 15 to 18
	well-done, 20 to 25

How do you roast lamb?   Of lamb, James Beard says, "You have to take the shape of the particular cut into consideration more than you do with beef." For example, the leg (*gigot* in French), crown, and saddle are roasted at a lower temperature than the rack; baby lamb, higher than the rack.

Because legs of lamb vary greatly in thickness, this is important in evaluating the roasting time. A meat thermometer is really the only satisfactory method. Use the preceding chart as an approximate gauge only, and to give you a notion when to put the roast in the oven. I feel compelled to add, I subscribe only to "pink" lamb.

To prepare lamb for roasting (any cut—unless recipe specifies otherwise), rub with freshly ground pepper, place on a rack in a shallow roasting pan. About 15 minutes before roast is done, salt, then salt again when you take the last thermometer reading.

What is a saddle of meat? A cut of meat that includes both loins, a saddle of lamb or mutton, for example.

What is a rack of meat? A rib section of meat. Rack of lamb, for example. One of the most luxurious cuts.

What are English lamb chops? Double lamb chops, rolled around a kidney, and skewered, then broiled. In England, served with pickled walnuts.

What are French lamb chops? Rib chops, the tips trimmed, then broiled or pan-fried, served with a paper frill on the end of each tip.

What is "baron" of lamb? Both loins and both legs of the animal. The term also applies to mutton. Originally, it meant beef only. The story goes that Henry VIII, particularly pleased by a piece served to him and on being told it was the loin, proclaimed it "Baron Sirloin." Other authorities credit the legend to Charles II and James I. In all probability, the name derives from the French, *sur*, meaning over or above, and *longe*, meaning loin. Whatever, the cut is known, in England to this day, as a sirloin or a baron of beef.

What is the difference between mutton and lamb? Mutton is the meat from sheep between 1 and 2 years of age, while lamb is the meat from young animals. Baby lamb is meat from 6- to 8-week-old animals; spring lamb, from 3- to 5-months-old animals; and lamb, meat under 1 year old. The U.S. grades for both mutton and lamb are: Prime, Choice, and Good.

Are shish kebab and shashlik the same thing? Yes. Both *shish* and *shash,* from the Turkish, mean skewer; *kebab,* or *kabob,* means meat cut into small pieces, grilled or broiled. Thread the pieces of meat (in Turkey and the Near East, it is usually mutton) on a skewer and you have shish kebab in the Near East; shashlik in Russia; and *en brochette* in France.

What are the best pork cuts to roast and how long should they be roasted? The three most desirable cuts, in this order, are: the loin, the leg (fresh ham), and the shoulder. As is true of all pork, they must be cooked thoroughly in order to kill the trichina, the source of that dread disease, trichinosis, which may well be lurking in under-done pork. Allow 30 minutes per pound or until a meat thermometer registers 170° F. (With the bone in it, it will take a somewhat shorter time than if boned.) Once removed from the oven, the roast will continue to cook several minutes. We strongly advise using a meat thermometer, because you can determine exactly when the meat is properly cooked but still succulent. Over-done pork becomes stringy and tasteless.

Pork roasts from a medium or small animal are more desirable because the meat is usually firmer and better flavored. In buying loin of pork, make sure the butcher cuts through the chine (back) bone to make it easier to carve. Unless you have scales at home (and all cooks should have), remember to ask your butcher to give you the exact weight so you can gauge the cooking time precisely, assuring yourself of delicious meat.

What are the various types of hams and how are they prepared? Smoked pork (ham) falls into two groups: cook-before-eating and fully cooked. If fully cooked, the meat needs no further cooking, it can be eaten "as is," although many good cooks cook it, in a slow oven, for an hour or so, then glaze it properly, in the belief it improves the ham. That's my opinion, too. If it's a cook-before-eating ham (it may have been partially cooked), it needs further cooking before it is served, hot or cold.

COOK-BEFORE-EATING HAMS Regular hams: Whole, shank, and butt halves. Whole hams weigh from about 10 to 18 pounds (butchers will cut in half, if you wish). Shank halves contain bone and part of the leg bone, although it costs less per pound than butt, it has a higher proportion of meat.

Country-style hams: A Southern-type ham that must be scrubbed, soaked, and simmered before baking and glazing in the oven.

Ham slices: These are cut out of the center of a whole ham to whatever thickness you like—2 to 3 inches is about right. Stud with cloves, cover with maple syrup, and bake in a slow oven for an hour.

FULLY COOKED HAMS Fully cooked, whole hams, leg bone in, weigh from 8 to 12 pounds. Fully cooked, rolled hams, boneless, can be bought whole, halved, or in smaller pieces. Fully cooked, formed hams weigh from 7 to 10 pounds, whole, although usually available halved or quartered. Fully cooked, Virginia or Smithfield hams are dry salt cured, smoked over hickory, then hung to develop flavor and texture, crowned with coarse black pepper. A ham is not a Smithfield unless it's processed in Smithfield, Virginia, and aged at least 6 months. To serve, slice paper thin.

CANNED HAMS Cured, but not usually smoked: Skinned, trimmed, boned, weigh from 1½ to 10 pounds. Although ready-to-eat, they can be baked whole or sliced paper-thin and pan-fried, or cut thick and baked. Unless label specifies otherwise, canned hams should be refrigerated. Once opened they *must* be refrigerated.

SMOKED SHOULDER AND LOIN CUTS Smoked picnic (or picnic ham): Cut from the shoulder, very smoky flavor, available whole, 4 to 8 pounds, or in halves. Smoked shoulder roll (or butt), weighing from 2 to 4 pounds; simmer or bake the whole roll, or bake, pan-fry, or broil slices. Smoked loin roasts and chops, usually fully cooked; best to heat, however.

OTHER HAM ITEMS Sliced cooked ham: Available by the pound or, in some areas, packaged. Ham loaf: a mixture of ground ham or smoked pork and fresh pork. Must be cooked.

How are smoked loin roasts and pork chops cooked? Cook roasts exactly as you would cured and smoked ham; broil or pan-broil the pork chops.

What is fresh ham? Meat from the leg of a "porker" that has not been cured and smoked. A most delicious cut that can be roasted, plain or stuffed. If to be stuffed, have the butcher make a pocket in the meat to hold the stuffing. Although the butcher will undoubtedly want to skin the leg, don't let him. The crisp skin of fresh ham, properly cooked, is perfectly delicious. Always score the skin before roasting. Allow about 30 minutes per pound for fresh ham, or until a meat thermometer reaches 165° to 170° F.

How do you carve a ham or leg of lamb? Smoked ham, fresh ham (this is pork before curing), and leg of lamb, with the bone in, can all be carved the same two ways: American style and French style.

To carve smoked or fresh ham, or leg of lamb, American style: Before placing the meat on the platter, cut off several slices, parallel to the bone, on the under side to make a flat surface for the meat to rest on. Turn the meat over, fat side up and, holding it firmly with a fork, slice down to the leg bone, beginning at the shank end, then cut along the leg bone parallel to the bone to loosen the slices. For more servings, turn the meat over, and here, too, slice at right angles to the bone. These meats, carved in this fashion, are usually sliced ⅛ to ¼ inch thick.

To carve smoked or fresh ham, or leg of lamb, French style: Place meat on serving platter with shank end at carver's left. Holding the bone with one hand (most skillful carvers use their hand) or steadying it with a fork, make a straight cut down to the bone near the shank end; make a second cut, somewhat higher up, slanting it slightly, to meet the first cut. This wedge, which is mostly fat, is discarded. Now, start slicing, with a long, thin knife, at a 30-degree angle to the bone, keeping the slices very thin and even. Lift the carved slices, with the knife, to one side of the platter or to the dinner plate. About the middle of the roast, or the broadest part, start slicing from one side to the middle. In other words, half slices, for the obvious reason that the whole slices would be too large to fit comfortably on a dinner plate. Continue this pattern, alternating from side to side. For more servings, turn the ham over and slice parallel to the bone.

Is there any easy, handsome glaze for a baked ham? The easiest of all, and one used by many professional chefs, is apricot jam. A half hour before the ham has finished baking, take it out of the oven, cut off any rind, score the fat, diamond-fashion, and place a whole clove in each diamond. Meanwhile, heat a jar of commercial apricot jam, push warm jam through a fine sieve to purée, then spoon the apricot purée over the entire surface of the ham. Return to a 350° F. oven for about half an hour or until glaze has set. This gives the ham a glorious, golden, professional finish.

What are the various types of bacon and how are they used? Bacon comes in many forms, the best known, undoubtedly, is the cured, smoked bacon slices, available in ½-, 1-, and 2-pound packages. As a matter of interest, bacon must be fat to be good—"the leaner, the better" is a fallacy. It can be too lean. All sliced bacon can be used interchangeably. It's simply a matter of which kind you prefer. Over and above the standard sliced, we have the following.

Wafer-thin or thin-sliced bacon: more slices to a pound than in the more familiar sliced bacon, packaged in 8, 12, and 16 ounces; thick-sliced bacon: fewer slices to a pound, available in 1½- and 2-pound packages. Pre-fried or pre-cooked bacon: requires heating for 1 to 3 minutes, available packaged and canned. Packages contain 5 to 6 ounces (18 to 20 slices); canned, about 7 ounces, the equivalent of 1 pound of uncooked bacon. The packaged requires refrigeration. Beef bacon: government regulations forbid its being called "bacon," so the generic name is "breakfast beef," available in ½-pound packages, about 12 to 14 slices. Slab bacon: sold by the pound, with the rind on, for home slicing. It keeps better than sliced bacon, which is one of its major advantages. It is not, as too many people think, more flavorful than sliced; it's the same bacon. Bacon crumbles and bits: completely cooked and crumbled, it is ready to use in casseroles, sandwiches, etc.

Is Canadian-style bacon the same as Irish bacon? Not quite. Canadian bacon is really the boned loin, all in one piece, that has been cured and smoked; Irish bacon includes the loin or "muscle," as it's called by butchers, and the pork that we, in America, use as strip or sliced bacon which comes off the side. It, too, is cured and smoked, but with a heavier smoke. Both of these types of bacon can be baked whole, or cut (usually rather thick) and fried. Both are available imported and domestic.

What is the best way to cook bacon? There is no best.

To pan-fry: Place bacon slices, unseparated, right from the refrigerator, in a cold skillet. Turn heat to low. As the bacon gets warm, the slices will separate. Cook, turning strips frequently, until evenly brown. Do not allow the fat to get hot enough to smoke. Drain on absorbent paper.

To bake: Arrange separated slices on a rack in a shallow pan.

Bake in a preheated 450° F. oven for 10 to 15 minutes or until nicely brown.

To broil: Place separated slices on broiling rack. Broil in a preheated broiler about 3 inches from the heat unit. Turn once to cook and brown evenly.

What are the various types of sausages and how are they used? There are around 250 types of sausage products on the market. Here is an edited list of the most popular.

COOK-BEFORE-EATING SAUSAGE   All are made of selected cuts of fresh meat, primarily pork but sometimes beef, that has not been cured; all must be used within 1 or 2 days of purchase, kept under refrigeration, and cooked thoroughly. Fry, broil, or bake.

Pure pork sausage: spices added, sold in bulk (hot or mild), link, patty or roll form.

Bratwurst: coarsely ground pork frequently with veal, and seasonings.

Bockwurst: composed of meat and eggs finely ground, with the occasional use of milk; highly perishable.

Smoked, country-style pork sausage: coarsely ground pork stuffed into a casing without being cooked, then smoked and cooked.

READY-TO-SERVE SAUSAGE   All are fully cooked, and should be used within a week after purchase.

Frankfurters (origin, Frankfurt, Germany): also called franks, wieners (origin, Vienna, Austria), hot dogs, are finely ground beef and pork mixture (recipes differ somewhat from packer to packer). The kosher variety is all beef, with or without garlic. Certain localities prefer frankfurters artificially colored; others like a natural smoke color. Cocktail franks are miniatures, available frozen and in cans; Vienna sausages are made in links, then cut into pieces and canned.

Smoked linked sausages: fresh pork and lean beef, chopped fairly coarse, seasoned, in links, then smoked and cured.

Bologna: similar to franks, available large for slicing; in rings to serve heated; in sticks for home slicing.

Knackwurst: also called Knoblauch or Garlic Sausage. Made the same way as franks but contains garlic. In short, chubby links.

COOKED SAUSAGE   Prepared from fresh, uncured meats, with

the occasional use of some cured meats. Sometimes, but not always, smoked after cooking. Must be refrigerated.

Liver sausage (Braunschweiger): made from livers and pork which have been cooked and, in some instances, smoked.

Liver cheese (liver loaf): similar to the sausage, with better body for slicing, molded into a brick shape.

Blood sausage (Blutwurst): contains beef blood and sometimes bits of fat pork and tongue.

Keilbasa (or Polish sausage): fine pork blended with beef, delicately seasoned with garlic. Stuffed into casing, made into links, then smoked and cooked in the smokehouse.

SEMI-DRY SAUSAGE   Ready to eat, these sausages have a long storage life, if refrigerated. Semi-dry simply means that less than 20% of the natural moisture has been removed.

Soft summer sausage: Usually all beef, or predominantly beef, mildly flavored, smoked in varying degrees. Excellent cold, in sandwiches, fried or grilled with eggs, red cabbage, or sauerkraut.

Cooked or cotto salami: usually 50% pork and beef, heavy with garlic. Available in varying sizes from 10 to 14 ounces. Good luncheon meat or julienned in green salads, cole slaw, or potato salad. Yildiz (all-beef salami) is made the same way.

Mortadella (Italian-type bologna): made from beef and pork with chunks of pork fat and garlic. Available from 4 pounds up to 8 pounds. Use in sandwiches, on cold plates, or baked with a sauce.

Lebanon bologna: coarsely ground, all beef, with a heavy smoke. Its sour, tangy taste and almost black color are characteristic. By the piece, it weighs about 8 pounds. Made only in Lebanon, Pennsylvania. Excellent in sandwiches, on cold plates, grilled or fried with baked beans, and in hot potato salad.

Kosher salami: all beef, rabbinical-inspected meat, and produced under rabbinical supervision. Available from 14 ounces to 6 pounds. Generally used in making sandwiches or served on cold plates.

DRY SAUSAGES   These sausages have more than 20% of the natural moisture removed and, like the semi-dry, have a long storage life, if refrigerated. There are two kinds: salamis and cervelats, differentiated by the fact the salamis are heavily seasoned while the cervelats are much milder.

THE SALAMIS   Genoa salami: The most popular, called the "king" of all salamis, the best of which are all pork. Available in 4- and 5-pound pieces. Use in sandwiches, on cold plates, for antipasto, in lasagna, noodles, spaghetti, and other Italian recipes calling for salami.

Sicilian-type salami: there are two types—lola and calabrese salami.

Lola, all pork, mildly seasoned, with garlic, is easily identified by being closely wrapped with twine. Usually available in 14-ounce sizes. Good in sandwiches or salads and, sliced very thin, as an appetizer. Calabrese salami, all pork, very hot with hot peppers. Use for sandwiches, antipasto, cold plates, in casseroles or Italian specialties.

Cotto salami: Pork and beef, highly seasoned, contains garlic. Bright, cherry red, cooked and heavily smoked. Available in 8 to 11 ounce sizes. Can be used in all the ways other types of salami are used.

Easter nola: pork, mildly seasoned, with black peppers and garlic. Used in sandwiches, salads, and many famous Italian dishes.

Frizzes: all pork, flavored with black peppers and some garlic. Good for sandwiches, cold plates, and many Italian dishes.

Hot pepperoni (*caserta pepperoni*): pork, sometimes with beef, with chili peppers and paprika. Each pepperoni contains two links, weighing about 12 ounces. A delicious snack, it's often used on pizzas. Very good sliced thin, diced, then fried with scrambled eggs.

Sweet pepperoni (*dolce salsiccia*): pork, mildly seasoned with salt and black pepper. Two short, chunky links, weighing 8 to 12 ounces. Can be used interchangeably with hot pepperoni.

Goteborg: predominately beef—as its name indicates—of Scandinavian origin. Seasoned mildly with salt, pepper, and thyme. Use as you would any mild dry sausage.

Holsteiner: predominately beef, heavily smoked. Made in rings weighing ½ pound. Popular with the Belgians, Germans, Dutch, and in American farm communities. Use on cold plates, in sandwiches, salads, etc.

Dry cervelat: a hard summer sausage, mildly seasoned, heavily smoked. Available in 8 and 12 ounces. Everybody loves this good sausage. Excellent with a drink or in sandwiches. To cook, slice very thin, add to a hot cream sauce and serve on toast.

Chorizos: A Spanish pork sausage, made from graded, coarsely chopped pork. Seasoned with imported Spanish pimiento and sweet red pepper. Lightly smoked. Available looped in 4-inch links. Commonly used in soups and as a flavoring for vegetables.

How do you heat frankfurters or hot dogs?   They are, of course, thoroughly cooked when you buy them, but the flavor improves when heated—even if they are eventually served cold.

To heat in water: Drop into simmering water and allow to heat through for 5 minutes or so after the water comes to "simmer" again. (Do not boil or pierce skins.) Lift from water with tongs.

To broil: Brush with vegetable oil, then broil 3 inches from heat, 5 minutes on each side. Or split lengthwise, not quite through, and broil, cut side up, until lightly browned.

To pan-broil: Cook in a small amount of hot fat in a skillet, turning occasionally, until lightly browned. Or split lengthwise, brown cut sides first, then the skin sides.

Can fresh sausage meat be frozen?   No. The flavor will be impaired and the texture changes.

How do you cook fresh sausage or uncooked smoked sausage?
Pan-fried: Place links or patties in a cold frying pan. Add 2 to 4 tablespoons of water, cover tightly, and cook slowly for 5 to 8 minutes. Remove cover, brown slowly until well-done.

In the oven: Arrange in a single layer in a shallow baking pan. Bake in a preheated 400° F. oven 20 to 30 minutes or until nicely done. Turn once or twice to brown evenly, siphon off the drippings as they accumulate.

What is a cassoulet?   A famous French dish composed of white beans and a combination of such meats as pork, sausage, goose, mutton, or other poultry, sometimes game. The invariable rule about cassoulets, whatever the origin and the other ingredients, seems to be that it is a dish of white beans cooked in a pot with some form of pork or sausage.

What are chitterlings?   The small intestines of the pig, fried. An American corruption of the English, chitlings, means rags and tatters. Seems appropriate. It means, too, the "pluck" (heart, liver, etc.) of young lambs or calves.

What is feijoada?   Pronounced fay-zhway-dah, it is the national dish of Brazil. The main components are black beans, collards, farina, several meats, onion rings, fresh orange slices, and rice. Roast pork usually accompanies the beans. Each is served separately.

Casa Brasil, one of New York's most interesting and smallest (it seats only 20) restaurants, serves feijoada, exclusively, every Wednesday night. Other nights Dona Helma, the proprietor, offers a more varied menu—equally superb.

What is jambalaya?   A Creole dish that consists of smoked pork sausage or ham, green peppers, shrimp, tomatoes, onion, garlic, parsley, rice, and seasonings. The name comes from the Spanish, *jamón*, meaning ham.

What are canned luncheon meats made from?   Usually pork shoulder, sometimes with ham or beef added, delicately spiced. Although ready to eat, they can be fried, baked, or used combined with a sauce.

What is prosciutto?   A delicious, highly seasoned Italian ham, sliced very thin and served with breads such as pumpernickel and rye. Or, as a first course, with melon or fresh figs. The only accompaniment needed is a peppermill. Germany's Westphalian ham is comparable. A domestic prosciutto-type ham is now available in the U.S.

What are rillettes?   Like *rillauds*, or *rillots*, or *rillons*, they are combinations of pork, both lean and fat, cut in small pieces, cooked in lard with seasonings, very common all through France. Comparable to *pâtés*, except they are coarser.

What is scrapple?   *Ponhaws*. as the Pennsylvania Dutch called it, was originally a way to use up scraps of pork after the hogs were slaughtered. Today, it is cooked pork shoulder, liver, cornmeal, and seasonings, chilled until firm, then cut into slices, floured, and fried.

Are short ribs and spareribs from the same animal?   No. Short ribs are from beef; spareribs, from pigs. Short ribs can be braised or marinated, then roasted; spareribs can be broiled, or marinated, then roasted. Allow around 5 pounds or so of either for about 4 people.

Doesn't anybody ever eat the tenderloin of pork?   Yes, but you'll have to hunt to find a recipe. It's so small, it takes 2 or 3 to make a decent meal for a family. The *Joy of Cooking* offers a couple of recipes, one of which suggests cutting the tenderloin into 1-inch pieces, rolling them in seasoned flour, then sautéeing in butter. Finish the dish with heavy cream.

What are the various cuts of veal and how are they prepared? Anyone who has ever eaten veal in France will remember the young, whitish-pink, unbelievably good meat for which we have no equivalent. Most of the veal we get is baby beef, not meat from a milk-fed animal under twelve weeks old. A superb, white veal, under the name of *plume de veau,* is currently being developed in the East. It is expensive but worth tracking down if you're fond of veal. Mrs. Julia Child (the French chef of TV fame) suggests, "You train yourself, when shopping for veal, to look carefully at its color. Once you are aware of what good quality should look like, you can avoid the frankly reddish pieces. You will be more likely to find the better qualities of veal in markets catering to a European clientele."

Most cooks agree that the double loin of veal, which corresponds to the saddle, and the loin (sometimes called tenderloin), which is a boned rack, are the best cuts for roasting. If you can get young, white veal, the rump makes a delicious roast, and the cut which corresponds to the eye of the round in beef, is also excellent.

Because veal has no natural fat covering, such as other meats, and no marbling of fat inside the meat, roasted cuts need barding with fat (fresh fat pork, if available, or blanched bacon) or larding. Unlike beef and lamb, veal is always roasted well-done or until the juices run clear yellow with no traces of pink—about 175° F. on a meat thermometer or 30 to 40 minutes, per pound, depending on the thickness of the meat, in a preheated 325° F. oven. Most veal cuts are best braised.

Veal should never be broiled. Thin cuts, such as scaloppine or veal birds, are delicious sautéed, and ground veal can be pan-fried.

What is blanquette de veau? It is a famous French dish that is nothing more than a glorious veal stew made with onions, mushrooms, eggs, and cream which, when served, is a creamy white (hence, blanquette). Purists season it with white pepper, rather than black, to keep it white. *Blanquette d'agneau* is, of course, a lamb stew. These are noble dishes worthy of your most important dinner parties.

What is osso buco?   Veal shanks, served with a mixture of vegetables, specifically tomatoes, seasonings, and wine.

Is scaloppine the same thing as a veal cutlet?   No. Scaloppine are small squares of veal, sliced exceedingly thin, then pounded, usually cut off the leg. Correctly, a cutlet is a veal chop but it depends on what country you're in. *Escalope* is the French equivalent of the Italian *scaloppini* and, to further confuse matters, the English have corrupted *escalope* to collop, a term you may occasionally run into. Germans and Austrians call the same cut *Schnitzel*.

What is vitello tonnato?   Veal cooked with tuna and many seasonings, served cold with a sauce made with good mayonnaise, the concentrated, strained broth from the cooked meat, lemon juice, and capers. A superb buffet supper dish with cold, parsley rice. Chicken can also be prepared this way: thus, *pollo tonnato.*

What is Wiener Schnitzel?   Breaded veal cutlets, sautéed in butter. Schnitzel à la Holstein is a veal cutlet, sautéed in butter, served with a fried egg on top.

What are variety meats?   Liver, brains, heart, kidneys, sweetbreads, tongue, tripe, etc. All excellent sources of essential nutriments, usually more economical than other cuts of meat and, when prepared properly, make delicious eating.

Do brains and sweetbreads need any special care before cooking? They do, indeed. Wash in cold water, then soak in cold water for several hours, changing the water several times. This softens the filaments that cover them and dissolves any patches of blood. With the help of a small knife or, better, with your hands, pull off as much of the membrane that encloses them as you can without breaking the flesh. Soak them again for about 2 hours in several changes of acidulated water (1 tablespoon of vinegar to 1 quart of water). Again, peel off as much more of the membrane as you can. With sweetbreads, you now separate the two lobes from the tube with a knife; with brains, cut off the white, opaque bits at the base. Both should be blanched if they are to be sautéed; unnecessary if they are to be braised. Blanching will help to preserve them if they are not going to be cooked within a day. But they *must* be used within 24 hours because they are highly perishable.

How are brains prepared? They can be braised, sautéed, or cooked and served in a sauce. They are extremely perishable and should be used immediately after purchase, or should be precooked. *Cervelles au beurre noir* is one of the classic and more delicious ways of serving calf's brains.

What are sweetbreads? The thymus glands of a young calf (in French, *ris de veau*). A great delicacy, they are used in innumerable ways in cookery. Handle and prepare as you would brains.

How is heart cooked? Braised or cooked in a liquid, because it is one of the less tender of the variety meats.

How are kidneys prepared before cooking? The membrane and hard parts should be removed. Lamb kidneys can be split or left whole; beef kidneys, less tender than other kidneys, should be made into a stew or braised. Because they are inclined to be strong, it is advisable to soak them in water, with vinegar, for a couple of hours, before proceeding with the recipe. Lamb chops, with a kidney in the center, broiled, are an elegant and delicious extravagance.

Is there any way to make it easy to grind liver? Yes. Cook the liver slowly, on both sides, in 2 or 3 tablespoons of fat, for 5 minutes. This softens the tissues and makes grinding much easier.

How can you buy tongue? Fresh, pickled, corned, smoked, or canned. The fresh usually has to be ordered, since most markets don't keep it on hand as they do the others. A delicious meat, for which more people should cultivate a taste.

What is tripe? The stomach of beef cattle. The smaller section is called honeycomb tripe. Widely used as food in France, *Hering's Dictionary of Classical and Modern Cookery* cites more than two dozen French recipes. *Tripes à la mode de Caen* and *tripes à la lyonnaise* are two famous dishes.

What is Philadelphia pepperpot? Its base is tripe, and it's made with

a vast quantity of seasonings, veal bone, marrow bone, and vegetables. Served with dumplings, cooked in the simmering soup. It is
said to have been improvised when supplies were low at Valley
Forge. Available, today, canned.

What is venison? Formerly it applied to the meat of any animal killed
in the chase and used as food. Today, it is more usually applied to
the meat from deer. If you are lucky enough to get a young deer that
has eaten well, you're in for a treat. But if, on the other hand, it did
the chasing, you may find it tough going. In which case, braise or pot
roast the meat.

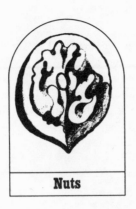

Nuts

How do you judge nuts in the shell?   The shells should be clean, free from cracks, scars, and holes and the kernels should not rattle, if shaken. Rattling indicates dried-out kernels. Walnuts in the shell are a favorite for cracking and snacking around a big fire, especially at holiday time. The English eat them with port.

What's the best way to protect nuts from turning rancid?   In the shell, store at room temperature, unless for a prolonged period; otherwise refrigerate. Kernels (those you have opened yourself) should be frozen. Once cans, jars, or bags have been opened, refrigerate or freeze, depending on how soon they will be used.

How do you freeze nuts?   Place kernels in a tightly covered freezer container or plastic bag (all air squeezed out), tied tightly. After thawing, allow nuts to dry out before using. Unlike other foods, nuts can be refrozen successfully.

How can you buy almonds?   In every conceivable form. In the shell; whole natural; whole blanched; sliced natural; blanched, slivered, and toasted; sliced blanched; diced and roasted; ground blanched; smoked (to serve with drinks). And every one has a good use. The whole, natural or blanched, make beautiful garnishes; the sliced, natural or toasted slivered, are good for mixing into things; the diced, roasted, can be added to almost any batter, mixed with or sprinkled over other foods; and the ground blanched can be turned into stuffings, used in place of flour in European cakes, etc.

197

How are almonds used in cookery?   It would take a whole cook book
to cover all the ways. Here are a few examples: with cooked rice
and currants or onions, or in bean salads; salted almonds with drinks;
in sandwiches; in candies; in pastry; in place of flour in cakes; in
macaroons; in pies; as a garnish on cakes; with chicken; etc. Next
time you serve rice as a vegetable with chicken, try this simple, good,
little recipe.

   Almond currant rice: Brown ⅓ cup slivered almonds slowly in ¼ cup
butter. Add ¼ cup currants. Combine with 1 cup hot, cooked rice, toss
until well mixed. Serves 4.

What is the easiest way to blanch almonds?   Bring a saucepan of water
to a boil, drop the almonds in slowly, so as not to stop the water's
boiling, and boil for about 1 minute. Drain. Then slip off the skins
between the thumb and forefinger. This works more effectively, I
find, than covering the nuts with boiling water and allowing them
to stand. If you are going to use the almonds immediately (and need
them thoroughly dry), place for a few minutes in a moderate oven,
in a large pan.

How do you sliver almonds?   Blanch, if necessary, and slice with a
very sharp, small knife while they are still warm and damp. But it's
much easier to buy them already slivered and toasted.

What are bitter almonds?   The kernel of the fruit from the bitter
almond tree, which yields a fragrant oil used in the preparation of
pastry and confections, commercially called almond extract. They are
not edible as food, as is the sweet almond.

What are burnt almonds?   An unfortunate name for sweet, blanched
almonds, roasted to a golden brown. It probably stems from the days
of uncontrolled ovens when the almonds, more often than not, were
burnt.

What are green almonds?   Young, sweet almonds marketed while their
shells are soft and their outer skins are green and tender. The white,
creamy kernels, considered a great delicacy, are peeled and eaten
fresh.

What is a Jordan almond?   An almond coated with hard sugar, in white or pastel colors, known in France as *dragées*. Apparently they originated in Rome, as early as 177 BC, and were used as a token of rejoicing on the occasion of a birth or a marriage in patrician families. The custom still exists in France and in many Mediterranean, Middle Eastern, and North African countries. At the time of King Hussein's marriage a few years ago, the guests at the wedding received mother-of-pearl boxes filled with Jordan almonds. How they came to be called Jordan almonds is a mystery. In this country, dragée means the little silver-coated "bullets" used to decorate cakes and candies.

What does amandine mean applied to cookery? Prepared with almonds. *Amandine* is the French for almonds.

Are Brazil nuts ever used in cooking? In innumerable ways: in fruit cakes, puddings, tarts; ground, in place of flour; as a garnish on cakes, etc. Out of the shell, they are delightful, and will remind many beyond the age of say, forty, of Christmas stockings with a "pigtoe" in the toe.

How do you crack Brazil nuts? As the saying goes, "It's a hard nut to crack." To facilitate cracking, freeze them. Then crack open with a hammer. Brazil nuts are available in the shell or out, in transparent bags.

Are cashew nuts ever used in cooking? Yes, although most of us are more accustomed to eating them roasted or salted with drinks. The Cashew Export Council of India has many suggestions, including: spiced, curried, with broiled chicken, cashew butter over vegetables, with baked fish, in frostings, etc.

Cashews, imported from Brazil and India, are available plain, roasted and salted, whole or in pieces, packed in cans, jars, or plastic bags. You'll find them in stores specializing in quality foods.

How do you shell chestnuts? With a small, sharp knife, peel a tiny strip of shell off one side of each chestnut. Place chestnuts in a pan of cold water, bring to a boil, and boil 1 minute. The trick in getting the outer and bitter inner shell off is to work with the chestnuts while they are warm. So, once they have been boiled, peel them one by one. Any that refuse to co-operate should be dropped back into boiling water for a moment.

How many cups does 1 pound of chestnuts yield? 35 to 40 whole, raw chestnuts, or approximately 1 pound, will yield 2½ cups peeled chestnuts.

How do you cook chestnuts? Once shelled, they can be cooked in a well-seasoned stock, then puréed, seasoned with salt, pepper, butter, cream, a pinch of sugar, and served as a vegetable; or they can be braised whole, in a good stock and, again, served as a vegetable; when called for in *entremets,* the raw nuts are usually cooked in sweetened milk or a vanilla syrup, then puréed.

Can you buy fresh coconut? Yes. They're available, imported, to some extent all year, but the peak months are mostly September through December. In choosing coconuts, look for those that are heavy for their size and full of milk. Shake the coconut and you will hear the milk sloshing around. Those without milk, moldy, or with "wet" eyes should be avoided. (Coconut is available flaked, grated, and toasted, of course, all year).

To open a coconut, put it in a 350° F. oven briefly or in the freezer (zero temperature) for an hour. Pierce a couple of the eyes with an ice pick and a hammer, or comparable implement, and drain off the milk. Finally, drop the coconut from a good height on a hard surface (the porch makes sense) to crack it open. It will break into many pieces, which makes it very easy to remove the shell, then peel the skin off the meat. If you haven't a good, solid porch, crack it open with a mallet or hammer.

Fresh coconut makes the most wonderful coconut cake; it's splendid (the milk, too) in a curry; it makes a nice baked pudding and marvelous ice cream. Children love to drink the milk, *au naturel,* right out of the nut.

Are hazelnuts and filberts the same thing? Yes. The hazelnut is the wild nut and the filbert, the cultivated. All those commercially marketed are designated filberts. Filberts, whether used as an ingredient in a recipe or eaten out of hand, are usually used with the skins left on. The skin can, of course, be removed, but most people find the flavor and texture of the skin attractive. The elegant filbert, available both shelled and unshelled, is generally considered best if the nut is lightly toasted before using. To toast: spread whole filberts in a shallow pan and bake in a 400° F. oven 10 to 15 minutes. Stir or shake the nuts occasionally during baking. To skin: toast as directed, then rub toasted nuts in a towel or between your hands to rub off skins.

Filberts are only marketed whole, in plastic bags (3 ounces to 6 ounces, depending on the packer) and, although available the year round, you'll probably discover they are easier to find during the fall and running into Christmas. They keep well refrigerated and can, if the necessity arises, be frozen most satisfactorily.

What are marrons?   Chestnuts. Available raw, fresh in the winter, they are also imported, canned, in these forms: sweet purée (*crème de marrons*), used in making dessert sweets; whole in water (*marrons entier au naturel*), used as a vegetable, in stuffing, chopped as a garnish; whole or chopped in vanilla-flavored syrup (*marrons au sirop*), used in making desserts; unflavored, unsweetened purée of chestnuts (*purée de marrons au naturel*), used in stuffings, desserts, and vegetable sauces.

What does nougat mean?   Essentially, a sweet composed of nuts, usually almonds, and sugar. According to some authorities it is the same as pralin. Actually, it can be many things, including a type of confection called white nougat (*nougat blanc*), the celebrated nougat of Montélimar. And there is a cake made with walnut oil called nougat.

What are dry-roasted peanuts?   Peanuts that have been oven-roasted, as against deep-fat fried. In addition to peanuts, other nuts are available dry-roasted: cashews, pecans, blanched almonds, Spanish peanuts, mixed nuts. Obviously, dry-roasted nuts would tend to have fewer calories than fried. In cans or jars, vacuum-packed.

Is there a low-calorie peanut?   Yes. In the processing of these nuts, a high percentage of the fat is replaced with water. Low-calorie nuts are available in jars, vacuum-packed.

What are Spanish peanuts?   Small peanuts with red skins. Available dry-roasted or oil-roasted, salted, vacuum-packed in jars, cans, or transparent bags.

Are pecans a native nut?   Yes, native to the South, and known to the Indians as *pecaunes*. They didn't come north of the Mason and Dixon Line until after the Civil War. So, it is the South that can take credit for such American delicacies as pecan pie, pralines, and pecan rolls. Pecans are available in the shell, in bags or bulk (unlike some other nuts, they are relatively easy to crack), whole, in pieces, and roasted, plain, or salted; in plastic bags, vacuum cans, or jars.

What are hickory nuts? There are many varieties, but the "shagbarks" are the most desirable and they are sold under the name of pecans.

What are pine nuts? Also known as Indian nuts, *pignon, pignolia,* the more familiar name is *piñon* (rhymes with canyon), they are the seeds from a species of pine tree that grows extensively in the American Southwest, Italy, and France (where our imports hail from). Whitish, cylindrical, and about ¼ of an inch long, they are either roasted or salted, or used plain in cookery, much as you would use almonds—in confectionery and pastries. You often see them as a garnish on Italian cookies. They are also used in meats, salads, sauces, and rice dishes in Mediterranean countries. Generally available in jars.

Are the shells of pistachio nuts naturally red? No. The true color is just off-beige. In Turkey and Iran, where pistachio trees grow, the nuts are roasted in the sun in a salt brine, which turns the shells a pinkish color. American importers attempted to imitate this color, and in the process came out with the now-familiar "shocking" red. As a matter of interest, the pistachio fruit grows in clusters, like grapes, on trees as large as our apple trees, and the nuts we eat are actually the seeds of the fruit. Pistachio nuts, artificially colored, are available vacuum-packed or in moisture-proof bags, in shells; or *au naturel,* without coloring; in limited distribution, and very expensive, out of the shell in jars.

In what forms are walnuts available? In the shell, in transparent bags, of 1 and 2 pounds. Shelled, in 3-ounce to 2-pound clear bags; and in 4-ounce and 8-ounce vacuum cans.

How are walnuts used in cooking? Pies, cakes, puddings, cookies can all be made with walnuts. The toasted nuts added to salads (marvelous in chicken salad), Brussels sprouts, green beans, etc. Ground walnuts, in place of flour, make many spectacular confections, including a walnut roll with a whipped cream filling.

Are black walnuts like butternuts?   No. We have two species of native
North American walnut trees: black and white. The bark of the tree
determines the name of the nut. However, white walnuts are better
known as butternuts—our native Indians called them *wussoquat*—
familiar and beloved by our "foremothers." A very rich nut, it was
used by New England cooks in custard pies, in rice puddings sweetened with maple syrup, and in frostings. Unless you have a butternut
tree on your property, you will probably have to forego the pleasure
of cooking with them.

Black walnuts are available, in the shell, in bulk and vacuum-
packed cans. They, too, make a marvelous addition to a cake or frosting. However, the shell, hard as that well-known rock, is formidable.
Once cracked, the meat usually has to be picked out—often a de-
terrent to the cook.

What are English walnuts?   They are not, as one might logically think,
a type of walnut grown in England. The Persian walnut, brought to
England by the Romans, came to be known as Circassian walnut and
was used extensively by English furniture makers. It was later,
erroneously, called "English" walnut—and that's the circuitous route
by which English got tacked onto the nuts.

What are pickled walnuts?   Green walnuts that are eventually cooked,
then bottled in spiced vinegar. They are not, as some people believe,
black walnuts, but rather the common walnut with which we are all
familiar. Long a favorite relish in England (where they are made),
pickled walnuts make an interesting addition to a "kipper breakfast."
They also go well with roasts and cold meats. Available in fine food
stores.

Poultry

Are poultry and fowl the same thing? Yes. They both mean any domesticated bird used for food. However, fowl is often used, especially by old-time cooks, to designate a mature hen, as distinguished from a broiler or roasting chicken.

Do you wash poultry before cooking? No. Some people have the unfortunate habit of running cold water through the cavity of the bird, which can do nothing more than help to destroy flavor. If there should be any need for wiping (never washing)—and today, this would be most unusual with the kind of beautiful, clean birds we get—simply wipe with a clean, damp cloth.

Are frozen turkeys and chickens as good as fresh? Not in my opinion. In general, few frozen foods are as good as fresh. However, we have to accept the facts of life and learn to use these foods with imagination. Care in thawing and preparation are of extreme importance.

Is it true hen turkeys are more tender than Tom turkeys? No. Once, when it took 8 to 12 months to raise a turkey for the table, this may have been true but today, practically all the turkeys, whether girls or boys, in the market are young—from 3 to 6 months old. Hence, tender and delicious, when cooked properly.

How can you buy turkeys these days? Whole, ready to cook, fresh, fresh chilled but not frozen, or frozen, although the majority available are frozen; raw, boneless roasts in 2- to 8-pound sizes; turkey rolls in 2- to 10-pound sizes, or bought cut to fit your needs; pre-stuffed, frozen, ready-to-cook from the frozen state, usually weighing from

8 to 12 pounds; turkey parts, wings and legs particularly, but also some thighs and breast meat, frozen.

How long can you keep frozen chicken in the freezer? If it's in an actual freezer (one that is separate from the refrigerator, with its own door, and maintaining zero temperature), chicken can be stored 6 to 7 months; the giblets, 2 to 3 months. But, if it is in the section where the ice cubes are stored, you should limit the time to 2 weeks, since this section is not cold enough.

N O T E : Do not refreeze the chicken once it has been thawed, and cook it promptly after thawing.

How do you thaw frozen fowl? Preferably in its original wrapper in the refrigerator (allow a good long day for a 3- to 5-pound bird). But, if time is of the essence, you can thaw it in its original wrapper or, lacking that, a polyethylene bag that is tied securely, under cold running water. The point to remember, if you use this second method, is that the water must not reach the bird, or much of the juices and flavor will be lost.

What is meant by disjoint? To cut poultry (chicken, turkey, game, or other birds) into pieces at the joints.

What is an eviscerated chicken? One that has been completely cleaned and had the entrails taken out. This applies to all poultry. However, the heart, liver, gizzard, and the neck, wrapped in paper, are returned to the cavity of the bird for the cook to use.

What is meant by singe? It simply means to burn off any hairs or pinfeathers on fowl. You do this by holding the bird over an open flame, turning it quickly to singe any hairs or feathers. Actually, our poultry today is so clean the problem rarely arises. However, it might be necessary with wild game birds.

What does truss mean? To tie the wings and legs of poultry tightly in place so the bird holds its shape while cooking and looks shapely when presented at the table.

What's the best way to truss a chicken? There are many ways, but we find the easiest is the way our butcher does it. First, however, rub the inside of the neck and cavity with a mixture of salt and pepper and the cut side of a lemon, add a bit of thyme, a sprig or two of parsley, and a knob of butter.

To truss: Place the bird on your work table with legs facing you. Fold the wing tips under, akimbo, and pull the neck skin under. Take a good long piece of lightweight white string and slip it under the body, holding the neck skin in place. Bring one length of the string along the right side of the body, across the cavity, and loop around the left leg; do the same with the other length, looping it around the right leg. Then draw the two together tightly and tie. Clip off the ends. Before roasting, rub the entire bird generously with softened butter. All birds can be trussed the same way.

Is a broiler the same thing as a frying chicken? Yes. Designated by the Poultry and Egg National Board as broiler-fryers, they are young, all-purpose birds, weighing from 1½ to 4 pounds, that can be broiled, sautéed, deep-fat or pan-fried.

What are capons? Castrated cocks, weighing from 6 to 7 pounds or better, especially desirable for roasting when a large bird is in order.

What are hens? Also called stewing chickens and fowl (the name varies according to the region), they are mature females, less tender, less expensive than roasters and, generally, heavier. Don't choose one weighing less than 5 pounds. When poached properly, the way we recommend cooking them, they are the basis for many magnificent dishes calling for cooked chicken meat—chicken salads, chicken pie, jellied chicken, etc. We further recommend poaching them whole, rather than cut up (regardless of their ultimate use) for greater flavor, tenderness, and succulence.

The broth from a poached hen has endless possibilities. It can be cleared to make aspic; in itself, it makes a delicious soup, with or without the addition of fresh vegetables; obviously, it can be used in any recipe calling for chicken broth. Freeze, if you are not going to use it up fairly soon, or store in the refrigerator in a clean jar, sealed with its own fat or melted vegetable shortening.

What are squab chickens? Mere babies, weighing about 1 pound, which can be roasted whole in a hot, 450° F. oven, or split and broiled. Serve 1 to a person.

What is a supreme? The breast of chicken when it is removed, raw, from one side of the bird, in a skinless, boneless piece. One breast, both sides, contains two supremes. There are many delicious ways to cook them, but the point to remember is they must not be over-cooked.

To poach in clarified butter: Salt and pepper lightly, roll in flour, shaking off any excess; heat butter until it begins to color slightly, add the supremes (don't crowd the pan), cook for 3 minutes on one side, turn and cook 2 on the other. They are springy to the touch when cooked perfectly.

What are roasting chickens? Large birds, older than broiler-fryers, ranging from 3 to 5 pounds, best roasted, with or without stuffing, poached, or fricasseed.

Why is my broiled chicken sometimes dry and stringy? You cook it too long and you don't baste it enough. Buy one 2½-pound broiler-fryer for 2 people. Have the butcher split it and remove the backbone and neck (drop these into the next chicken stock you make). Twist the wing joints in the sockets so the pieces lie flat. Preheat the broiler. Rub the chicken well with softened butter, arrange on a greased rack, skin side down, and sprinkle with salt and pepper. Broil, 4 inches below the heating unit, basting every 5 minutes with melted butter, for 15 minutes. Turn, sprinkle with salt and pepper, and broil for 10 minutes, basting once or twice with butter. Test for doneness by pricking the leg or thigh with a fork. The juice that runs out should be clear yellow. If tinged with pink, broil a few minutes longer.

How do you test roast fowl for doneness? Take several folds of paper toweling (unless you have "hot" fingers, like chefs) and feel the drumstick. It should feel soft and the bone should move easily in its socket. Or prick the thickest part of the leg with a fork. Juices should run clear yellow without any trace of pink. With a poached bird (chicken, duck, turkey), the flesh of the leg will feel soft and the meat will have just begun to shrink from the tip of the drumstick.

Do you use a meat thermometer to test chicken? No. The test for doneness is extremely satisfactory and, further, it is difficult to insert a thermometer far enough into the flesh of a bird without touching bone.

At what temperature should chickens be roasted? Unless the recipe specifies otherwise, we recommend roasting at 350° F. in a preheated oven; the chicken should be at room temperature when put in the oven. If the bird is stuffed, allow a few minutes longer, but, here you should depend on the doneness test.

Ready-to-Cook Weight (in pounds)	Number of People It Will Serve	Approximate Total Cooking Time
¾ to 1	1	30 to 40 minutes
1½	2	40 to 50 minutes
3	4	50 to 60 minutes
4	4 to 5	1 hour, 10–20 minutes
4½	5 to 6	1 hour, 15–30 minutes
5¼	6 to 7	1 hour, 30–45 minutes

Can you roast two or more chickens in the same pan? Yes. But you should roast them in a pan generous enough for "elbow" room, at a higher heat (say 10 to 15 degrees higher) than normal. Otherwise they will, quite literally, stew in their own juices.

How long does it take to thaw a turkey in the refrigerator? From 1 to 3 days, depending on the size.

Do you roast fowl in foil? No, because this is steaming, not roasting. However, the method has two advantages: it eliminates basting and reduces the cooking time, which is sometimes important. For example, a 6- to 8-pound turkey, wrapped in foil, should be roasted at 450° F., in a preheated oven, for 1½ to 2 hours (a saving of half an hour). See the temperature chart for roasting turkey without foil and gauge all other weights accordingly.

At what temperature should turkey be roasted? At the same temperature you roast chicken, 350° F. in a preheated oven. Since turkey is normally stuffed, you should, as with chicken, allow extra roasting time for a stuffed bird. Use this timetable as a guide and always test for doneness (page 208):

Ready-to-Cook Weight (in pounds)	Number of People It Will Serve	Approximate Total Cooking Time (in hours)
6 to 8	6 to 10	2 to 2½
8 to 12	10 to 20	2¾ to 3
12 to 16	20 to 32	3¾ to 4

Why do turkey legs sometimes seem dry after roasting? The turkey is inclined to be dry by nature and the legs, which cook more quickly

than the breast, will dry out during the long roasting time, unless protected. Many good cooks cover the entire bird with about 3 layers of
cheesecloth soaked in butter, basting right through the cheesecloth.
This not only helps to keep the turkey moist, but also helps to brown
it beautifully and evenly.

How do you stuff fowl? Chicken, turkey, squab, pheasant, etc., in fact
all birds, are stuffed the same way.

Prepare large birds by rubbing both the neck and cavity with a cut
lemon; small ones, just the cavity. With large birds (not squab, Rock
Cornish game hens, squab chickens, etc.), I like to stuff both the neck
and the cavity in the belief the roasted bird looks handsomer. Spoon
some of the stuffing into the neck, and pull the neck skin under the
bird, then spoon remainder of the stuffing into the cavity. Fasten
the opening with a metal skewer or a toothpick. At this point you
are ready to truss the bird properly.

Can poultry be stuffed the day before roasting? It is not recommended, but if the bird is refrigerated, then brought to room temperature before going in the oven (with turkey, for example, this will
take a good long time), it sems to us perfectly safe. The reason it is
not recommended is because of the possibility of bacteria develop-
ing. It has always seemed to me that any bacteria with enough forti-
tude to survive all that time in a hot oven deserved to live.

Can chickens and turkeys be cooked on a rotisserie? Yes. The size of
the bird is only limited by the size of the rotisserie. Rub the inside of
the chicken or turkey with a cut lemon, plenty of butter, salt, and
pepper. Truss, insert spit rod, and balance. Brush with equal parts
of butter and white wine from time to time. Follow manufacturer's
directions for temperature and roast until done.

Can the rack (carcass) of a chicken be put to any good use? It certainly can. You can make good chicken stock with it. Place the rack,
gizzard, and neck (freeze the liver to use some other way) in a
heavy pan along with an onion stuck with two cloves, a bay leaf, a
few peppercorns, a stalk or two of celery with their tops, a few sprigs
of parsley, a scraped carrot, and a good dash of salt. Cover with cold
water and bring slowly to a boil. Simmer, covered, for a couple of
hours or until broth has boiled down to about half. Remove rack and

any bones, strain, and pour into a jar that has been scalded in boiling water. Refrigerate.

If enough chicken fat does not rise to the top to seal the stock completely, cover with melted vegetable shortening. It is important for the stock to be sealed securely; otherwise it will turn sour. Sealed with chicken fat only, it will keep several weeks in the refrigerator; sealed with melted vegetable shortening, it will keep almost indefinitely (as homemade jellies do). Frozen, it will really keep indefinitely. It's practical to store the stock (or broth) in pint jars rather than in large ones. To use, remove and discard congealed fat.

Stock from the rack will not make as sturdy and rich a broth as stock made with the whole chicken. However, it's handy to have on hand to use as a base for soups, to cook vegetables or rice, or to add to any recipe calling for chicken stock. An inexpensive, useful backlog.

Does a tiny blood clot or pink flesh indicate fowl is insufficently cooked?   No. Slight pinkness of the meat or miniature clots sometimes found in the legs or thighs of roasted birds are perfectly normal. For the record, darkened bones are one of the best indications of a young bird.

How do you carve a turkey, chicken, and capon?   All are carved exactly the same, with one exception (see Step 5). The bird should be on a warm platter, generous enough for its size, and the platter should be placed in front of the carver with the bird's legs to his right.

The seven steps are:

1) Holding the bird firmly with a two-pronged fork, cut down between the thigh and the body, using a sturdy, fairly short, sharp knife, starting with the leg nearest you. Pull the leg away from the body with a fork or your hand, and cut the leg from the body at the joint.

2) Cut the leg in two at the second joint, either on the platter or a separate plate, to separate the thigh from the drumstick.

3) Holding the drumstick with your hand, slice downward into attractive pieces. Then slice the thigh.

4) Cut off the wing, pressing the wing tip down with a fork so you can see the joint, and sever it from the body with the point of the knife.

5) Holding the body firmly with the fork, begin to carve the breast on an angle in thin slices. With a large turkey, continue until the

widest part of the breast is reached, then carve the front and back
ends alternately (this makes the slices just the right size to be
inviting); with chickens and capons, this is not necessary, since
the breasts are much smaller.

6) The second side of the bird is carved the same way as the first but,
correctly, you do not turn the bird around.

7) Serve both dark and light meat to each person at the table with a
spoonful of the stuffing, if any, and gravy or sauce. The gravy
should be spooned onto the plate, not over the meat or stuffing.

Is smoked turkey what the name says? Yes. It is cooked and smoked.
Serve cold, sliced, on a buffet, or as a canapé with toast. Very rich,
so it goes a long way. Best not to attempt to combine it in other
cooked dishes.

What is a turkey roll? Boneless turkey meat, made into a roll in such
a way that slices provide both white and dark meat in natural proportions. The roasts, as they are sometimes called, are marketed in
sizes from 2 to 10 pounds and should be thawed, before roasting, in
the refrigerator (it will take 1 to 2 days) or under cold water running in original wrapper. Remove the wrapper to cook, leaving the
string on.

To roast: Rub with salt and pepper, place in a pan on a rack in a
preheated 350° F. oven, brush with melted butter. Roast, basting
occasionally with melted butter, until a meat thermometer inserted
in the center registers 170° or 175° F. A 5- to 7-pound roast will take
from 3 to 3½ hours.

*Why is it necessary to remove giblets from fresh fowl immediately after
purchase?* Because the entrails, especially the liver, deteriorate very
quickly and if left in the cavity of the bird (where the butcher
usually tucks them) will contaminate the flesh. Giblets can be frozen
and used later; they can be cooked immediately and used within a
couple of days; or they can be cooked, then frozen. If the bird was
frozen when purchased, you should not refreeze the thawed giblets
a second time. In this case, they can be cooked and used at once;
or cooked, then frozen again for future use.

Are the giblets and gizzard the same thing? No. Giblets encompass
all the edible entrails of any fowl, of which the gizzard is only one

part. Giblets include gizzard, heart, and liver. Normally, the gizzard, heart, and neck of the bird are used in making giblet gravy. The liver is usually reserved to use some other way.

How do you cook chicken livers?   Quickly. In clarified butter over high heat, so they are a rich brown on the outside and a delicate pink inside.

Why do chicken livers sometimes taste bitter?   Because the green gall, which is extremely bitter, has not been removed, as it should be.

What is pâté de foie gras?   Foie means liver, and gras, fat. In cookery, the words are used together, meaning preserved, seasoned, fattened goose or duck livers. Foie gras or goose liver is available fresh, in loaves, or tinned. The fresh must be kept, in the original package, under refrigeration and eaten within 2 weeks of purchase; the tinned does not need refrigeration until about to be served, when it should be well chilled—allow several hours. Do not freeze.

How should you present pâté de foie gras?   Unmold the chilled foie gras carefully from the can, place on a board, and slice with a warm or wet knife. Arrange the slices attractively on a bed of fresh, crisp lettuce, water cress or port-flavored, chopped aspic. Place this dish on crushed ice to keep the foie gras cold. Serve with toast.

What is arroz con pollo?   A Spanish dish consisting of sautéed chicken, cooked with rice, tomatoes, saffron, and vegetables.

What's Brunswick stew?   As all-American as the flag, it apparently originated in Brunswick County, Virginia, and is an amazing mixture of chicken, beef or veal bones, ham bone, squirrel, seasonings, and six different vegetables. Modern versions have, in a sense, "killed" the squirrel. It is a specialty of the very fine inns of Williamsburg, Virginia, where it is served in tin bowls as it was in the time of its Colonial origin.

What is chicken cacciatore?   Essentially, an Italian stew. Chicken pieces, browned in olive oil and garlic, then simmered with seasonings, wine, tomato paste, etc.

What is chicken Kiev? Chicken breasts, flattened, each rolled around sticks of ice-cold, sweet butter to enclose it completely, then dipped into flour, beaten egg, and bread crumbs and fried in deep fat.

What is chicken Marengo? Chicken stew, really, made with chicken, cut in parts, seasonings, wine, fresh lemon juice, and loads of fresh parsley. Fresh lemon is also served on the side.

What is chicken Tetrazzini? Diced, cooked chicken combined with mushrooms, seasonings, wine, Mornay sauce, Parmesan cheese, and cooked spaghetti.

What is coq au vin? A classic French recipe consisting of chicken cooked in red wine with onions, mushrooms, and bacon. In *Mastering the Art of French Cooking,* the authors say, "it may be called *coq au Chambertin, coq au riesling,* or *coq au* whatever wine you use for its cooking. The traditional accompaniments are parsley potatoes and buttered green peas."

What is Country Captain? Although generally assumed to be of American origin, it is actually, Cecily Brownstone, Food Editor of the Associated Press, reports, East Indian. According to *Miss Eliza Leslie's New Cookery Book* (circa 1857), it was introduced to the British by a captain of the sepoys, the native East Indian troops. Country Captain is really a curry, made with chicken parts, seasonings, vegetables, and currants. Served with chutney and toasted almonds.

Can you buy fresh ducks these days? If you're next door to a duck farm. The bulk of the ducks coming into the markets are frozen. Although Long Island ducklings dominate the field, Massachusetts, Wisconsin, and the Far West are now raising ducks in good quantity. Thaw, as you would any fowl, in the refrigerator, in the original package. Ducklings average about 5 pounds each.

Can you buy duck parts? No. There have been some efforts to market parts but, to date, this has not gone very far. However, it's child's play to cut up a duck with poultry shears.

To broil ducks: Cut the ducklings in half with poultry shears, cutting from the vent at the tail along the side of the breastbone to the neck opening. Turn the duckling and cut down the center of the back until it is halved. Rub the skin with salt and freshly ground pepper. Preheat the broiler, place the ducks, skin side down, about 4 inches from the heating unit. Broil 20 minutes on one side, then turn and broil only long enough to brown and crisp.

Can duck be poached? Of course. Poach as you would chicken. Skinned and sliced, it makes a handsome and delicious dish in aspic.

How many will a duck serve? Two trenchermen can eat 1 without a pause. One nice 5- to 6-pound duckling can be stretched to serve 4, but they should be on diets or you a dextrous carver.

Is caneton à l'orange like à la bigarade? It's the same thing. Both mean duck or duckling (*canard* is the French word for duck, *caneton* for duckling) served with an orange and lemon sauce, garnished with a julienne of orange and lemon peel.

What is Peking Duck? One of the most famous and delicious dishes in the Chinese cuisine. Also the breed name of duckling raised on Long Island. Once the duck is roasted (the method is quite complicated), the skin and meat are each cut, separately, into tiny squares, and arranged on a platter. To eat, a piece of meat and skin is placed in the center of a "doily"—this is a steamed roll, very light and feathery —with a scallion and a sweet sauce. The doily is then rolled up and eaten while warm.

Is it possible to get a good goose these days? Yes, but you have to be a regular curmudgeon to get it, and here's why. Nobody tells you the best geese come from North Dakota and Wisconsin and all geese available in the open market are frozen and, further, markets are inclined to deliver the goose without the original wrappings, which show the address of the processor. Your only hope of a Cratchit-quality goose is to insist on knowing the source and on its being sold to you in the original wrapping. You thaw it out, don't let the market do it.

Are the pheasants in the market fresh or frozen? Frozen, farm-raised. It's a wonderful little bird, cooked properly, and will serve 4. Because it's inclined to be dry, it should always be well barded with pork.

Are quail available in the markets?   Yes, frozen, eviscerated quail, in pairs. You can also buy canned whole quail, stuffed with *pâté de foie gras*, in a sherry sauce; smoked quail meat; and quail eggs.

What are salmis in cookery?   Salmis is an abbreviation of the French *salmigondis* (salmagundi, meaning a mishmash). Essentially it's a *ragoût* of game or wild fowl.

What are Rock Cornish game hens?   A special breed, introduced several years ago, that is a cross between a Rock Cornish and a White Rock. They are small birds, available frozen, weighing around 1 pound or better each. Usually roasted, with or without stuffing, serve 1 to a person. A much over-rated bird.

What are squabs?   Young squabs (*pigeonneaux* in French) are young domestic pigeons of a breed raised especially as a table bird. Available fresh or frozen.

Sauces

If it's a sauce, is it a gravy? Although the French word for gravy is *jus*, which can be translated as juice or gravy, there is a difference. Gravy starts, of course, with the juice in the pan, but in this country, it is more often than not thickened with flour. A sauce can start with the juice in the pan or it may be composed of ingredients entirely unrelated to the dish with which it is to be served. Sauce is, broadly speaking, more elegant than gravy.

How can I make smooth gravy? The tendency in this country is to make gravy thick and, as a consequence, lumpy, so it looks and, frankly, tastes like glue. Or, to put it more graphically, a lot of uncooked flour held together with a little fat.

The secret to a good gravy is to keep the thickening agent to the very minimum, adding only enough to give the gravy or sauce a little body. Most sophisticated people do not make a gravy to serve with roast beef, but serve it *au jus*. However, for those who like a gravy, here's how.

To make beef gravy: Pour off the fat from the roasting pan, leaving only the juice behind, season with salt and pepper, a sprinkling of flour, and cook, whipping constantly with a *fouet* until the gravy has taken on color. Then add, if you have some on hand, some beef broth or a bouillon cube dissolved in boiling water. Failing that, potato water, and failing that, boiling water. Cook, whipping constantly, until it is perfectly smooth and thickened slightly. Taste for seasoning. Strain into a hot sauce boat.

To make chicken gravy: Cook the giblets ahead of time. Cover the giblets with water and wine in these proportions: ⅔ water, ⅓ dry white wine. Add a teaspoon of salt, 3 or 4 peppercorns, a bit of parsley, 1 onion stuck with 2 cloves, and 1 carrot. Bring to a boil and boil for 1 minute. Skim off the scum, cover the pan, and reduce the heat. Simmer for 1 hour. Strain off the broth and reduce to 1 cup. Taste for seasoning. Add the giblet broth to the pan juices, and thicken, if you like, with a *beurre manié*. You can also add the chopped giblets. This same recipe can be used for turkey gravy.

How can you prevent a "skin" forming on a sauce? Professional chefs dot the surface with softened butter. However, a piece of plastic wrap placed right on top of the sauce, sealing it so no air can reach it, is equally effective.

Can you salvage a mayonnaise that has curdled or separated? Yes. Rinse out a bowl in hot water, then dry. To it add 1 teaspoon of prepared mustard and 1 tablespoon of the curdled mayonnaise. Beat together with a wire whisk until creamy and thick. Then add the remaining mayonnaise by teaspoons, beating vigorously after each addition until creamy. The important thing to remember is that you must add the curdled sauce bit by bit.

What does Allemande mean in cookery? À la Allemande means "in the German style," but sauce Allemande—a Velouté sauce made with chicken stock, enriched with egg yolks, cream, a "nut" of butter, perfumed with the essence of mushrooms, and finished with a little nutmeg—has nothing whatsoever to do with Germany or things German. Carême baptized it Allemande because its color reminded him of "Gretchen's" fair hair. It is also known as *sauce blonde* and *sauce Parisienne*.

What is arrowroot? A thickening agent used primarily when you want the finished sauce to be clear and transparent. It is mixed with a cold liquid—depending on the dish you are making—then cooked, with a minimum of stirring, until the sauce is clear. Allow about 1 tablespoon to ¾ to 1 cup of liquid. Sauces thickened with arrowroot reach their maximum thickness at 158° to 176° F. on the thermometer. Further heating causes marked thinning.

What is Béchamel? In this country we call it white sauce. It is made with a white roux plus milk and is the base for innumerable recipes:

cream soups, soufflés, hot hors d'oeuvres, etc. It can be enriched with butter; with cream to make *sauce crème;* with eggs and cream to make *sauce Parisienne;* with cheese to make *sauce Mornay;* with tomato purée to make *sauce Aurore.* Onions, herbs, capers, or curry can each be added to the basic sauce to make a new sauce.

A thin Béchamel is made in these proportions: 1 tablespoon of all purpose flour to 1 cup of liquid; a medium (general purpose) requires 1½ tablespoons of flour; a thick, 2 tablespoons of flour; and a soufflé base, 3 tablespoons of flour.

What is a beurre manié?   A raw or uncooked roux—a mixture of butter and flour kneaded together. In some cases, with more flour than fat. Used to bring a sauce to the right consistency, it is added in little balls, at the last minute, to a sauce that is to be served right away, not to a sauce that is to be stored and/or reheated. After adding the beurre manié, the sauce should be cooked an additional 8 to 10 minutes so it won't taste raw and floury.

What is beurre noir?   Black butter. Actually, it's not black but, rather, dark brown. To make it, brown the butter and, just before serving, add capers and a little vinegar. It is served with eggs, calves' brains, broiled fish, etc.

What is drawn butter?   Nothing but melted butter. To do it properly, place the amount of butter you will need in a small saucepan and allow it to melt, gradually, in a warm spot on the stove—not over direct heat, which will cook it. Old cook books give "drawn butter" as a mixture of melted butter and flour, seasoned, with hot water added; then cooked until somewhat thickened. We can only assume it was a tasteless way of stretching the butter.

What is lemon butter?   As is often true in cookery, it can be several different things: (1) it is a sauce in which lemon juice, seasonings, and butter are combined and served hot with fish or vegetables; (2) an extremely rich cream made of eggs, lemon, sugar, and butter, and used as a spread on bread or toast or as a filling for tarts and pies. This is also known as lemon curd.

What are savory butters?   In French, *beurres composés,* they are butters which have been creamed or melted, then mixed with some other ingredient, to serve with fish, vegetables, meat, eggs, etc. To give you a few examples: *amandine,* melted butter combined with slivered toasted almonds, served with fish; anchovy, mashed anchovy fillets worked into softened butter, sometimes with a bit of garlic, served with steak or fish; chive, freshly chopped chives combined with melted butter, served with fish, meat, vegetables, or eggs.

What is bread sauce?   Milk and bread crumbs, with onion, cloves, and seasonings, cooked briefly, and served with wild game, such as partridge or pheasant, and in England (where it is traditional), often with turkey and chicken. Better than it sounds.

Do chasseur and forestier have the same meaning in French cuisine? They are not unlike. The main ingredient in *sauce chasseur* or "hunter" sauce is mushrooms (with shallots, herbs, and sometimes tomatoes added), and any dish prepared *au chasseur* (oeufs au chasseur, for example) is finished with minced mushrooms; *à la forestier,* from *forêt* (forest), indicates a garniture of *morilles* (morels) specifically, but if they are out of season it is not unusual to substitute cultivated mushrooms.

What is the meaning of chaud-froid?   From the French, meaning "hot-cold." Actually, it's a sauce prepared hot and eaten cold. The rich sauce, usually stiffened with gelatin, is used to coat cold chicken, game, tongue, etc. Essentially an aspic, although not clear, it's a most elegant way to present food, especially for buffets.

What is the difference between white and red clam sauce?   The base is the same: wine, garlic, onions, seasonings, etc. To make it red, you add tomato purée.

How is cornstarch used in cookery?   It can be used in place of flour (1 tablespoon is the equivalent of 2 tablespoons of flour). It is commonly used in puddings, pie fillings, fruit sauces, etc. The finished result is more translucent than when flour is used, but not as clear as arrowroot. Do not use when high temperatures are called for.

Do degrease and deglaze mean the same thing?   No. But often, in cooking, deglazing follows degreasing. Degrease, from the French *degraisser,* means to remove the fat from a hot liquid; deglaze, from *deglacer,* means to dilute the juices in which meat, fish, poultry, or game have been cooked.

To degrease: The two easiest ways are (1) congeal the fat by chilling the hot liquid, then scrape or lift the fat off and discard. The major disadvantages to this method is it takes time and would normally apply when you have large amounts of liquid, such as broth; or (2) dump a couple of trays of ice cubes into the hot liquid. When the fat congeals around the ice cubes, lift them out and discard. Since the ice will have diluted the juices somewhat, boil them down rapidly to concentrate the flavors. You would use this method only with a comparatively small amount of liquid, such as the juices in the roasting pan.

To degrease fat from simmering liquids: You need a long-handled spoon and the best you can do, while it's simmering, is to skim off a thin layer of the fat. Once the simmering is over, it's somewhat simpler, since the fat rises to the surface and you can remove the bulk of it with a spoon, blotting up the fat globules that remain with paper towels.

To remove fat from roasting pan while meat is roasting: It can be accomplished with a spoon by tilting the pan to allow the fat to collect in a corner, but it's safer and much more satisfactory to siphon it off with a bulb baster.

To deglaze: Degrease the pan, add whatever liquid is called for, bring the mixture to simmer, scraping the bottom and sides of the pan to incorporate all the coagulated juices. Cook, stirring, until you have a rich sauce to complement the dish. This is an important technique in making all sauces to accompany meat, fish, etc.

What is sauce espagnole? Craig Claiborne, in the new, superb *The New York Times Menu Book,* a companion to *The New York Times Cook Book,* writes, "There is nothing more French than the sauce known as *espagnole.* It is one of the foundation sauces of French cuisine and is nearly as important as wine, shallots, butter, and cream. In most recipes written in English, *espagnole* is translated as 'brown sauce.' Brown sauce is easy to prepare, but it is time-consuming. It frequently is combined with a reduction of butter, shallots, and wine as an accompaniment to grilled meats, poultry, and game. It is also used to enrich stews and *ragoûts.* There is nothing that is a perfect substitute for brown sauce, but the closest approximation is canned beef gravy, which may be used in any recipe calling for brown sauce."

Should sugar be used in making French dressing?   Correctly, no. And for the record, there is no such thing in France as French dressing. The sauce with which the French dress salads is called *sauce vinaigrette*. A Frenchman would swoon at the very thought of adding sugar to a vinaigrette, but many American cook books "call for" sugar in French dressing which, realistically, we should think of as an American salad dressing. Being a purist, I would not use sugar but, as is true of many things in cookery, it's a matter of taste. In this instance, your taste.

What is garlic dressing?   Sauce vinaigrette mixed with minced fresh garlic.

Is a gribiche sauce like a rémoulade?   Very much. They both "call for" a mayonnaise base (in the case of the gribiche, made with hard-cooked egg yolks) combined with mustard, gherkins, capers, chervil, and tarragon. The gribiche, however, is finished with a julienne of hard-cooked egg whites and the rémoulade with anchovy essence. Broadly speaking, they can be used interchangeably.

What is Hollandaise?   Perhaps the most famous of all sauces—absolutely gorgeous—made with butter, egg yolks, lemon juice, salt, and pepper. Although the name would indicate it originated in Holland, there is no evidence to support it except the fact the Dutch housewives make and use it more than the French. It is served tepid with vegetables, eggs, or fish. Other members of the Hollandaise family include: *sauce Mousseline* (also known as *sauce Chantilly*)—a combination of Hollandaise and whipped cream, served with fish, soufflés, asparagus; *sauce Maltaise*—Hollandaise made with lemon juice, orange juice, and orange rind, served with asparagus and broccoli; *sauce Choron*—a bearnaise made with tomato, served with fish; *sauce Mousseline Sabayon*—Hollandaise with cream with a white wine fish *fumet*, served with fish; *sauce bearnaise*—Hollandaise combined with an essence made of vinegar, wine, shallots, herbs, and seasonings, served with steaks, fish, chicken, eggs, etc. Blender Hollandaise is extremely good but it does not, in our opinion, match the sauce when made by hand. If Hollandaise curdles, and this is one of its idiosyncrasies, it can be salvaged.

In discussing the historical origin of the name of sauce Hollandaise with Roy Andries de Groot, author of the recently published and fascinating cook book, *Feast for All Seasons*, he pursued my query and wrote me as follows: "I was lunching recently with a visiting Dutch friend, a brilliant and knowledgeable gourmet and I put it to him. He pointed out at once that there have been various cross-tides of immigration between France and Holland. For example, in 1544, William the Silent, the first dominant ruler of the newly-independent provinces of Holland, inherited by marriage the principality of the pre-Roman city of Orange in Provence. That city gave its name to the ruling house of Holland and remained a Dutch possession for more than 100 years, with much travelling back and forth by Dutchmen and Frenchmen, until Louis XIV returned it to France. When that autocratic monarch, in 1666, began revoking the Edict of Nantes, thousands of persecuted Huguenots fled to Holland. Apparently, two points about the Dutch cuisine struck these French travellers most forcibly: First, the superb richness of the butter made from the milk of Frisian cows; second, the fact that large quantities of this butter were melted and poured over all kinds of cooked fish. The idea caught on in France and, from about 1690 onwards, fish served with melted butter was always known as 'Poisson a la Hollandaise.'

By the 1750's both Spanish and French provincial cooks knew how to make mayonnaise by thickening olive oil with egg yolks. So it was a natural gastronomic progression for them to assume egg yolks could be made to thicken *la beurre* Hollandaise. The word comes from the old French, *moyeunaise*, which, in turn, derives from *moyeu*, meaning a yolk of egg.

What is mock Hollandaise?   1 cup of good mayonnaise, heated in a double boiler, mixed with ½ cup heavy cream, whipped. A quick substitute for the "real McCoy." Serve as you would Hollandaise, over asparagus, broccoli, cauliflower, etc.

Should Hollandaise sauce be served hot or cold?   Neither. Correctly, it is served tepid. If Hollandaise must stand a bit before serving, place container in a pan of hot, not boiling, water—not over direct heat or it will curdle. Try to keep water at the same temperature during this waiting period. Serve in a warm bowl, if not spooned over something. Left-over Hollandaise can be stored in the refrigerator successfully for several days and heated to lukewarm by this same hot-water method. It can also be frozen, brought to room temperature, then heated in the same gentle way.

What does à la king mean? A dish made with chicken, fresh mushrooms, green pepper, pimientos, egg yolks, a rich cream sauce, sherry or madeira, served on toast triangles or in heated patty shells. Quoting *The American Heritage Cookbook*, "There are innumerable stories about the origin of the chicken à la king—all of them equally authoritative. One version says it was created by Foxhall Keene, suggested to Delmonico's, and first served in that restaurant as chicken à la Keene. Another authority insists that it was created by the chef at Claridge's Hotel in London in 1881 for the sportsman J. R. Keene (Foxhall's father), whose horse Foxhall had won the Grand Prix in Paris. There are other well-substantiated stories that the dish originated in Florida, on Long Island, and at the Waldorf."

What does liaison mean? Literally, joining. It's a term used by professional cooks for thickening agents to bind ingredients together to bring sauces and soups to the right consistency. All-purpose flour, arrowroot, cornstarch, potato flour (also called potato starch) and egg yolks are all used, at different times, in different ways, as thickening agents.

What is Lorenzo dressing? Vinaigrette sauce mixed with chili sauce and chopped hard-cooked eggs. Eggs Lorenzo are poached eggs on a crabmeat canapé, coated with Mornay sauce, then placed in the broiler for a minute or two; Lorenzo salad consists of romaine, watercress, pear, apple, and red beets.

What does lyonnaise mean? It stems from Lyonnais, a region of France, famous for the excellence of its cuisine. Lyon, the major city, is considered the gastronomic capital of France. Any dish designated as lyonnaise or à la lyonnaise indicates it originated in the region: lyonnaise sauce is a sauce based on onions; lyonnaise potatoes (with which you are undoubtedly familiar) are boiled, peeled potatoes, sautéed slowly until brown, then combined with sautéed onions and seasonings.

Are mayonnaise and salad dressing the same thing?   No. Mayonnaise, when made in the classic manner, is an uncooked emulsion of egg yolks and oil with seasonings. One of the great French sauces, it can be served plain or varied with fresh herbs to make *mayonnaise aux fines herbes;* with a purée of spinach, watercress, parsley and fresh herbs (chervil and tarragon) to make *mayonnaise verte;* with an-chovies, pickles, herbs and capers to make *sauce rémoulade.* Salad dressing, also known as boiled dressing, is American to its very core. Its base is eggs, milk, flour, butter, sugar, and seasonings. Unlike mayonnaise, it is cooked and mildly sweet.

What is aioli?   A sauce made with garlic (*ail* is the French for garlic), oil, egg yolks, and seasonings. Served with boiled fish, hot or cold, sometimes cold meat, salads, and vegetables. Very potent with garlic.

What are some of the great classic meat sauces?   Here is a limited edition: *sauce Bordelaise* (a red wine sauce, garnished with beef marrow and parsley, served with meat dishes); *sauce chasseur* (mean-ing hunter—a highly flavored sauce composed of brown sauce, mush-rooms, shallots, herbs, sometimes tomatoes. Good with veal scallops); *sauce Périgueux* (a brown sauce with madeira and truffles, served with fillet of beef, etc.); *Cumberland sauce* (English Currant jelly, orange and lemon, port wine, a little thickening. Served hot or cold with ham, mutton, venison); *sauce Robert* (brown sauce with wine and mustard, served with pork, boiled beef, etc.).

How is mint sauce made?   By steeping some fresh, chopped mint leaves in vinegar, with a little sugar.

What is pesto?   The famous sauce eaten by the Genoese with all kinds of pasta. It can be made only with fresh basil.

What does à la Provençale mean?   A dish made with tomatoes and garlic, sometimes with garlic alone. Provence is a part of France famous for its culinary specialties in which garlic plays a major role.

Is sauce ravigote a hot or cold sauce?   It can be either, but they are different sauces. The hot ravigote is a reduction of white wine and vinegar, combined with a Velouté, shallot butter, garnished with chervil, chives, and tarragon; the cold ravigote is a combination of oil and vinegar (essentially a vinaigrette) mixed with chopped capers, onions, parsley, chervil, tarragon, seasoned with salt and pepper. Brains are served with either a hot or cold ravigote; eggs in aspic, and cold, cooked crabs with the cold sauce, also calf's head.

What is Roquefort dressing? Sieved Roquefort mixed with vinaigrette sauce.

What is a roux? A mixture of fat and flour that is cooked before it is combined with a liquid so the finished sauce can be stored and/or reheated and still keep its consistency. A *roux blanc* (white) should be cooked slowly for 6 to 8 minutes without allowing it to brown; a *roux brun* (brown) is also cooked slowly until it turns a rich, nut brown.

What is Tabasco? The original, and still best known brand, of the hot pepper sauces, it is used widely in cooking when a recipe calls for a good, hot seasoning. Adds zip to a Bloody Mary.

What is soy sauce? Madame Grace Chu writes in *The Pleasures of Chinese Cooking:* "The one ingredient that most characterizes Chinese cookery is a dark, salty liquid that goes under the name of soy sauce. All types of soy sauce are made from soybeans, water, and salt, although the sauce comes in many grades and shades of color from dark brown to darkest brown." It is always served with the food in Chinese restaurants. Actually, it is the Chinese cook's substitute for salt.

How is Thousand Island dressing made? The original recipe called for thin mayonnaise mixed with chili sauce and chopped red and green peppers. The American version is a different kettle of fish and the variations on the "theme" are endless. Essentially, it's mayonnaise mixed with chili sauce, chopped green peppers, chopped pimientos, and chopped olives (stuffed or not).

What is Russian dressing? The true Russian salad dressing is Thousand Island dressing (the original recipe) with the addition of caviar. American recipes do not "call for" caviar, but vary Thousand Island dressing by diluting the mayonnaise with vinaigrette sauce and adding minced onion.

Another version is made with mayonnaise mixed with grated fresh horse-radish and whipped cream. And a recipe for a hot Russian sauce is bordelaise sauce with caviar, chopped fresh fennel, and capers.

How do tomato sauce, tomato paste, and tomato purée differ? They are alike in two respects: they are all made from fresh tomatoes and they are all used as an ingredient in cooking. They differ in concentration of flavor, consistency, and seasonings. Tomato sauce, which is of pouring consistency, is seasoned with salt, pepper, and spices; tomato paste, the most concentrated tomato product produced, has only salt added; tomato purée, with about the same consistency as tomato sauce, is unseasoned. All three products can be used interchangeably if flavor concentration and consistency are taken into consideration. For example, 1 8-ounce can of tomato sauce can be used instead of 1 cup of purée; 1 6-ounce can of tomato paste mixed with 1 cup of water is about the equivalent of 2 8-ounce cans of tomato sauce. Storing these products is a problem with many housewives because they will keep for only 5 or 6 days, once opened, unless frozen. To store, spoon what's left over in the can into a clean glass jar, with a tight-fitting lid, and refrigerate or freeze.

What is the difference between sauce vinaigrette and French dressing? None. Literally translated, vinaigrette means vinegar sauce. According to *Larousse gastronomique*, the culinary bible, vinaigrette sauce or French dressing (as it's commonly called in this country) is made in the proportion of 1 tablespoon vinegar (or lemon juice) to 3 tablespoons oil, with salt and pepper to taste. However, the French sometimes add fresh green herbs, minced, and mustard. A sauce made of vinegar, oil, salt, pepper, capers, fresh herbs, and minced onion is known both as vinaigrette and cold ravigote.

Are white sauce and sauce Velouté the same thing? No, but close relations. White or cream sauce (known as Béchamel in France) is made with milk (sometimes with the addition of cream). Sauce Velouté (which means velvet), is made with chicken, veal, or fish stock in place of the milk. When cream is added to a Velouté, it becomes *sauce suprême.*

Seasonings

Can fresh and dried herbs be used interchangeably? Of course, but the proportions are different. Dried herbs are much more concentrated than fresh. If a recipe calls for 1 teaspoon dried herbs, you should use 3 teaspoons, or 1 tablespoon fresh herbs, chopped. Just remember the ratio is 1 to 3.

Why do some of my herbs lack flavor? They're too old. Dried herbs should be stored away from light and used up fast. If you sniff an herb and it doesn't answer with conviction, discard it and buy some more.

Are allspice and pickling spice the same thing? No. Allspice is the flavorful berry of an evergreen tree with a fragrance resembling a blend of cinnamon, nutmeg, and cloves. "This is the spice Columbus missed twice," report the authors of that excellent book, *The Spice Cookbook,* "when he made his way through the Caribbean." It was eventually discovered by the Spaniards, who thought it was pepper and, erroneously, named it "pimento"—the name that still clings to it in Jamaica, where allspice grows lavishly. As a result, the U.S. Customs Department continues to list it as pimento on its records. (Hence, the confusion between allspice and pimiento, the canned red peppers). Allspice is available both whole and ground. In the ground form, it is used in fruit pies, cakes, spice cake, and it is indispensable in making mince meat, plum puddings, etc.

Pickling spice, a blend of 10 to 16 different whole spices (of which allspice is one, depending on the packer), is used in pickling, but it can also be used, and is, in other cooking, such as certain fruits and vegetables.

What is anise and how is it used?   A spice that will remind you of the taste of licorice candy. Although it is used principally in the manufacture of liqueurs (Pernod, for example), the anise seed, sold whole, is also important in the preparation of certain cookies, cakes, breads, and sauces. A pinch of anise is delicious when used to flavor fresh fruits. Add ¼ to ½ teaspoon to 1 cup of simple syrup and pour over a fruit compote. Anise is also delightful, used sparingly, mixed with cole slaw.

You can grow your own anise from seed, if you like. It's nice to have in the summertime. To use anis seed, by the pinch, it must be crushed. Put a few seeds between sheets of wax paper and give it a good bang with a rolling pin or some other heavy weight.

Is there more than one type of basil?   Yes. Lemon-scented basil; one that smells like tarragon; another like fennel. But the familiar one, common basil, is generally referred to as sweet basil. Mrs. Elizabeth David, in *Italian Food*, writes, "If I had to choose just one plant from the whole herb garden, I should be content with basil." When bruised, the fresh leaves are reminiscent of cloves. Basil has a special affinity for tomatoes, broiled or fresh, but it complements many other foods: seafood, potatoes, cooked cucumbers. Unless you grow it yourself (which is quite easy to do), you may have difficulty finding the fresh. It is, of course, generally available dried; in the summer, you may be able to pick it up, fresh, in good vegetable markets.

What is bay leaf?   The pungent leaf from the evergreen sweet bay or laurel tree, known botanically as *Laurus nobilis*. As Craig Claiborne says in his fine *Herb and Spice Cook Book*, "like wine, thyme, and leeks, bay leaf is a foundation flavor of *la cuisine française* and it is virtually impossible to conceive of French cuisine without it." It is used in meat, fish, and poultry cookery. Bay leaf should be used with a cautious hand because it is strong stuff. As a rule of thumb, you would use 1 leaf in a stew to serve 6 people. A half a leaf means just that. Break it in two. Bay leaves are always removed from the dish before serving. Dried leaves are readily available.

What is a bouquet garni?   It means a bouquet of herbs, tied with a bit of string, then placed in a simmering sauce or stew. Specifically, parsley, thyme, and bay leaf. However, if celery, garlic, or other seasonings are added, it is still a bouquet garni. Dried herbs, if used, should be wrapped in a piece of wet cheesecloth, then tied—for easy removal at the end of the cooking time.

Is it true that capers are the seeds from nasturtiums?   No. The confusion probably arises from the fact that capers resemble nasturtium seeds. Capers (they are always referred to in the plural) are the flower buds from a shrub, *Capparis spinosa*, which grows along the Mediterranean, in the East Indies, and in the Orient. Capers, widely used in Mediterranean cookery, add a unique flavor to hot or cold sauces and are a great addition to many salads. Usually bottled in vinegar, they are sometimes available packed in salt.

What gives rye bread its particular flavor?   Caraway, the spice that "will cure hysteria." Germans, Austrians, and Hungarians use it extensively. The seeds are used in sauerkraut, boiled cabbage, cole slaw, beef stews, pork dishes, and it's almost the *raison d'être* for that lovely English cake called "seed." "Comfits," candy-coated caraway seeds, are sometimes available in the U.S. And it's caraway, along with cumin and anise, that perfumes certain liqueurs. Caraway seeds can be bought for planting. It is a biennial.

What is cardamom?   A member of the ginger family and next to saffron, the most valuable spice in the world. Also spelled cardamum and cardamon, used for years in the Far East, it has been adopted by the Scandinavians. It's one of the flavors that make Danish pastries taste so good. Used in curry dishes and baking, it can be used interchangeably with cinnamon. Available both whole and ground. If the recipe calls for crushed cardamom, pound it in a mortar and pestle or between sheets of wax paper.

Is celery seed the same thing as celery salt?   Not exactly. The seed is actually a spice from a wild variety of celery (no connection with the celery stalks we know), known as smallage. Celery salt is a combination of ground celery seeds and ordinary table salt. The seed is a good substitute for fresh celery in sauces, soups, and vegetable dishes. The two can be used interchangeably, if you take into consideration the salt content of the celery salt. As a matter of record, celery salt changes the flavor complexion of a Bloody Mary—for the better.

How is chervil used? Originally known as sweet Cicely, it's not a well-known herb in this country, but used widely in Europe, as an alternate to parsley, in soups, in salads, especially potato, and is one of the classic *fines herbes*—the others being tarragon, parsley, and chives. Like fennel, it is reminiscent of anise. Available dried.

Is chili powder one kind of pepper only? No, it's a blend of chili peppers, red peppers, oregano, cumin, and garlic powder. Although the use of chili peppers, in combination with oregano, has been traced back to the Aztecs, the mixed, blended chili powder we know was invented by Texans early in the 19th century. Obviously, chili con carne comes automatically to mind, but chili powder can be added to many dishes to give a real hot "bite."

Are cinnamon and cassia the same thing? There are two types of cinnamon: *Cinnamomum cassia* and *Cinnamomum zeylanicum* (Ceylon cinnamon). The reddish-brown, pungent, sweet cassia cinnamon is the kind you will find in the markets, designated simply as cinnamon (the term, cassia, is used in the spice trade only). The milder Ceylon cinnamon is popular in other parts of the world, particularly Mexico. One of the spiciest of our spices, what would cooking be like without cinnamon? With fruits, in vegetables, cakes, apple pie, Indian pudding, etc. Available in sticks or ground.

How do you use cloves? It's almost impossible to count the ways. An exquisite spice, it is a downright essential in stock; with baked ham, American-style; in pickling; in certain sweet dishes, such as cakes, puddings, pumpkin pie, etc. Cloves are also an important ingredient in punches and drinks. And how would we make pomander balls without those "little brown nails?" Available ground or whole.

What is a condiment? Literally translated, it means seasoning. Today, it means prepared sauces or brightly flavored accompaniments for foods: for example, chutney, pickles, mustards, etc.

What is coriander and how is it used? An ancient spice, it is used extensively in the Far East, in curries of all kinds. You'll find it used, too, in Mexican and Latin American dishes. In this country, it goes into pot roasts, with game and game sauces, and is mixed with cheese. Like juniper, it is also a flavor ingredient in gin, and like anise, it, too, is candied to make "comfits." Available whole or ground, sometimes fresh in Filipino markets.

How is cumin used?   It is an essential ingredient in all kinds of curries and is used extensively in Latin American cooking. Although caraway is its cousin, there is a distinct difference in the flavors of the two spices. You'll find it's very good sprinkled over cooked rice or potatoes, or mixed into bread dough. As a gauge, ½ teaspoon will season a chicken stew that serves 6. Available ground or whole.

What exactly is curry powder?   In *Classic Cooking from India*, Dharam Jit Singh says, "Curry is a word which comes from the Hindustani, *turcarri*. In the colloquial, it is shortened to "turri," which in the Anglo-Saxon usage is called "curry." It means a sauce or gravy and, in India, the curry is made freshly each time, in every household—a blend of many spices. The curry powders available to us contain as many as a dozen spices, including: cassia, turmeric, cardamom, coriander, mustard, various peppers, cloves, fennel, mace, and allspice. Obviously, it is used to make curry dishes (fish, meat, or fowl), soups, curried eggs, etc. Even fruit, when served to accompany meat, is sometimes curried. In buying curry powder, choose a good, lively, established blend.
   N O T E : Although they make a number of interesting and delicious chutneys and pickles in India, they do not, as is our custom, serve a whole raft of condiments with their curries. Nevertheless, here is a small list of foods that accompany a good curry well: raisins, plumped up in cognac; toasted, slivered almonds or peanuts; shredded coconut, fresh or canned; chutney; chopped scallions or chives.

Are dill seed and dill weed the same thing?   The seed is the dried fruit of the plant and the weed is the leaf of the same plant. In *An Herb and Spice Cook Book*, Craig Claiborne says, "dill seeds are best known as an ingredient for dill pickles, but there are few dishes from sauerkraut to apple pie to which the seed would not add interest." The feathery leaves of fresh dill, extremely popular in Scandinavian countries, are excellent with eggs, light cream cheeses, poached salmon, and other dishes.

Fresh dill is sometimes available in vegetable markets, but you can always stick a few seeds in the ground and enjoy the fresh "feathers" from your own garden.

Is fennel an herb or a vegetable?   It's both. Similar in flavor to anise or licorice, called *finocchio* in Italy, *fenouil* in France, almost all of the plant is edible. The seeds are used in sturdy sauces, such as spaghetti; the chopped leaves or the seeds in stuffings for pork or pig, chicken, goose, etc.; the bulb (or root) raw, eaten like celery with salt, or sliced in salads, also cooked as you would celery or asparagus. The seeds only are available commercially, but fresh fennel is found in Italian vegetable markets in season. It has a decisive flavor, so use it sparingly.

What is file powder?   Dried sassafras leaves used originally, it is believed, by Louisiana's Choctaw Indians. It is used in a great many Creole recipes for thickening soups and stews. The flavor, Dr. Sturtevant remarks in his *Notes on Edible Plants*, is "much relished by those accustomed to it."

What is meant by fines herbes?   Unless the recipe specifically calls for other herbs, it is a mixture of parsley, chervil, chives, and tarragon. At one time, fines herbes meant mushrooms and shallots, but today this combination is called a *duxelles*.

Are garlic salt and garlic powder the same?   Not exactly. Garlic salt is a mixture of pure garlic powder and ordinary table salt; garlic powder is pure garlic in powdered form. To use, $\frac{1}{16}$ teaspoonful of garlic powder should be sufficient for a dish serving 4 to 6 people; about twice that amount of garlic salt, taking into consideration what other salt has been added to the dish.

Do you use dehydrated garlic in any form?   No. For the plain and simple reason there is nothing to compare with the real thing, and since fresh garlic is available, the year round, why fool around with a substitute?

In what ways is ginger available?   Four: ground, the whole root, crystallized, and preserved (these last two are considered confections, although the crystallized, chopped, in a syrup, makes a delicious dessert sauce). Ground ginger, gingerbread, and gingersnaps are almost synonymous. Generally used in baking, it can add "snap" to many other foods, such as: soups, sauces, hamburgers, spareribs. Ginger root (whole roots are known as "hands" in the trade), available in Chinese stores, used in minute quantities, gives character to many Chinese dishes, and is excellent in pickling and syrups. Whole dry ginger is now available.

GINGER ICE CREAM SAUCE

Mix 1 cup of water, ¾ cup of sugar, and the juice of half a lemon together in a saucepan. Cook over a moderate heat until syrup spins a thread or reaches 230° F. on a candy thermometer. Take off the heat, stir in 3 tablespoons finely chopped candied ginger, then bring up to a boil again.

Serve hot or cold over vanilla ice cream. Makes 1 cup. You can make this up in a quantity and store, because it keeps beautifully.

Are ground and whole ginger interchangeable in recipes?   Not really. "The whole ginger root," and we quote from that excellent book, *The Spice Cookbook*, by Avanelle Day and Lillie Stuckey, "is preferred when making flavored syrups and pickling vinegars. About half an hour of cooking is required to release the flavor. A half-inch lends a delicious aroma to chicken or beef stock, or tongue. Ground ginger may be used in all baked dishes, or as a last-minute seasoning for soups or sauces."

Is juniper what flavors gin?   It's one of the flavorings used in making gin. It was originally the very essence of Holland gin, where it was known as *genièvre*, the French name for juniper. From *genièvre*, the English got gin. Juniper berries are commonly used in *choucroute à l'Alsacienne* and the bittersweet taste goes well in game marinades. The berries are called for, to some extent, in Swedish cooking.

Can you substitute mace for nutmeg?   Yes. Ground mace for ground nutmeg. Actually, they are "sister" spices. The lacy red membrane which surrounds the nutmeg, the seed of the fruit of the tree, is known as mace. Somewhat more pungent than nutmeg, mace is available both in the ground form and, in limited distribution, in blades. The blades are used in jellying primarily because they do not, as would the ground mace, cloud the jelly. But they can also be used in any recipe calling for mace or nutmeg if there is some liquid—a stew, for example. Whole nutmegs which must be freshly ground on a grater (small graters are available for just this purpose) is generally considered more desirable because it gives a fresher, brighter flavor than commercially packed ground nutmeg. When using mace, you should take into consideration its somewhat stronger flavor.

Are marjoram and oregano alike?   Oregano, until recently known as wild marjoram, and sweet marjoram are cousins, both members of the mint family. Marjoram is sweeter, more delicate; oregano much lustier, pleasantly bitter and assertive. You would not use them interchangeably. Marjoram adds a delightful fillip to vegetables, such as lima beans, peas, snap beans, etc., and it is excellent with lamb.

Oregano, origano in Italian, the herb that launched a zillion pizzas, is indispensable in Spanish, Italian, and Mexican cooking. Excellent with tomato dishes, eggplant, and innumerable Italian dishes. But remember to use it with thoughtful taste buds, it's potent. Available dried.

Is wild marjoram ever used in place of sweet?   Not here, but it is in Italy. Sweet marjoram, like bay leaf, is one of the old "strewing" herbs.   It is used in stuffings for meat and poultry, in soups and sauces, cooked vegetables, and the fresh leaves are excellent in salads. Available dried or ground. An annual, it can be raised successfully in the garden.

Except in sauce and jelly, where is mint used?   Of course, in Mint Julep and with vegetables, such as carrots and peas; with fish; in salads and soups; and to make sherbets. A chicken or boned leg of lamb, stuffed with fresh mint, is a memorable taste experience. Of the many kinds, spearmint, which spreads like wildfire in gardens, is the common variety. Sometimes available in good vegetable markets fresh, always dried.

What is monosodium glutamate?   To explain it as simply as possible, it is a natural substance found in most of the foods you eat, but in greater amounts in meats, poultry, fish, and vegetables. Technically, one of the amino acids which make up protein that build and repair body tissues. First discovered in the Orient, it is used commercially to enhance the natural flavor of foods. Unlike salt or sugar (although it looks like both), it has no individual taste. Known in the professional world as MSG, it is used widely by leading food processors. The Ac'cent brand is most familiar to Americans and Aji-no-moto to the Japanese. A splendid Chinese cook we know, who has used it all her life, suggests that the best way to learn to use monosodium glutamate properly is to begin with sauces and soups, and to use small amounts: for example, ⅛ teaspoon to 2 cups. Monosodium glutamate is not, as many people think, a meat tenderizer.

What is mustard?   A condiment known to man since prehistoric times. There are two basic types of mustard seeds: *Brassica alba,* white or yellow seeds, and *Brassica juncea,* dark brown seeds also called "Oriental" mustard. Mustard comes in three forms: whole seeds, powdered, and prepared. The name, interestingly enough, comes from the fact the French first mixed the crushed seeds with *must* (an unfermented wine).

Why does homemade mustard sometimes taste bitter?   Because it has not been allowed to season sufficiently. The minimum seasoning time is 10 minutes after the mustard has been prepared. The standard recipe is simply dry mustard mixed with enough tap water to make a thick, smooth, creamy paste. Don't use hot water, because it will stop the enzyme action. Make only as much as you can use at one time and discard any that is not used up.

What is paprika?   A vibrant, beautiful red powder that comes from the dried pods (fruit) of the plant species, *Capsicum annuum.* Actually a member of the pepper clan that ranges from the sweet "bell" peppers to the very hottest chilis. Incidentally, it is extremely high in Vitamin C (ascorbic acid)—one of the richest of all sources. Paprika is used to garnish light-colored dishes, such as eggs, poultry, fish, potatoes, pastas, salads, and salad dressings; and to flavor sausages, soups, goulashes, chicken dishes, etc. The highest quality paprika has an exquisite taste and varies in strength from mild to decidedly hot. Connoisseurs consider Hungarian paprika the finest. Hungary has recently introduced a sweet paprika, now available in the U.S. In addition to Hungarian, there are these other paprikas: American (sweet and mildly pungent); Spanish (a sweet paprika in a wide range of color values); Yugoslavian (similar to the Hungarian); Moroccan (similar to the Spanish); and Bulgarian (a mild paprika). All paprikas should be stored in a cool, dry place, away from light.

What is Italian parsley like? Unlike the more familiar curly parsley, it has a plain, flat leaf, very dark and glossy, with a rich flavor. Considered more attractive than other plain-leaved types.

What is freshly ground pepper? Black or white peppercorns ground in a peppermill or grinder as needed. The sweet spiciness of fresh pepper makes all the difference in the world in the flavor of any dish.

Is there any difference between black and white pepper? To this extent only; black pepper has a lustier aroma than white and is good in anything and everything. White pepper, somewhat more subtle, is preferred by European cooks, and is usually "called for" in foreign recipes, especially if it is a "white dish." Both black and white peppercorns come from the *Piper nigrum* vine, which can live only in the steaming tropics. The black peppercorn is a whole berry when picked and somewhat under-ripe; white peppercorn is a pealed or decorticated berry, which was allowed to remain on the vine until completely ripe. Until a few years ago, the grind of pepper known as the table grind was pretty much standardized. According to the American Spice Trade Association, the advent of outdoor cooking spurred a rush to coarse grinds, probably because it wouldn't blow away. Now, coarse ground pepper and even cracked (very, very coarse) pepper, along with the ubiquitous peppermill, which calls for peppercorns, have become standard equipment in the sophisticated American kitchen.

Are red pepper and cayenne the same thing? Technically, no, although the chances are the container you buy will say "red pepper and cayenne." Red pepper originally was the product of certain varieties of hot, red-colored peppers, while cayenne was a ground blend of small, extremely hot peppers, ranging in color from yellow to red. Today, in the packaged product, the traditional distinctions are not always followed. Red pepper and cayenne can be, and are, used interchangeably, but the important thing to remember is they are really "piping" hot and should be used with a judicious hand.

Do the poppy seeds used in cooking come from the same plant that yields opium? Yes, but they do not have any opium content. The poppy seeds cannot form until after the plant has lost all its opium potential. What makes poppy seeds so interesting in cookery is the tiny droplet of sweet, faintly fragrant oil in each seed. Poppy-seed rolls are no doubt familiar to you, but you may not know how delicious the seeds are sprinkled over noodles or rice, broiled fish, or cooked green beans. They can also be an important ingredient in pastries and desserts.

N O T E : Because of their oil content, poppy seeds are inclined to turn rancid after a certain length of time. We suggest you store them in the refrigerator.

What is rosemary like? An extremely fragrant herb but, in *Italian Food*, Mrs. Elizabeth David advises, "to treat it with caution." Her point is that the oil which comes from the leaves is very powerful and can kill the taste of a food. With that in mind, it's extremely successful with lamb, pork, chicken, certain fish, stuffiings, and mixed into dumplings. The spiky leaves of the dried herb should be crushed well. Burpee's says it's a half-hardy perennial that can be raised, from seed, successfully in home gardens.

What is saffron, and how is it used? Saffron, a spice, is the dried, orange-colored stigmas of the autumn crocus. Each blossom, which has only three stigmas, has to be picked by hand. The American Spice Trade Association tells us it takes 75,000 flowers to yield 1 pound, which explains why it is probably the most costly spice on earth. It is widely used in cooking in Spain, Italy, and southern France. Two old English recipes, saffron cake and saffron bread, are probably familiar to you, by name at least. Such famous Spanish recipes as paella and arroz con pollo both call for saffron, and it is frequently used to flavor and color rice. Delicate and delightful as saffron is, it should be used with a light hand; otherwise it gives a medicinal flavor. The saffron threads should be soaked in cold water or added to boiling liquid, depending on the recipe.

Small historical note: Henry VIII was so fond of saffron he forbade the ladies of the court to use it as a hair dye. Because it was once used to dye fabrics, we now have the name, saffron color.

What do you think of sage? It seems to me one of the least appealing of the herbs, but perhaps that's because cooks sometimes use it too

lavishly in the Thanksgiving turkey. But, as Craig Claiborne asks in
An Herb and Spice Cook Book, "Where would homemade sausage be
without it?" It does make a good seasoning for pork, admittedly, and
poultry. But the cook should remember it's powerful stuff. Available
ground or in leaves, dried. Like so many herbs, sage can be grown
with great success right in one's own garden.

What is kosher salt?   A highly purified, evaporated salt with a large,
jewel-like crystal. Very pretty and sparkly. The name kosher is a
misnomer, which probably comes from the fact that the salt is inspected by a rabbi and conforms to Jewish dietary laws. You perhaps
know that the dining table symbolizes the altar (in the temple) and
it is written in the Bible: "On all thy offerings shalt thou have salt."
That is why it is an accepted custom in orthodox Jewish homes to
sprinkle the first piece of bread with salt for the blessing. Historically,
salt and bread have always been the traditional gift for a house-
warming with people everywhere. Most good cooks of our acquaint-
ance use both kosher salt and regular table salt—keeping an open,
wide-mouth jar (for easy access) of each, right on their work tables.
Because the large kosher crystals absorb moisture very slowly, if at
all, it's nothing short of marvelous in high-humidity weather and, for
the same reason, ideal (also elegant) if you serve salt from salt cellars
at your table. As an ingredient, kosher salt is perfect for salads, since
the greens are less apt to wilt; for meats and fresh fruits, because they
stay juicier. French people living in this country say it is an excellent
substitute for *gros sel* (meaning coarse salt), used widely by chefs
and home cooks in France. Kosher salt should not be confused with
ice cream salt, a heavy, really coarse salt, made specifically to use in
freezing ice cream.

What is Malden salt?   Sea salt, used extensively in England, that is
bought in blocks and must be crushed before using, either in a mortar
or a salt mill. Sometimes it can be tracked down in stores featuring
specialty foods. Kosher salt seems to us a good substitute.

Why do some people salt and pepper food before tasting?   Because
they don't know any better. Any cook who presents what he believes
to be a perfectly seasoned dish cringes when a guest dashes it with
salt and pepper before even taking a mouthful. Everyone's "salt and

pepper tolerance" varies, so it's quite possible that even a flawless dish to one person's tongue needs more salt or pepper to another's. But salting and peppering before tasting verges on bad manners, because it tends to reflect on the cook's culinary prowess.

Is summer savory like winter savory?   They can be used interchangeably, although winter savory is somewhat more potent. Chances are you won't run into the winter variety—the commercially packed herb is summer savory. It is sometimes called the "bean herb" because it goes so well with peas, beans, and lentils. It is also excellent in stews and stuffings. Summer savory, an annual, can be grown successfully in the garden.

How do you use sesame seeds?   Quoting from that splendid book, *An Herb and Spice Cook Book,* by Craig Claiborne: "They play an important role in pastry making, are an excellent addition to green salads and French dressings in general, and toasted and blended with butter they make a most palatable spread." Mr. Claiborne goes on to say: "Sesame seeds were introduced into the United States during the days of slave trading, but they did not achieve their extraordinary and deserved status in this country until a decade or so ago. One of the first uses of the seeds in America was as an ingredient in benne wafers." They were known to the African slaves as "benne seeds," hence the name of the benne wafers, so familiar to Southerners.

What is spice Parisienne?   A very popular seasoning in France. We have a very good facsimile, by the same name, made by Spice Islands.

Is tarragon a native of France or Russia?   Apparently Russia (Siberia), but the tarragon (*estragon*) nurtured by the French is a far superior herb. "Seductive, deeply satisfying to the palate," Craig Claiborne writes in *An Herb and Spice Cook Book,* "it is an essential in béarnaise, tartare, and ravigote sauce, and complements poultry, veal, and eggs." It is used widely in making tarragon vinegar, so delicious with green salads. Always available dried but, in the summer, can sometimes be found in markets catering to Europeans.

How is thyme used in cooking?   Along with bay leaf, almost an indispensable ingredient to the French cuisine, it is used widely in stuffings, soups (New England clam chower is a good example), meat and fish dishes, and with certain vegetables, especially onions. The herb is always available dried, but look for some fresh lemon thyme and use it with sole fillets. A hardy perennial, it grows well in gardens.

What is turmeric? If you'd ever eaten a good mustard pickle, you'd know. Its primary use is in pickles and it is, more often than not, the spice that gives curry powder its brilliant hue. It is sometimes "called for" in special curry dishes. But if you'd like to experiment you can string along with *The Spice Cook Book* whose authors suggest it can be used with "chicken, fish, pork, in rice, creamed eggs, in butters to serve with corn, snap beans, and steamed green cabbage." If you're bored with potatoes in the same old garnish, dress them in turmeric butter (ground turmeric to taste creamed with butter), a speck of cayenne, and some chopped chives. As a rule of thumb, start with ¼ to ½ teaspoon to serve 4.

What is a vanilla bean and how is it used? The dried pod of the vanilla plant. From it we get vanilla extract, the flavoring that bestowed its name on an internationally famous dish—vanilla ice cream. Chefs, generally, prefer the pod (it should be split), to flavor the milk in sauces, in rum and cognac to be used in cooking, tucked into a jar of granulated sugar, to perfume it for cooking, etc. The pod is reusable—just take it out of the liquid, rinse, dry, and put away. In buying vanilla by the bottle, don't be beguiled into buying imitation products, because that's exactly what they are.

What are the different types of vinegars and how are they used? You know, of course, the pale gold apple or cider vinegar, with a distinct odor of apples, which is used in salad dressings, some cooking, and sometimes in pickling, although white, or distilled vinegar, is more common for pickling. Then, there are the wine vinegars, red and white, usually used only in making salad dressing. The flavored vinegars include tarragon, chili, shallot, and garlic—all used in salad dressings. In addition to apple vinegar, there are other fruit vinegars, such as pear (fairly new on the market and delicious), pineapple, and guava. These last two are more frequently made in the home. Also, there is a homemade raspberry vinegar, actually an old-time American drink. Very refreshing on a hot summer's day.

Can I make my own herb vinegars?   If you have loads of fresh herbs and good quality cider vinegar. Pack them into a bottle or big jug, then fill with the vinegar, covering the herbs completely. Allow to mellow as long as possible—certainly several months. As you use the herb vinegar, keep adding more of the cider vinegar, and you'll be able to prolong the life of the vinegar indefinitely.

Soups

Are stock, broth, and bouillon all the same thing? Essentially, yes, and cooks use the terms interchangeably. Broth, which means brew or stock, is the liquid obtained from simmering together meats, bones, or fish trimmings with vegetables, seasonings, and water. This liquid, strained and reduced, is the base for soups, sauces, and aspics, and is also used to braise and to cook vegetables. Bouillon is simply the French word, now anglicized, for stock or broth. But as Narcisse Chamberlain insists, correctly, stock never goes to the dinner table.

What is double consommé? It is *consommé simple* (the French term for strained stock, broth, or bouillon) that has been clarified to remove all extraneous matter and reduced to concentrate flavors. The clear liquid is used as soup, hot or cold, to make aspics, etc.

What is glace de viand? It is stock, broth, or bouillon boiled down, or reduced, to a syrup that becomes a firm jelly when cold. It has important uses: a small amount can be added to a sauce or a soup to add extra flavor or it can be dissolved in hot water and used in place of stock. Because it is so concentrated, a small amount is easily stored; 3 quarts of broth will make 1½ cups.

When are fruit soups served? In Sweden, sometimes for breakfast or lunch but, more often than not, as a dessert. Mainly of German origin, fruit soups are made with fresh and/or dried fruits, cooked in water or wine or a mixture of both, sweetened, thickened slightly, served cold. Almost any fruit or berry is used.

Germans usually serve it as a dessert with a little molded semolina

245

pudding in the center of the soup plate. Hungarian cherry soup, though sweet, is served toward the beginning of the meal, as a regular soup course.

What is birds' nest soup? One of the most exotic of the Chinese delicacies, made with chicken broth, water chestnuts, mushrooms, ham, and cleansed birds' nests. Edible nests of swifts are composed essentially of the mucus secreted by the birds' remarkably developed salivary glands. The pleasure of this soup lies mostly, however, in the broth used in its preparation.

What is a bisque? The term used for a purée of lobster, crayfish, or other shellfish, in a thick, richly flavored cream soup.

Do you know a good recipe for Black Bean Soup? The best Black Bean Soup I ever tasted comes from the Coach House, in New York.

THE COACH HOUSE BLACK BEAN SOUP

4 cups black beans	3 leeks, finely sliced
3 stalks celery, finely chopped	4 bay leaves
3 large onions, finely chopped	1 tablespoon salt
½ cup (1 stick) butter	½ teaspoon freshly ground pepper
2½ tablespoons flour	1 cup dry madeira wine
½ cup finely chopped parsley	2 hard-cooked eggs, finely chopped
Rind and bone of a smoked ham	

Pick over and wash the beans, cover with cold water, and soak overnight. Drain. Place beans in a large kettle, add 5 quarts fresh, cold water, bring to a boil, then simmer for 1½ hours.

Meanwhile, melt butter in a second large kettle and sauté the celery and onions for about 8 minutes or until tender. Blend in the flour smoothly, add the parsley and cook, stirring constantly, for 1 minute. At this point, stir in the beans and all their liquid. Add the rind and ham bone, leeks, bay leaves, salt, and pepper. Simmer over a very low fire for 6 hours.

Remove and discard rind, ham bone, and bay leaves. Force the bean mixture and broth through a fine sieve. Stir in the madeira, bring to a boil. Remove from fire immediately and mix in the finely chopped eggs.

Serve in hot soup plates with a thin slice of fresh lemon floating on top. This makes a generous quantity of an extraordinary soup that should accommodate even a large, hungry family for at least 2 meals.

What is borsht? A Russian soup (also spelled borsch or bortsch), and there may well be as many versions as there are Russians. In *The New York Times Cook Book,* Craig Claiborne gives two: The Ukrainian and the Russian, remarking that, "the only ingredient that is constant is beets." Essentially, true borsht is a peasant soup made with meat (beef or pork and smoked meats), beets, cabbage, onions, a variety of other vegetables, and seasonings. The Russian version, but not the Ukrainian, is served with sour cream.

The borsht you will meet in most restaurants, considerably more refined, is usually served cold with sour cream.

What is bouillabaisse? A famous soup of Provence, France, composed of many kinds of fish seasoned with olive oil, garlic, saffron, and tomatoes. The true bouillabaisse, as any Provençal will tell you, is that of Marseille, and all others are mere echoes of this great dish. Italy, Spain, and other Mediterranean countries have similar "fish soups" for which there are partisans.

At Sloppy Louis', down on New York's Front Street, next door to the famous Fulton fish market, Louis Morino serves a bouillabaisse of such excellence, sophisticated New Yorkers who can't get all the way downtown themselves, frequently send their chauffeurs to pick up a few quarts.

What is boula-boula? It's a combination of cream of pea soup and green turtle consommé, served in individual casseroles, with a garnish of whipped cream, run under the broiler for a minute to gild the cream. Paul Steindler, chef-propriétaire of La Popotte Restaurant in New York, says, "It's a silly soup, because you can't taste anything."

What is chowder? It stems from *la chaudière,* meaning cauldron or big copper pot, and now means a sturdy, nourishing soup made from fresh fish or shellfish or both, vegetables, and seasonings. The most famous of the American chowders is New England clam chowder.

What is the difference between Manhattan and New England clam chowder? We can do no better than quote from that excellent source of Americana, *The American Heritage Cookbook,* which says, "The most famous of American chowders is Clam Chowder, with its two essential ingredients: Clams and salt pork or bacon." But "essential" is a prickly word. Every New Englander worth his salty independence has his own version of what is essential to clam chowder.

The most notable heresy is Manhattan clam chowder, which calls for water rather than milk—and tomatoes! Down Easters are so nettled over the tomato question that the Maine legislature once introduced a bill to outlaw forever the mixing of clams and tomatoes."

What is cockaleekie? A well-known Scotch soup made with an old cock and leeks—hence, the name—and seasonings.

Is a court bouillon the same as a fish stock? No. Court bouillon is a seasoned broth in which whole fish or shellfish are to be cooked, whereas a fish stock, made of fish bones, vegetables, and seasonings, is used as a base for fish sauces or aspics. A court bouillon is made with water, seasonings, onions, carrots, herbs, and wine, sometimes vinegar, boiled together for a given time, then strained.

What is a fumet? Fumet means bouquet and aptly describes the rich stock made of fish and fish bones, herbs, wine, and seasonings. It is used as the basis for a fish Velouté sauce or as a poaching liquid for fish. A fumet can also be made with mushrooms, chicken, game, truffles, etc. It is actually a concentrated broth or stock—richer than normal ones—with one particular flavor dominating.

What is gazpacho? Although new, more or less, on the American menu, it was made as far back as Mary Randolph's time and, in her *The Virginia Housewife,* designated as a salad. It's a cold soup, of Spanish origin, made of fresh tomatoes, oil, seasonings, garnished with diced fresh tomatoes, green peppers, cucumbers, chopped chives, and fried croutons. The variations on the recipe are almost endless. In the United States, eggs are frequently added to the basic recipe.

What is a madrilène? A rich chicken broth, cleared, then cooked with fresh tomatoes and a few sweet red peppers. Served well chilled and lightly jellied.

Is marmite a soup or a dish? It's both. Marmite means a pot or saucepan, but *petite marmite* means both a small meat pot as well as the consommé it contains. Petite marmite is a rich beef consommé, garnished with diced vegetables and small pieces of boiled beef, served in individual earthenware soup bowls, traditionally with slices of fried French bread spread with blanched beef marrow, served separately.

What is minestrone? "The hefty, rough and ready midday soup of northern Italy," as Mrs. Elizabeth David describes it in *Italian Food.* There are many versions but, broadly speaking, minestrone is essentially vegetables, a good broth, pasta or rice, and seasonings, with Parmesan cheese.

What is mulligatawny soup? A sturdy, cold-weather soup, meaning "pepper water," that apparently originated in India when the Union Jack flew. The key flavor ingredients are spices, coconut, and curry, in a strong beef or vegetable broth, with turmeric rice.

What is a purée mongole? A thick purée of split peas, blended with tomatoes, sometimes garnished with a julienne of root vegetables. More or less like American split-pea soup, which is often garnished with a julienne of ham.

What is Scotch broth? A thick soup made of mutton, barley, seasonings, and vegetables.

What is a Senegalese soup? A rich, cold soup made with a good chicken broth, curry, and other seasonings, and heavy cream. Like many soups, there are innumerable versions. The recipe that follows seems to us one of the best.

PAUL STEINDLER'S SENEGALESE SOUP

5 tablespoons butter	1 tablespoon tomato purée
1 small onion, coarsely chopped	2 heaping tablespoons commercial
1 carrot, coarsely chopped	almond paste
1 stalk celery, coarsely chopped	1 tablespoon red currant jelly
1 heaping teaspoon curry powder	3 tablespoons flour
3 small cinnamon sticks	Salt
2 bay leaves	Freshly ground white pepper
1 teaspoon whole cloves	2 cups heavy cream
3 or 4 cans 10½-ounce size condensed chicken broth	Toasted coconut

Melt 2 tablespoons of the butter in a heavy saucepan; add the vegetables. Cook over a moderate heat, giving mixture an occasional stir, until the vegetables have taken on a little color. Stir in the curry powder until well blended. Then add cinnamon sticks, bay leaves, cloves, broth, tomato purée, almond paste, and red currant jelly. Mix well, bring up to a boil, then simmer for 1 hour. Skim off any foam that rises to the surface. Knead the remaining butter together with the flour. Add, bit by bit, to the soup, stirring until well blended. Cook for about 5 to 6 minutes or until soup has thickened slightly. Strain, taste for seasoning, and refrigerate.

Just before serving, combine with the heavy cream. Serve well-chilled in soup cups with a sprinkling of toasted coconut. Serves about 8.

The basic soup can be made ahead of time, even several days, and re-frigerated or frozen.

Are soupe bonne femme and vichyssoise the same?   They are both made with leeks and potatoes, but there the similarity ends. In soupe bonne femme, the peasant soup of France, the vegetables are chopped; in vichyssoise, they are puréed. Soupe bonne femme has milk added to it just before serving, and is served hot; vichyssoise has heavy cream added just before serving, and is served cold. Vichyssoise—correctly, crème vichyssoise glacé—was introduced to New York society in 1910 by Chef Louis Diat, when the famous roof garden at the old Ritz-Carlton opened. Actually, it was adapted by M. Diat from soupe bonne femme.

Vegetables

How long should you cook frozen vegetables? In general, you should follow the cooking instructions on the package exactly. As is true of all vegetables, over-cooking is death to the flavor and texture. We prefer our vegetables, fresh or frozen, under-done somewhat, and suggest you experiment with the cooking time, rather than take the prescribed method as gospel.

Can you substitute canned vegetables for frozen? Certainly, if the vegetable is to accompany the main course or is used in a cooked dish. Remember, canned vegetables, or those packed in glass containers, are already cooked and need heating through only. Then drain thoroughly and, if served separately, season and dress with butter or a sauce.

When do you add herbs to cooked vegetables? There's no hard and fast rule about this, but most food authorities suggest adding them, whether fresh or dried, after the vegetables are drained. There's a possibility that certain herbs cooked with the vegetables might give a bitter taste. In soups, stews, etc., the herbs are added at the beginning of the cooking. Fresh herbs should always be chopped fine, of course, to bring out all their volatile flavors.

Do you approve of using baking soda when cooking green vegetables? No, although it is done by many cooks, even presumed good ones. It will keep green vegetables green but, at the same time, it destroys nutrients and makes the vegetables mushy. The French, who have made an art of cooking vegetables, do two things to maintain color: First, they blanch all green vegetables by dropping them into a large

251

kettle of rapidly boiling, salted water. Second, they "refresh" all green vegetables. As *Mastering the Art of French Cooking*, that incredibly valuable source of information, says about blanching: "Success is entirely dependent on having a great quantity of boiling water—7 to 8 quarts for 2 to 3 pounds of vegetables. The more water you use in proportion to your vegetables, the quicker the water will return to the boil after the vegetables have gone in, and the greener, fresher, and more full of flavor they will be. Baking soda is never necessary when you cook green vegetables the French way." Always cook them without a cover. To "refresh" simply means to plunge the blanched vegetables into a large quantity of cold water to stop the cooking fast, to set the color, and to preserve both texture and flavor. This is done if the vegetables are not to be served immediately or if they are to be served cold. Vegetables cooked ahead of time, in the French manner, can be reheated in hot water just before serving.

How do you julienne vegetables such as carrots and potatoes?   Slice a thin strip off one side of the vegetable, lay cut side down on your board, then cut lengthwise into very thin slices. Cut slices into ⅛-inch strips, the strips into whatever seems a suitable length.

How do you dice root vegetables?   Cut like julienne, then cut the strips, a bundle at a time, crosswise, to make a dice.

What is meant by crisping?   To place vegetables or salad greens in ice water to chill and crisp. Bread and crackers are crisped, by heating them in the oven until crisp and/or brown.

What does chiffonade mean?   Chiffon means "rags"; chiffonade, "ragged." Originally, it meant specifically sorrel and lettuce, julienned and cooked in butter, and used as a garnish for soups. A chiffonade salad is composed of shredded greens, beets, and hard-cooked eggs, with a vinaigrette dressing.

What are légumes?   The French for vegetables but, in English, the word for the fruit or seed of pod-bearing plants. In short, dried vegetables such as lima beans, white pea beans, etc.

What does à la Grècque mean?   Correctly, dishes à la grècque should mean of Greek origin. In practice this is seldom the case. Sometimes a dish called à la grècque on a menu really is of Greek origin, but more often than not the name is given to dishes of French invention.

Many vegetables are prepared à la Grècque, which simply means to cook the vegetables to the crisp stage only, in water to which ¼ cup olive oil, 1 crushed clove of garlic, the juice of 1 lemon, a few sprigs of parsley, a pinch each of thyme and tarragon, a bay leaf, and 3 or 4 crushed peppercorns have been added. The vegetables, drained and cooled, are then served with a vinaigrette sauce or mayonnaise. Artichokes; asparagus; celery hearts or stalks; cauliflowerets; eggplant, peeled and cut in fingers; leeks, mushroom caps; tiny white onions; young green onions (scallions); zucchini, cut in slices, all lend themselves to à la Grècque method of cooking.

Is printanier the same as jardinière? Printanier (spring-like) is a soup garnish (carrots, turnips, in julienne, peas, French beans); but printanière (with an "e"), like jardinière (of the garden), is a meat garnish. Glazed carrots and turnips, cut in small shapes, peas, French beans, cauliflower, arranged in separate groups around the meat.

Is the Jerusalem artichoke the same as the French? No, not even related. The Jerusalem artichoke somewhat resembles the potato, but is sweetish and more watery. There are two types: one long with a red skin; the other round, knobby, and white. They are generally boiled, although some people enjoy eating them raw, with salt, like radishes. It's not a vegetable one would spend much time tracking down.

How can one tell if a French artichoke is fresh? A fresh French or "globe" artichoke is heavy in the hand, with the leaves clinging tightly into a compact head; the stem is firm. If the leaves are open and the stem rubbery, the artichoke is growing old. A real test, which you can obviously make only at home, is to break the stem off with your hand. If fresh, the break will be clean without any fibers; if old, it will be noticeably fibrous. In season from October to June.

How do you prepare and cook whole artichokes properly? Break off the stem, then, using a heavy, sharp knife, trim the base and break off the small leaves at the base. Lay the artichoke on its side and slice about ¾ of an inch off the top. Trim the points off the rest of the leaves with a pair of scissors. Wash under cold running water.

Tie a thick slice of fresh lemon on the bottom of each artichoke (this helps to keep the heart white). Have ready a large kettle of boiling, salted water. (Do not use aluminum or iron because it turns artichokes grayish.) It should be large enough to accommodate all the artichokes comfortably. Add the artichokes, bring up to a rolling boil as quickly as possible. Cover the tops of the artichokes with a double layer of cheesecloth (this helps to keep the tops moist). Do *not* use the pot cover. Boil slowly, uncovered, for 35 to 45 minutes, or until a leaf will pull out easily. Lift out of the kettle and drain upside down.

Serve hot or warm with melted butter, lemon butter, or Hollandaise sauce. Serve cold with vinaigrette sauce, sauce ravigote, or mayonnaise.

How do you remove the "choke" from an artichoke? Spread the leaves apart carefully so you can reach the interior easily, then pull out the center cone of leaves, all in one piece. This will expose the hairy choke. Scrape out the choke with a teaspoon. Underneath you'll find the heart. To present the artichoke with professional *éclat*, turn the cone of leaves upside down and place in the hollow on top of the artichoke.

How do you eat a whole, cooked artichoke? To eat, pull off a leaf and, holding the tip in your fingers, dip the bottom of the leaf into the sauce (hot or cold), then scrape off the flesh between your teeth. Eventually, you will come to the heart which is covered with the "choke," a hairy center growth (a fine cook would have removed this before serving). Lift the choke to one side and eat the heart with a knife and fork, dipping the pieces into the accompanying sauce.

How do you prepare artichoke hearts? Break off the stem as close to the base of the artichoke as possible. Holding the artichoke upside down, break off the leaves, one by one, working around the artichoke until you come to the pale yellow part and you can feel and, to some extent, see the little ridge formed by the heart. Slice the entire cone off with a sharp knife, then with a small, sharp knife, cut off the ends of the leaves, making the heart look shapely. As you finish each heart, rub the entire surface of the heart with a cut lemon, and tie a thick slice of lemon on the bottom. Drop the prepared hearts into a pot of boiling, salted water. When the water comes up to a boil again, turn heat down to moderate and cook for 30 to 40 minutes or until a knife will pierce the hearts easily. If the water boils away, add more so the hearts are always completely covered. Cool in the water.

If they are not going to be used at once, they can be refrigerated for a couple of days in the liquid in which they cooked.

To serve, remove the choke carefully with a small spoon, and trim off any bits of leaf that remain. Artichoke hearts can be served cold with vinaigrette sauce; reheated in butter and filled with a suitable filling; or served in a seasoned fresh cream and lemon sauce.

Are artichokes only available fresh?   No. The hearts are packed frozen and in cans. Of the two, the canned seem to me the best. The canned need draining only, the frozen must be thawed and cooked. Artichoke hearts are available packed in a vinegar liquid, or better, in a seasoned oil marinade; also available pickled for hors d'oeuvre.

How do you judge fresh asparagus?   The stalks should be firm and crisp, the tips, compact and tightly closed. We recommend buying asparagus loose, rather than by the bunch, because you can choose each spear and spears all of a size. Allow 6 to 8 spears per person.

Should asparagus be peeled before cooking?   If you would have fresh, green, appetizing asparagus, peel it. But it is not only a matter of appearance. Peeling shaves off the tough outer flesh and makes the whole spear edible. Cut off the tough root ends; then with a small, sharp knife or a potato peeler, peel from the tips down, rolling the stalk around as you work. Done properly, the stalks will be all of a size and, except for tips, all of a color. Wash thoroughly in cold water. Drain. Line up the tips and tie in bundles with soft string. Lay the bundles in rapidly boiling, well-salted water in a flat skillet and cook, uncovered (this keeps the color) until tender but not limp. Test with a knife. Young, fresh asparagus will cook very quickly, in a matter of minutes. Drain and serve in a dish lined with a fresh linen napkin to absorb the asparagus liquid.

Is frozen asparagus available in spears only?   No. You can get the cut asparagus frozen, too.

What is the meaning of Argenteuil in cooking?   Argenteuil is the name of a district, northwest of Paris, famous for asparagus. Thus, the many dishes designated as Argenteuil are made or garnished with asparagus in one form or another.

Is the avocado a fruit or a vegetable? A fruit. There are two types, the leading variety being the California fuerte, distinguished by its leather-like skin (hence, its old name "alligator pear") and the Florida Lula which has a smooth, or slightly corrugated, skin flecked with yellow dots. The fruit varies in color by variety, from light green to almost black and it also varies widely in size. But no relationship has been found between skin color and flavor or between size and flavor. The skin may be thin and smooth, thick and smooth, or leathery and rough. Avocados are one of the fruits that ripen perfectly off the tree but should be eaten only when well ripe. At this point the fruit yields to gentle pressure by the fingers. If purchased when hard, it will take a few days at room temperature to ripen properly. If, by chance, you choose an avocado with brown irregular markings, known in the trade as "scab;" simply ignore them. They are superficial and in no way affect the flesh of the fruit. Fully ripe avocados should be refrigerated if not eaten promptly. Available the year round but especially plentiful from January to April.

Avocados have been called, colloquially and variously, "midshipman's butter," "vegetable butter," and "butter pear."

How do you prepare avocados? Cut the fruit in half, remove the big seed, and serve in the "shell" (½ avocado to a person) with lemon juice or vinaigrette sauce in the shell. Or peel and then combine with fresh grapefruit or orange sections, dressed with Vinaigrette; or make the famous Mexican guacamole and serve as a salad or as a dressing with salad greens. Avocados can also be served "on the half shell" filled with vinaigrette sauce, *madrilène,* crabmeat, or mixed fruit. Sometimes, they are sliced thin and floated on a hot consommé. They are rarely cooked.

Since avocados are inclined to darken once cut and exposed to air, this can be prevented if the cut surfaces are sprinkled with or dipped in lemon or lime juice. The Mexicans have a theory that if the seed of the avocado is placed in the middle of any mixture in which avocado plays a role, it will keep the flesh from discoloring. It has been our experience the citrus juice or a seal of foil or Saran is more effective.

What is guacamole?   A Mexican recipe calling for very ripe avocado, combined with chili powder, salt, lemon juice, minced onion, to taste. This is the basic recipe but diced ripe tomatoes, sliced ripe olives and crisp, crumbled bacon are sometimes added. It is usually served as a dip, traditionally with tortillas, fried crisp. However, it can also be used as a dressing for tomatoes or green salads.

What are bamboo shoots?   A basic ingredient in Chinese, Japanese, and other Oriental cooking, they are the inner, white part of the young shoot of the bamboo plant. We can buy them in this country ready to use in cans, peeled, and in chunks. Any left-over from a cooking bout can be stored, covered with cold water and sealed, but the water must be changed every other day.

What are bean sprouts?   An Oriental vegetable, the tender shoots of the curd bean, an important ingredient in chop suey, chow mein, and some of the classic Chinese and Oriental dishes. Available canned and, in Chinese markets, fresh.

What is barley and how is it used?   A hardy grass cereal, related to wheat, essential in the brewing of beer and in the distillation of Scotch whisky. As a food, its rich, nutty flavor is excellent, in place of potatoes, with meat. But it takes a good long time to cook until tender—1 to 1½ hours. Also used in making casseroles, soups, etc.

What are the various types of dried beans and how are they used?
   Black or turtle beans: Imported from South America, white inside, oval-shaped. In the U.S. South they are used primarily in soups, but in South America in many bean dishes.
   Black-eye and yellow-eye beans: Oval, with either a black or yellow "eye," called cow-peas in the South. Black-eyes are the very heart of Hopping John, an old Southern dish, traditionally served on New Year's Eve.
   Chick-peas: Also known as Spanish or *garbanzo* beans, chick or *cecci* peas. Good in stews, soups, etc.
   Cranberry beans: Known in Ohio and Indiana as "shellouts," similar to pinto beans, except markings are pink rather than brown. Popular in New England, where they are used interchangeably with young limas in making succotash.
   Lima beans: Both large and small, flat and kidney-shaped. In the

South, large limas, mottled with purple, are called "calico" or "speckled butter beans." Often used in combination with meat, such as lamb.

Pinto beans: Pale pink, speckled with brown. Can be used interchangeably in cooking with "pink" beans (which are a brownish red, rather than pink); also called "red Mexican" or "red miners." Both pintos and pinks turn red-brown when cooked. Popular in the Southwest in hearty stews.

Red beans: Also known as Mexican "chili beans," darker red than pink beans. Essential in making chili con carne and other Spanish dishes.

Red kidney beans: Bright, red-purple, red kidneys are used in France, England, the Scandinavian countries, and are very popular in the U.S. They, too, are used in chili con carne, as well as soups and salads.

Soybeans: About the size of a pea, they are used extensively both as food and to make oil. The color ranges from yellow and green to brown and black, or mixtures. The flavor is so distinctive, many people do not like it. Used in combination with other vegetables in casseroles.

White beans: Include marrow beans, great northern beans, navy beans, and pea beans. The "marrows'" are the largest of this popular group and the pea, the smallest. They can be used interchangeably in cooking, generally in baked beans, whether Southern, New England, or Western style.

How do you prepare dried beans? They must always be soaked to replace the water lost in drying. Packages usually give complete instructions. The two accepted methods are:

Quick: Cover the washed beans with water in a large, heavy kettle. Bring to a boil, cover, and cook 2 minutes. Allow to stand 1 hour. Then follow recipe directions.

Overnight: Cover the washed beans with water, put the top on the kettle, and allow to stand 6 to 8 hours. To forestall the possibility of souring, bring to a boil and cook 2 minutes, before soaking them.

Are Boston baked beans really of American origin? Yes, but the Indians get the credit, not Bostonians. When the Pilgrims landed in Plymouth, in 1620, they found the squaws baked beans, first soaking to make them swell and soften the skin (done to this day). They then baked them with deer fat and an onion, in a stout clay pot, overnight in a hole lined with hot stones, covered with sod. Pilgrim housewives adopted the method because their religion forbade all worldly activities on Sunday, including cooking; thus, the custom of cooking beans Saturday night for Sunday. Later, even with religious laws relaxed, baked beans on Saturday night became a New England tradition. The recipe changed to some extent, pork replacing the deer fat, brown sugar and seasonings being added. Beans baked in the same, old, New England way, before being canned are just around the corner in your nearest market.

What are broad beans? A fresh bean (also known as faba or fava and English broad bean), they are used extensively in Europe. In general, they can be prepared and served as you would fresh lima beans, although they take slightly longer to cook. Broad beans are edible in three stages: First, when the pods are so small the flower has just withered; cook whole or cut into two or three pieces. Second, when the beans are about as big as a good-sized pea. In the third stage, when the beans are considerably bigger, they should be shelled to cook; at this stage, the skin has an unpleasant taste.

When are fresh lima beans in season? The year round, with the peak season from June to September. The pods should be clean, well-filled, fresh, and dark green. Weighed in the pods, 2 pounds will give you about 2½ cups shelled. Do not shell until you are ready to cook them. Meanwhile, refrigerate, in a polyethylene bag, all air squeezed out. Baby limas or Fordhooks (larger and fatter than the "babies") are available frozen.

Frozen fresh limas are also available in various sauces, such as cheese, tomato, and butter. Also in succotash, the corn-lima combination we inherited from the Narragansett Indians—called by them, *misickquatash.*

Are snap beans and green beans identical? Yes. Just as a matter of interest, there are two types of snap beans: the bush and the pole and, within these types, there are green-podded and yellow-podded varieties. Some beans are round-podded, some oval, and some flat. Available the year round. That's the whole story except there is no longer such a thing as a "string" bean.

How to cook green beans: French-style: Bring a good, big pot of salted water to a rolling boil. Add the beans. (3 pounds will serve 6 to 8). As soon as the water comes to a rolling boil the second time, reduce heat to low, and cook, uncovered, for 10 to 15 minutes. Test a bean by eating one at the end of 10 minutes. Correctly, beans should be tender but still somewhat crisp to the bite. Drain immediately.

If they are to be served at once: Dry them off quickly, shaking the pan over a high heat for a couple of minutes. Add seasonings and butter and place in a hot serving dish.

If they are to be served later or cold: Run cold water over the drained beans for several minutes to cool them quickly, stop the cooking, and retain the color. Drain and pat dry with a towel. To reheat and serve: Toss the beans in hot, melted butter, season, cover the pan, and let them warm up over a low heat. Do not cook. To serve cold: Toss them in a good vinaigrette sauce.

In addition to fresh, beans are available canned, whole, whole vertical pack, French-style, and cut. Yellow beans are available cut. "Dilly" beans are packed in vinegar (used as a cocktail snack). Also frozen whole, cut, or French-style.

What are flageolets? Very small, green haricot beans, similar to baby limas, grown in France and considered by epicures the most delicious of all beans. They are available fresh, canned, and dried in France, but we import only the dried and canned from both France and Belgium. Puréed, they make a delicious garnish for lamb or mutton. Dried flageolets must, like other dried beans, be soaked before cooking. Canned flageolets can be jazzed up with a little minced onion cooked in butter or, if you like, crumbled crisp bacon.

How can you stop fresh beets from bleeding? Cook them in their skins, with the roots, and about an inch of the top on. Leave them in the hot water until just ready to use. Beets of average size take about 40 minutes to cook. They are very easy to peel, the skins just slip off. Usually available the year round, they are at their peak from June through October. Canned beets are always in the market and seem to us one of the best of the canned products.

How can you tell when broccoli is fresh? The buds should be compact (open flowers indicate it is old); it should be a rich, dark green—sage green or purplish-green, depending on the variety. Stalks and stem branches should be tender but firm. Toughness, woody stalks and branches, yellowed or wilted leaves are all indications that it's not fit for anybody's table. At its best from October through April.

How do you prepare and cook fresh broccoli?   The problem with broccoli is that the buds cook more quickly than the stems. For that reason it makes sense to divide the tops into flowerets; peel the stalks, right down to the white flesh, then cut into short lengths. Drop the stems into boiling, salted water for 5 minutes, then add the flowerets and cook another 5 minutes. Drain at once, place in a napkin-lined dish to absorb the liquid, and serve with melted butter or Hollandaise sauce on the side.

What determines fresh Brussels sprouts?   They should be firm, compact, fresh, and a good, bright green. Puffy or soft sprouts are usually of poor quality and flavor; wilted or yellow leaves indicate aging. They're on the market all year except in June and July, but the peak months are October through December. They are also available frozen.

How do you prepare and cook Brussels sprouts?   The major point to remember is not to cut the stem ends too short, or the outer leaves will fall off in cooking. However, you should pull off any wilted or yellow leaves. Blanch as you would green beans in boiling salted water for 10 to 12 minutes, or until the point of a small, sharp knife will pierce the stem end easily. Drain at once. Season with salt and pepper and toss in melted butter.

Fresh sprouts, hollowed out, filled with crabmeat mixed with mayonnaise, make an attractive hors d'oeuvre.

What is the difference between red and green cabbage?   Color, obviously, and the method of cooking. Red cabbage must always be cooked with something acid (apples, red wine, vinegar) to retain the color, otherwise it turns out a rather horrid grayish-purple. Combined with apples, red wine, brown sugar, and vinegar and braised, it is excellent with roast goose, duck, or pork.

Of the green cabbages, there are four. Danish (sometimes called Hollander): firm head, round, oval, or a bit flat. Domestic: not quite as compact as Danish; the leaves generally crinkled or curled. Pointed: conical head with smooth leaves. Savoy: greenish-yellow with a curly leaf, more delicate than the other green cabbages. These types can all be used interchangeably in cooking, remembering that young cabbage cooks more quickly than winter cabbage. Cabbage can be shredded or quartered and then boiled; shredded, then creamed or braised; and it can be shredded to make cole slaw. Cabbage should be cooked quickly in a small amount of water only until it is *al dente*.

In choosing cabbages, judge on the basis of firmness and weight. They should be fairly heavy for their size. Defects are easy to detect; the commonest are worm injury and decay, yellowed leaves and burst heads.

The cabbage family, often maligned, is one of the best of our vegetables, so rich in Vitamin C that, weight for weight, it ranks with oranges and grapefruit.

What is Chinese cabbage?   Also known as celery cabbage, it resembles cos lettuce or romaine, compact with slightly wrinkled, fresh green leaves. It makes a delicious salad, but can be cooked as you would other green cabbage.

Is cold slaw or cole slaw correct?   Cole, although you occasionally, and incorrectly, see it spelled and hear it pronounced cold. Cole has nothing at all to do with temperature; it is the generic name for any plant of the *Brassica* genus, which includes cabbage. Slaw derives from the Danish word for salad.

Cole slaw is finely shredded cabbage mixed with a boiled dressing that is quite sharp with vinegar. Another version: Sweeten 1 cup of commercial sour cream with sugar, season with salt, freshly ground pepper, and vinegar to taste, combine with shredded cabbage.

What is sauerkraut?   Kraut means cabbage, and sauer, sour. It is shredded cabbage, fermented in brine made from its own natural juices, with salt added. It is available canned, in jars, in pliofilm bags, and loose. Most German of German vegetables, it is served in innumerable ways. For example, cold, as a salad or relish; hot, with frankfurters or spareribs. Sauerkraut juice is also available.

What is choucroute garni?   Garnished sauerkraut. Sauerkraut cooked in pork or goose fat, garnished with ham, pork, or sausages, etc. (It varies from region to region.)

Where did the tops of carrots go?   They got chopped off, and a good thing, too, because when left on, they continue to live on the carrot root, sapping it of its moisture and causing it to shrivel. If carrots have their tops on, cut them off before storing, and the carrot roots will stay fresh longer.

Note, in buying carrots, the deeper the orange color the more Vitamin A tucked inside the good root. Note, too, that carrots that are rough, cracked, wilted, flabby, soft, or shriveled are not of a quality good enough for your dinner table. Baby carrots are delicious if you can find them.

Do carrots need peeling?   It depends on how they are being used. If in broth, as a flavoring agent that will be discarded, scrub only; if to be served as a vegetable, trim off the ends and peel with a potato peeler. Then slice, halve, or quarter, etc. Carrots can be braised in butter, with or without herbs, creamed, made into soup, or puréed.

How do you slice carrots and their ilk?   Slice a thin strip off one side and lay the cut side down on your board. This keeps the carrot *et al.* from slipping around. Then slice crosswise.

How do you make carrot curls?   First, peel the carrots, then with a vegetable peeler, shave strips, lengthwise, from long, straight carrots, working around the carrot. Curl each strip around your finger tightly as you finish each strip. Place on ice and refrigerate for an hour or better.

What does Crécy mean in cookery?   It means either made of, or garnished with, carrots. And especially, purée Crécy, carrot soup.

What does Saint-Germain mean in cookery?   A soup or garnish made with little, fresh peas.

When is cauliflower in season?   To some extent, the year round but, technically, it is a winter vegetable and the best cauliflower, with white or creamy-white heads, firm, compact, without brown spots or bruises, is available from September through October and into the winter months.

What's the best way to cook cauliflower? The whole head can be cooked, although some cooks are of the opinion it is best to separate the head into flowerets so they will cook more quickly. Simply drop the flowerets into boiling salted water and boil slowly, uncovered, for 9 to 10 minutes, or until the point of a sharp knife will pierce the stems easily. Drain immediately. Cauliflower can be served with, or in, innumerable hot sauces: fresh cream, Hollandaise, mousseline, etc., or gratined.

How do you judge the freshness of celery? Like snap beans, a rib should snap easily, all the heads should be fresh, crisp, clean. Soft, pliable branches indicate pithiness; very hard branches, that it may be stringy or woody. If you're suspicious about the interior, separate the branches and look inside.

Is a stalk of celery the same thing as a rib? No. A rib is one part of a stalk. A stalk and a bunch are one and the same. So, the next time a recipe calls for a stalk of celery, use a rib.

Can celery be cooked? In innumerable ways: braised; boiled until just tender, then dressed, *à la Grècque;* cooked and creamed or served with Hollandaise, etc.

What is Pascal celery? A variety of green celery which now constitutes the bulk of the celery sold in this country, in contrast to a few years ago when all available celery was blanched. The joy of a good bunch of celery is that every part of it is usable. The leaves can be added to the stock pot (don't let the market man cut them off, as they are prone to do when your back is turned), the big outer ribs cooked, and the hearts served fresh, stuffed or plain. Refrigerated, covered in a polyethylene bag, fresh celery keeps extremely well. Available throughout the year. As a change from the ubiquitous parsley, occasionally use a bouquet of celery leaves to garnish meats or fowl.

What is celeriac? A root vegetable and a member of the celery family, also known as celery root and celery knob. Widely used in France and Germany as a vegetable, cooked, and as a salad, raw, it is perfectly delicious either way. Since it is in good season in the winter months and into April, we suggest you try it. Don't be put off by its knobby appearance, which is far from attractive.

CELÉRIAC REMOULADE

Pare 3 medium celeriac using a sharp knife, then cut into slices about ¹⁄₁₆ of an inch thick. Cut the slices into strips about as thin as a toothpick. Combine 1 cup good mayonnaise with 1 tablespoon Dijon mustard and fresh lemon juice to taste. Mix in the celeriac thoroughly and refrigerate until serving time. Properly covered and refrigerated, the rémoulade will keep well for quite a spell. Serves 4 to 6.

PURÉED CELERIAC

Peel 4 big celeriac and 2 medium potatoes. Cut into quarters. Drop into boiling, salted water in separate pots, cover, and cook until each is tender when pierced with the point of a sharp knife, approximately 20 minutes. Take care not to over-cook. Blend the celeriac in a blender with a little chicken broth or put through a potato ricer. Mash the potatoes and combine with the puréed celeriac. Season with salt and pepper to taste and fold in enough heavy cream to give the mixture a good consistency. Excellent with duck, goose, turkey, ham, or pork. Serves 6.

What's the difference between fresh white and yellow sweet corn? From a nutrition standpoint, white isn't in the same league with yellow, the Fresh Fruit and Vegetable Association tells us. In a national popularity contest, yellow would win hands down. However, there are many people who prefer white, finding it more tender and sweeter. The corn season has been stretched to the point where it is available virtually all year, although it is not in good supply from October through March.

How long can you store fresh sweet corn in the refrigerator? As short a time as possible after it has come from the garden or market. The maximum time is 4 days if you want any of the milky goodness left but, as any corn lover knows, the sooner it is cooked the sweeter and milkier it is. But note well, it must be refrigerated, wrapped in plastic bags, or it will lose half its flavor even in 1 hot summer day. In buying corn, look for fresh, green husks and bright, plump, milky kernels.

Two ways to cook fresh corn: First way, drop the husked ears into rapidly boiling water to which a tablespoon or so of sugar has been added (do not add salt, it makes corn tough). When water comes to a boil the second time, boil corn 3 to 5 minutes. Very tender, young corn will take only 3 minutes. Second way, place the husked corn in a big kettle of cold water, add a good pinch of sugar, bring up to a boil over moderately high heat. When the water reaches a rolling boil, remove corn, drain, and serve. If the corn must stand a few minutes, leave right in the kettle of water, covered.

Cooked corn-on-the-cob should always be served on a platter wrapped in a linen napkin to keep it warm.

What is shoe peg corn?   Quoting from Burpee's catalogue, "Very sweet, pure white kernels with tender skin that is a general favorite for home gardens, canning, and freezing. Popularly known as 'shoe peg' because of the appearance of the dry grains, which are thin and narrow." It is, happily, available in cans and is delicious.

What is polenta?   The basic polenta, an Italian dish, is simply corn-meal cooked in water with butter and salt, then mixed with grated Parmesan cheese.

How can you judge a good cucumber?   Firmness, bright color, a good "figure," all are good signs. Cucumbers that look withered or shriveled should be avoided. When serving fresh, sliced cucumber, leave the skin on, and flute the cucumber by pulling the tines of a fork down its full length, all around. Or, still with skin on, cut lengthwise, into long fingers. Here's a nice little recipe of Scandinavian origin:

MARINATED CUCUMBERS

Wash the cucumber, cut off the ends, then slice paper-thin, literally. Place in a bowl, sprinkle with 1 teaspoon of salt, 3 tablespoons of sugar, and add ⅓ cup white vinegar. Press the slices with the back of a spoon to make the mixture very juicy.

Chill in the refrigerator and serve, as a salad, with fish or meat. Marinated cucumbers will keep a good long time, refrigerated.

Is it true the skin of cucumbers is coated with wax   Yes, a harmless wax sprayed on to inhibit wilting. Once thought poisonous, the skins of cucumbers are good to eat and, in addition, decorative. If a recipe calls for sliced cucumbers, flute the skin with the tines of a fork before slicing. Our grandmothers automatically sliced off the stem ends, because the cucumber of that time was frequently quite bitter. She would then rinse her knife and peel the "cuke." Happily, this characteristic has been bred out of the cucumbers by modern horticulturists. There are two types of cucumbers: the table variety and the pickling variety. The "slicers," a rich, dark green, are white-spined, round-ended, 7 or 8 inches long; the "picklers" are small, black-spined fruits too small to be sliced. The former are available pretty much the year round, although not in great abundance in the dead of winter; the latter are readily available only during the fall or pickling season.

What are cornichons? French gherkins; miniature pickles marinated in a spicy wine vinegar. Used as a garnish, to flavor sandwiches, etc. Comparable to, except in size, our own standard sour pickles.

What are dolmas? From the Arabic, meaning "something stuffed." The dolmas you will probably meet along the culinary trail will be grape (vine) leaves stuffed with a mixture of chopped mutton, lamb or chicken, rice, herbs, onions, etc., poached in a rich broth, then served with a sauce made with some of the broth, egg yolks, and lemon juice. Rice-stuffed grape leaves are also served cold with a wedge of lemon in Mid-East restaurants as appetizers.

Does eggplant come in any color other than dark purple? Yes, as a matter of fact, it does. But the variety generally available is purple and it's so handsome, why look for anything else? A good eggplant is heavy in relation to size, a rich, uniformly dark color, free of scars or cuts. If wilted, shriveled, or flabby, it is of poor flavor and probably bitter. You can buy eggplants any month of the year, but their peak months are from March into June.

How do you prepare and serve eggplant? Either peeled or unpeeled, it is used in innumerable ways: combined with tomatoes and baked; in *ratatouille;* fried in batter; or just fried. They are also stuffed and baked.

There's a dish known as eggplant caviar, said to be of Middle Eastern origin, in which peeled, cooked eggplant is mixed with onion, garlic, tomatoes, seasonings, and sesame or olive oil. The mixture is served chilled as a first course.

What is ratatouille? Spawned on the Riviera, it's a wonderful vegetable mixture that can be eaten hot or cold, composed of garlic (to the extent you can take it), onion, zucchini, eggplant, green peppers, and ripe tomatoes, all cooked in olive oil, well seasoned. You can make a meal of it with good, crusty bread and a bottle of sturdy wine.

Will you please explain the difference between endive, escarole, and chicory? French or Belgian endive (also known as witloof and, in England as chicory) has a pleasant little "bite" and looks like large attenuated buds, in compact heads, shading from white to creamy yellow. Escarole, sometimes confused with chicory, or the curly endive, has long, slender leaves curly at the edges, and a slightly bitter taste. Chicory, sometimes called curly endive, a feathery green that grows flat, also has a tang. Here, imported French or Belgian endive is most frequently served as a salad, which is sad, because it is so delicious cooked. Both escarole and chicory are true salad greens, especially good when combined with less authoritative ones, such as Boston lettuce. All are in season except for the summer months.

   To prepare Belgian endive for salad: Discard any withered leaves, rinse under cold running water, drain and dry thoroughly. Split each into quarters, lengthwise, and arrange in a shallow salad dish. Dress with vinaigrette sauce.

   To braise Belgian endive: Allow 2 heads per person. Trim off the root without cutting the leaves and remove any discolored leaves. Rub the bottom of a heavy, ovenproof casserole with butter, add the endive, the juice of half a lemon, and enough chicken stock (your own or canned) to half cover the endive. Bring up to a boil, on top of the stove. Place a round of buttered waxed paper on top, cover, and cook in a preheated 325° F. oven for an hour or until the endive is tender when pierced with the point of a small, sharp knife and lightly browned. To serve, lift the endive to a hot serving dish, boil down the liquids in the pan until you have 2 tablespoons or so. Pour over the endive. Sprinkle with finely chopped parsley. Particularly good with veal.

What is meant by spring greens? The name covers a multitude of sins. Mustard greens, with bright, little yellow flowers, purple-green beet tops, and dandelion greens are all "spring" greens and are with us only in April, then they vanish for another year. Two other greens, also "spring," but less well known, are field salad (known, too, as marsh salad) and arugula (this travels under two other names:

rucola and rocket salad). Field salad, with its spoon-shaped leaves, has a slightly bitter flavor which may remind you of watercress. It is an excellent addition to the salad bowl. Arugula is quite distinctive and rather pungent. Best used in combination with less dominating salad greens.

What is the best green for making salads? There is no best. It's a matter of taste and what's in the market. We are extremely fortunate in the number of greens available to us. In addition to the "spring" greens, we have: Boston, also known as butterhead—very soft and delicate with a silky surface. Bibb, the most delicate of all, with a marvelous flavor and color and a head about the size of a tulip, but expensive. Romaine or cos, an elongated deep green leaf with a tightly folded head. Leaf lettuce, characterized by its loose, non-forming leaves. And, of course, iceberg, also called crisphead and Western iceberg. In buying iceberg lettuce, always squeeze the head to test for "springiness." In addition, there is escarole, chicory, and French or Belgian endive (known, too, as witloof).

Most salad greens are available the year round.

How do you take care of greens properly? All, except iceberg lettuce, should be washed under cool running water, wrapped in a fresh dish towel and dried completely. Then store it in a polyetheylene bag, with all air squeezed out, in the hydrator of the refrigerator. Iceberg lettuce should be cored, held under a strong stream of water, then drained thoroughly, core down. Special care must be taken with Bibb, both in washing and in separating the leaves, because it is extremely fragile. It is important for all greens to be dry before going into a salad, otherwise the dressing will not coat the leaves properly.

Why are the core ends of lettuce sometimes brown? When the lettuce is cut in the fields, a milky substance appears at the core-end which turns brown the minute it hits the air. Actually, it's nature's way of sealing the "wound." Every time you cut off the end, the same thing happens. It is a natural seal and does not indicate, as some people think, old lettuce.

Can you cook lettuce? Braised, it is perfectly delicious; or wilted, with bits of crisp bacon, a dash of mild wine vinegar, salt, and pepper.

Should salad greens be torn or cut? It makes very little difference. French chefs usually cut out the ribs. Whatever you do, toss your salad at the very last minute before serving or it will wilt, look extremely uninviting, and lose its crispness. Allow about 1 tablespoon of dressing per person—just enough to coat the leaves very lightly.

Are grits and groats the same thing? Yes. The seeds or kernels of oats that have been husked. Used in making gruel, to thicken broths or soups, and extensively, in other ways, in Southern cooking. Corn grits or hominy are made of white corn these days.

What is the difference between hominy and hominy grits? Hominy, also known as samp, is the kernel of white corn, the seed germ and outer skin removed; hominy grits are ground corn, either fine, medium, or coarse. Hominy, which must be soaked overnight before cooking, is used in casseroles in combination with other foods such as beans and pork, peas and frankfurters, or cheese; grits, more commonly used in breads, puddings, etc., and, of course, fried, need only about an hour's soaking prior to cooking.

Is fresh horseradish generally available? Yes. Not the most attractive looking of our root vegetables (its name is hardly less elegant), still, in a sauce, it makes an important contribution to such good dishes as boiled beef, tongue, cold meats, and game. Prepared horseradish is always available, but the fresh is essential in making many interesting sauces.

What is kohlrabi? A variety of cabbage, also called cabbage-turnip, with a turnip-like root growing just above the ground. The young leaves are often eaten as greens, but the root is the better part. It resembles turnip in flavor but has a more delicate grain. It is at its best when young and small—2 to 3 inches in diameter. To cook, cut into small dice and boil in salted water until just tender when pierced with the point of a small, sharp knife.

What are lentils? Probably one of the first plants cultivated by man, they are never eaten fresh but, rather, dried. In this country we use lentils in soups, but in Europe and the Near East they are served in stews, salads, and other dishes. Lentil salad almost always turns up on the French hors d'oeuvre table, and good it is. Puréed and served in place of potatoes, lentils make a splendid companion to fresh pork in any form. There are two varieties available in the U.S.: the French, gray outside, yellow inside, sold with the seed coat on; the Egyptian, reddish-yellow, smaller and rounder than the French, without the coating on the seed. They can be purchased packaged or, in bulk, by the pound. To cook, follow package directions, first picking them over carefully to eliminate any foreign matter or imperfect seeds. Why don't you try this French lentil salad sometime?

Wash 2 cups dried, quick-cooking lentils, then boil for 2 minutes in enough water to cover. Take off the heat, cover, and allow to stand for an hour. Add a good pinch of salt, 1 onion stuck with 2 cloves, and 1 bay leaf. Bring up to a boil, then lower heat and simmer, covered, until lentils are tender. Take care not to over-cook. Drain and cool.

Combine cooled lentils with 6 scallions or green onions, chopped, 1 cup chopped parsley, and ½ cup vinaigrette sauce. Toss thoroughly. Taste for seasoning. Chill. Serves 4 to 6.

Should fresh mushrooms be washed or wiped to clean?   As is true of many things in cookery, authorities differ about this. Some good cooks simply wipe the caps with a clean, damp cloth; others wash them under cool—not stone-cold—water, drain well, then dry them with a towel. The method is up to you.

How do you store mushrooms and about how long will they stay in good condition?   Refrigerate in tall, plastic containers, uncovered, and give them plenty of space. They like air around them. Do not wash before refrigerating and take care not to bruise them. Handled this way, the American Mushroom Institute tells us they will stay in prime condition for about five days. If you are not going to use them in that time, they can be frozen successfully. If they should turn brown before you get around to cooking them, peel, chop fine, sauté for 3 or 4 minutes, and serve with steak or other meat or mix them into a meat sauce or into soup.

What are the signs of old mushrooms?   They are usually very apparent: discolored, open caps and gills (the fluted formation between the cap and the stem) that are dark brown or black. Fresh mushrooms, available the year round, are clean, white to creamy-white, with closed caps.

Should mushrooms be peeled?　Not unless they are aging and somewhat shriveled, then we would peel them (this you do with your fingers), using the peelings and stems (if you're economy- and flavor-minded) in soups or sauces.

Are mushrooms ever served raw?　Yes. Stuffed, or in a salad. To stuff, take fresh, white mushroom caps, fill with cream cheese mixed with seasonings and minced chives; in a salad, sliced, with a few fresh greens, tossed in vinaigrette sauce. Our friend, James Beard, sometimes garnishes his salad with fresh violets.

What's the difference between a "fancy" and "extra fancy" mushroom?　None. They are mushrooms that measure an inch, or slightly better, in diameter, and the terms have nothing whatsoever to do with quality. Large mushrooms, ranging in size from 1⅝ inches to more than 3 inches, are best for stuffing. "Buttons" (about 1 inch in diameter) are always the least expensive. Therefore, best for chopping or slicing. If you've never stuffed mushrooms, here's an easy, delicious recipe. Serve them as a first course for dinner, as an accompaniment to meat, as an hors d'oeuvre (2 to a person), or for lunch as the main dish (4 to a person)—with some good French bread and a bottle of wine.

STUFFED MUSHROOMS

16 large mushrooms	1 tablespoon minced onion
¼ pound (1 stick) butter	1 tablespoon minced parsley
½ cup fine, fresh bread crumbs	Salt
made from day-old, firm bread	Freshly ground pepper
2 eggs, lightly beaten	Parmesan cheese

Break off the mushroom stems and mince; wipe the caps with a clean, damp cloth; heat 2 or 3 tablespoons of butter in a saucepan and sauté the minced stems lightly. Take off the heat and mix in the bread crumbs, eggs, onions, parsley, salt and pepper to taste.

Brush the mushroom caps with melted butter; arrange, cap side down, in a buttered, shallow, baking dish; stuff each cap, sprinkle with cheese, and dot generously with butter.

Bake in a preheated 375° F. oven for 15 to 20 minutes or until tender when pierced with the point of a sharp knife. Baste during the cooking with a little melted butter to keep them moist. Serve piping hot.

FRESH MUSHROOM SOUP

1 pound fresh, white mushroom buttons with stems, coarsely chopped
2 cans (10½-ounce size) condensed chicken broth

½ cup heavy cream
Salt
Freshly-ground nutmeg
Minced parsley

Puree the mushrooms, a small amount at a time, in the electric blender with some of the chicken soup. Pour into a heavy saucepan, add any remaining soup and the heavy cream. Season to taste with salt and freshly-ground nutmeg. Bring up to a boil over a low heat. Do not cook further. Serve immediately in heated soup cups with a garnish of parsley. Serves about 6.

What are cèpes? The French name for *boletus,* a type of wild mushroom, which is distinguished by small tubes or holes, in place of gills, under the cap. Extremely popular in France and Germany, they also grow wild in this country. Cèpes have a thick, white stem and a large rounded cap, yellowish to warm brown in color. Imported from France canned, sometimes dried, rarely fresh. The flavor is exceptionally vivid.

What are chanterelles? Also, known as *girolles,* they are a type of wild, trumpet-shaped, yellow mushroom. The flavor is excellent but they are frequently used as a garnish because they're so handsome. Imported from France in 8- and 16-ounce cans.

What are morels? A type of wild mushroom known by their deeply honeycombed caps—varying from oval to blunted conical—yellowish-brown when young but growing darker with age. Since they are hollow, they must be washed very thoroughly in several changes of water to remove any dirt or grit. Unlike other mushrooms, morels are never eaten raw; always cooked, and cooked a good long time. Dried morels, imported from France, are available in this country. Morels from the Great Lakes region, one of the sections in this country where they grow wild, are available, in season, in stores specializing in deluxe foods.

How do you use dried mushrooms? They must first be soaked in water or consommé, then squeezed dry. It takes about 10 minutes. Incidentally, even after they have been reconstituted, they will keep for several days in the refrigerator. We suggest you taste the mushrooms, since they are apt to be considerably more concentrated in flavor than that of cultivated mushrooms. Taking the flavor into consideration, use them as you would fresh, cultivated mushrooms. Imported Hungarian, Italian, and Chinese mushrooms are available in food stores specializing in fine foods (the Chinese in Chinese food stores). They are similar, except the Chinese, which are somewhat meatier and not quite as strong as the European.

If a recipe calls for fresh mushrooms, can I use canned? Yes. For 1 pound fresh mushrooms (20 to 24 whole mushrooms), substitute the contents of 1 6- to 8-ounce can of mushroom caps or crowns, drained well.

Can nasturtiums be eaten? Yes, and they're extremely good. Flowers and all. Just mix them in with a plain green salad to brighten things up.

How do you buy fresh okra? By the pound, and you should choose pods from 2 to 4 inches long. Larger ones are too tough and old to make good eating. Like beans and celery, they snap easily when fresh and tender. Okra can be kept for about 2 weeks.

Available fresh from April through October. Canned, the year round.

Are okra and gumbo the same thing? Yes. And the other names are gobo, gombo, and acra. Okra is the tapering pod of the okra plant which is used in making soups. Very particularly in the chicken and shrimp "gumbos" of Creole cooking. It is a natural thickening agent and performs this particular function in gumbos. However, it is delicious French-fried, creamed, or added to vegetable soup. Okra is available frozen, but the quality cannot match the fresh.

Can I make my own garlic olives? Sure. Drain the liquid off green olives, add a clove or two of garlic—peeled and split—to the jar and cover with olive or salad oil. And, if you like and have some on hand, add a bit of dried red pepper. Refrigerate for several days. By trial and error you can decide how much garlic to use. Use the oil to make salad dressings.

Is a head of garlic the same thing as a clove?   No. The head is a cluster of cloves encased in a tissue-thin white skin. The cloves, which usually must be peeled (unless recipe specifies otherwise), are used individually in the quantities called for in a given recipe.

Is garlic ever used in the shell?   Yes. Cooked, of course. Most chefs, when using it in a soup that will be strained, do not bother to peel the cloves. There are a number of French recipes calling for unpeeled garlic. For example, *poulet sauté à l'ail,* and there is another famous recipe, known as "chicken with forty pieces of garlic." In both instances, the garlic is served, the pulp being extracted by pressing with a fork. Garlic cooked this way makes a delicious little, almost-innocent bite.

How do you use garlic?   In all the classic ways: soups, stews, *bagna cauda* (Italian garlic sauce); *aioli* (classic French garlic sauce); any traditional Provençale dish; in roast leg of lamb; sometimes, a whisper in a salad; in mashed potatoes (*purée de pommes de terre à l'ail*). Actually, garlic is indispensable in hundreds of dishes but, as everybody knows, you either like or dislike garlic and there are no two ways about it.

How do you keep garlic?   As you know, it is beautifully prepackaged, so just store in a small container, uncovered, in the closet along with your salad makings.

Why do garlic dishes sometimes taste bitter?   Because the garlic was burned in cooking.

Is there an easy way to peel garlic and onions?   Not only easy, but tearless. Bring a pan of water to a rapid boil, drop in the garlic or onions. Allow about 5 seconds from boiling point for garlic; 10 seconds for white onions; 5 minutes for old, large onions. Drain and run under cold water, then slip off the skins and first layer (for onions) with your fingers.

How should you store onions? They should be kept as cool and dry as possible. High humidity tends to start root growth and decay.

What are the various types of onions and how are they used? We have six types, as follows.

Medium yellow: Pungent, good for chopping, boiling, stuffing.

Large yellow: Slightly milder than medium yellow, an all-purpose onion, excellent for stuffing and slicing.

Large Spanish or Bermuda: Relatively mild, excellent for slicing and French-frying.

Small whites: Fairly mild, best for boiling, to use in stews, casseroles, etc.

Pearls or picklers: Fairly mild and good only for pickling.

Medium or large red onions: The larger ones, of the Spanish type, are less pungent than the smaller ones. Good mostly for salads and garnishing, sliced into rings, because only the outside is red. All onions, except picklers, are generally available the year round.

Are green onions and scallions the same thing? Yes. An onion harvested very young. In buying them, avoid those with yellow, wilted, or discolored tops because this indicates the "necks" are flabby, tough, and fibrous. If you cut the tops off, they can be chopped fine, and used as a garnish in soups, sauces, etc. Green onions are delicious steamed in butter, or boiled and served cold with vinaigrette sauce.

How do you prepare green onions to serve fresh? Trim off the root ends, trim the green tops, leaving about 2 inches, and remove any loose skin. Wrap in a cloth wrung out in cold water and refrigerate. To serve cooked, prepare the same way, leaving the tops slightly longer.

Can you grow your own chives? Yes, if you have a garden. Also, you can keep a couple of pots going in your kitchen during the winter (just buy a packet of seeds and you're off). A gentle member of the onion family, these hardy perennials have distinguished themselves in cookery for something over 5,000 years. Chopped fine, they make not only a bright garnish, but add a mild raw onion taste to such things as cream or cottage cheese, dressings such as mayonnaise, salads, etc. In fact, almost anything, short of sweets.

Are leeks like onions? Leeks, chives, onions, garlic, and shallots are all members of the amaryllis family, but leeks are the most delicate and least pungent. Known in Europe as "the poor man's asparagus," they are often difficult to find in this country and are always expensive.

Leeks don't look like onions. If anything, they look like an enormous scallion, ½ to 1½ inches in diameter—with very little bulb and long, flat green leaves.

Prepare by cutting off the root ends and all but about an inch of the top, then peel the filmy skin from the white part. Soak thoroughly in cold water for half an hour or so. Because leeks are very gritty, they must be washed thoroughly. Run water into the tops, down through the stalks, making sure they are well cleaned. Leeks can be boiled, served hot with Hollandaise or a rich cream sauce; cold, *à la grecque* or vinaigrette; gratined with cheese; or braised; and, they are the very heart and soul of vichyssoise. Hot, they make an excellent accompaniment to roast beef, steak, or fowl. Actually, any place you would use asparagus.

Any ambitious gardener can raise leeks from seed.

This excellent recipe was adapted from *Mastering the Art of French Cooking.*

BRAISED LEEKS

12 fine fresh leeks	**½ tablespoon salt**
6 tablespoons butter	**Chopped parsley**

Trim off the roots, remove any withered leaves, and slit the green part of the leeks lengthwise. Wash thoroughly under running water, spreading the leaves apart. Cut enough off the tops to leave the leeks about 7 inches long.

Lay the leeks in a heavy pan, making 2 or 3 layers, and add enough water to reach to ⅔ the depth of the leeks. Add butter and salt.

Place over a high heat and bring to a boil. Partially cover, so steam can escape, and keep the water boiling at a good clip. As leeks soften, water will just cover them.

Cook for 30 to 40 minutes or until most of the liquid has evaporated and the white parts of the leeks are tender when pierced with the point of a small, sharp knife.

Lift out of the pan, place in a shallow, ovenproof baking dish that can go to the table. Add whatever juices remain from the cooking pan.

Just 30 minutes before serving time, cover the baking dish lightly

with foil, place in the middle of a preheated 325° F. oven for 20 to
30 minutes or until leeks have turned a light gold. To serve, sprinkle with
chopped parsley. Serves 6.

What are shallots?   The shallot is a member of the onion family, very
delicate in flavor, with only the slightest hint of garlic. Like garlic,
the bulbs separate into cloves. Widely used in France, they are currently growing in favor in this country. Our shallots, the bulk of
which come from Louisiana, can be found in some markets most of
the year. They are also available by mail order. Use in sauces, soups,
stews—in fact, in any cookery where you want a mild onion taste.
If they are not available, the white part of green onions (scallions),
minced, can be substituted in the same proportion as shallots called
for in the recipe.

Shallot is pronounced with the emphasis on the last syllable—
shall-*lot*—like "The Lady of. . . ."

How do you get nice crisp onion rings for salads, etc.?   Drop them in
ice water for an hour or so, then drain thoroughly and pat dry with
paper toweling.

Are onions that have sprouted still usable?   It depends on how much
they have sprouted. Obviously, the sprouts indicate the onion is still
"growing," and, inevitably, moisture is being sapped from the root.
If the onion is still firm, use it. If not, discard, but use the sprout,
which is really the same thing as a tender spring onion.

Is there any way to sauté onions without burning them?   Yes. Combine
water (allow ¼ cup or so for a small frying pan) and butter, add
thinly sliced onions, and cook over medium heat until water has completely evaporated and onions take on a nice golden color. Cook
books are inclined to say "sauté (onions) until they are golden
brown, stirring frequently to keep them from burning." This professional chef's "water" trick eliminates completely the necessity for
watching and stirring the onions. If the water evaporates before
onions are tender, just add a little more.

How can you keep whole onion intact when cooked?   Once it's peeled,
make an "X" with a small, sharp knife at the root end.

How do you peel, cut, slice, chop, or dice onions?

To peel: Slice off both ends cleanly with a good, sharp, sturdy knife, then peel off the skin with a small paring knife. Small white onions, not as easy to peel, can be topped and tailed, then blanched in boiling water for a minute or two. The skins can be then slipped off with a minimum of effort.

To cut: If the finished dish should have some traces of the onion showing, cut the onion lengthwise, from top to bottom, then slice each half in such a way, a small bit of the root end remains attached. But if you want the onion to disappear more or less into the dish, cut in two (as above), lay the flat side on the table and slice, starting at the crown end.

To slice: For complete slices, cut a very thin piece off the peeled onion, lay cut side down to keep the onion from slipping, then slice thick or thin, as you like.

To chop or dice: Cut the onion (shallots can be done this way, too) in half through the root. Lay one half, cut side down, root end to your left. Cut vertical slices from one end to the other, up to but not through the root. Then make horizontal slices from top to bottom, leaving the root still attached. Finally, cut down the length of the onion and you will have diced onions, all of a size.

Why do onions sometimes discolor noticeably when sliced?   Undoubtedly because you are using a steel knife. The acid from the onions comes in contact with the steel and causes it to stain the onions. Actually, this happens with many fruits and vegetables. To be on the safe side, it's best to use stainless-steel knives to slice or peel vegetables and fruits.

How do you make onion juice?   Cut a slice off the onion, then squeeze it as you would an orange, on a reamer.

How should parsley be stored?   Wash thoroughly and shake off as much water as possible. If it has long stems, cut them off. Store in a wide-mouthed jar with a screw top. Refrigerate. After it has stood for a while, drain well to get rid of any excess water and return to refrigerator. If parsley was fresh when purchased, it will keep as long as 10 days or even more. If you notice any yellow leaves as you use it, pull them off and discard. When you use parsley as a garnish with meats, make nice big bouquets, it's far more effective; or stick a good bunch in the tail of roasted birds.

How can you chop parsley? First, you need a good sharp French knife. Holding the knife blade at both ends, chop with an up-and-down motion, pulling the vegetable into a heap, with the knife, as you work. Parsley can also be chopped in the blender, but it makes it very fine, actually, minced. Remember, good sharp steel knives, kept sharp, are the *sine qua non* in cookery.

Do you measure minced parsley exactly as called for in recipes? Certainly not. Unless it's an important amount, such as ½ cup or more, chop up as many sprigs (not the stems) as look like the approximate measurement, and let it go at that. This is one case where a little more or less doesn't make one iota of difference, and if a recipe calls for "1 sprig of parsley," as they frequently and unfortunately do, don't be inhibited by such silly preciseness—throw in several. Cook dangerously.

Thrifty chefs make little bundles of the stems and use them in soups, etc.

Are parsnips a good vegetable? Those who like them, love them. Actually, there are few vegetables that taste better than parsnips, puréed; added to soups or stews; creamed, sautéed, or deep-fat fried. It's just too bad more people don't try them.

PARSNIPS PREPARED IN THE BEARD MANNER

Pare the parsnips and cut up in approximately the same size pieces. Cover with boiling, salted water and boil, covered, until tender when pierced with a knife. Drain thoroughly and push through a sieve or mash until free of all lumps. Beat in some heavy cream, a knob of butter, salt and freshly-ground white pepper to taste. Finish the purée with madeira wine.

Delicious with roast turkey, chicken or game.

When are parsnips in season? The year round. In choosing parsnips, look for smooth, firm, well-shaped roots. Avoid those that are soft, flabby, or shriveled, and large. Store at a low temperature.

What is pasta? The Italian name, used generically, for a whole family of "doughs" that come in countless shapes. There are two main distinctions to be made with regard to pastas. There are homemade pastas and "factory" pastas. Manufactured pastas are sometimes made with eggs, homemade pastas are always made with eggs. Although there will be those who disagree, I think the finest imported pastas are just about as good as the very best homemade. Green pastas are those made with spinach. If, instead, they have been dyed (and this happens), the color will "bleed" on cooking. So, make a note to read the label when you buy green pastas to determine how they were colored.

Contrary to popular opinion, pasta, whatever the type, is distinguished not by its taste but by its texture—determined by the special grind of durum wheat (semolina) used in making it.

Pastas are made in a bewildering number of shapes, some of the more fanciful—stars, melons, bow knots, wagon wheels, shells, snails, butterflies, roses, are used primarily to garnish clear soups. To most Americans, the most familiar are macaroni, available in an infinite variety of shapes, and spaghetti (meaning little string, from *spago*, string). Spaghettini is a finer string, and vermicelli (this translates into little worms), the finest of all. Linguine is similar to spaghetti, except that it's flat rather than cylindrical. Lasagna, meaning broadleafed, has flat or ruffled edges; and noodles can be very narrow or wide ribbons.

Actually, all pastas fit into four basic groups: ribbons, tubes, cords, and special shapes. All are made with the same kind of dough and all should, seemingly, taste the same, but the facts are that the variations in texture and thickness and the ways the various shapes absorp liquid, retain heat, and hold sauces produce different taste sensations.

Different shapes were originally evolved for different dishes and purposes, but many of them can be used interchangeably. The imaginative cook, with a good Italian cook book by her side, will undoubtedly find it amusing to experiment.

How do you cook pasta? It needs plenty of water in a good deep kettle. About 6 quarts to 1 pound (any type). Bring water to a rolling boil, add 1 teaspoon of salt per quart of water, add the pasta gradually so as not to stop the water boiling. The long pastas, such as spaghetti, should never be broken. Take handfuls, one at a time, and lower the ends into the boiling water. They will soften and curl into the kettle as the water softens them. Although many cooks say, "Do not stir," *Quality,* a magazine published by the Italian Foreign Trade Institute, recommends stirring the pasta once it has been added, then stirring occasionally during the cooking. Boil briskly, uncovered. The cooking time depends on the thickness, quality, and age of the pasta. After 4 minutes, taste a piece—it should be *al dente* (firm to the tooth). Continue taste-testing until it is very slightly resistant. Drain immediately through a colander and do not, as some cooks are prone to do, run under cold water. This accomplishes nothing except to cool the pasta.

Have ready a heated dish in which to serve it and serve immediately.

Can cooked pasta "wait"?   It shouldn't, but in a dire emergency, pour the pasta back into the kettle of hot water, add bits of butter to coat the strands and to keep them from sticking together. A half hour is the most time it should wait.

Can cooked pasta be kept and stored?   Yes. Cook and drain quickly, coat with oil, and refrigerate in a tightly covered container. To use, place in a pot of boiling water just long enough to heat through. Drain and use immediately.

N O T E : Do not store cooked pasta in a sauce, it softens the pasta and destroys the texture.

How can I keep pasta from sticking?   Add a little vegetable oil (olive, if you like) or bits of butter during the last few minutes of cooking. Allow about 2 to 3 tablespoons of oil, or the same of butter, to 6 quarts of water.

What are egg noodles?   A pasta made with eggs, available commercially, or they can be homemade. Those who make their own egg noodles (Mr. Craig Claiborne, Food Editor of the New York *Times,* is one) say no manufactured noodles can compare with the tender, fresh noodles made in your own kitchen. Not difficult, but it's helpful if you have a pasta machine (available in most good stores selling deluxe cooking equipment).

What is fettuccine?   It's the Roman name for home-made egg *tagliatelle* [noodles]. Served with melted sweet (unsalted) butter, Parmesan cheese, and freshly ground black pepper, it is associated in the minds of most travelers with Alfredo's, one of the great restaurants in Rome, where it is said to have originated.

To make fettuccine: Simply boil medium or wide noodles according to package directions, drain, add lots of soft or melted butter and lots of grated Parmesan cheese (preferably freshly grated). Toss gently, making sure butter and cheese are mixed in well. Season with freshly ground black pepper to taste. Serve with a sturdy red wine and crusty bread.

Are ripe olives always black? No. In addition to the ripe olives, both pitted and whole, there is a California "green ripe," with pits, more straw-colored than green, with some mottling. Available in cans and jars. Ripe olives are packed in cans only, in sizes ranging from small all the way up to super-colossal. Size has nothing whatsoever to do with the quality or the flavor—only with the price.

In serving ripe olives, the California Olive Advisory Board suggests draining them, drying, then rolling them around in a bowl with a few drops of olive or salad oil. This keeps them fresh and handsome for hours. *Note:* Olives are a fruit, not a vegetable.

OLIVE PASTE PROVENÇALE

Pound pitted ripe olives with anchovies, thyme, bay leaves, garlic, English mustard, and Worchestershire sauce. Push the paste through a sieve, bring to the right spreading consistency with brandy and oil. Place in a jar, cover with oil, and refrigerate. Use as a spread for canapes, or as a stuffing for leeks, tomatoes, or olives.

What are Spanish olives? A green olive imported from Spain, sometimes bottled over there; sometimes in this country. There are two sizes, the small Manzanilla and the big Queen. Both are packed in 4- and 8-ounce jars. The Manzanillas are available, pits in, unpitted, or stuffed. Mostly stuffed with pimiento, but also with anchovies, or tiny onions; the Queens are available, pits in, or stuffed with almonds or filberts.

Where do those little black, wrinkled olives come from? They come mostly from Spain (considered the best), with a few from both Greece and Italy. By the way, they are not all little, the sizes vary, but they all have small pits. Unlike American and Spanish olives, they have a good, sharp bite. Usually available, by the pound, only in fancy delicatessens or stores specializing in foreign foods.

Do you have difficulty finding fresh young peas? Yes. Like corn, peas are only perfect when picked very young from the garden and cooked as soon as possible. They're available, fresh, the year round, but you have to be a good "picker" to find them young enough to enjoy. Frozen *petits pois* seem to me a better choice.

Optimists on the search for good fresh peas in the market should look for uniformly light green color, slightly velvety to the touch, avoiding peas noticeably pale in color or swollen. If you can, open a pod or two and taste the peas. They should be tender, sweet, and not too big. Refrigerate, but use as soon after purchase as possible.

What are petits pois? A special variety of tiny sweet garden peas indigenous to France and imported, canned, from there. Although originally it meant a species of pea, we are inclined today to designate any small peas as *petits pois*. Some frozen peas in the U.S. travel under the name.

What are snow peas? Perfectly delicious members of the pea family, also known as edible-podded peas and sugar peas. The Chinese have used them in their cooking from time immemorial. Burpee's 1966 catalog says: "Sugar peas possess the tenderness and fleshy podded qualities of a snap bean and the flavor and sweetness of fresh green peas. Peas are not shelled." Sugar peas can be bought fresh in Chinese markets at a very fancy price, and they are now available frozen, packaged under the name pea pods. The quality cannot match the fresh ones. If you have a plot of ground, you can raise them yourself and know the infinite pleasure of eating them young and tender from your own vines.

How do split peas get split? It's nature's wonderful way. When dried and de-hulled, the peas have a natural break which splits them apart.

Are "bell" peppers and sweet peppers the same thing? Yes. They are often referred to as "bell" because of the shape. Peppers are classed in two groups: The sweet or mild and the hot. All peppers are green at first, changing to red when ripe—except one species which turns bright yellow. Sweet peppers either green or red can be used in salads, casseroles, stuffings and, of course, stuffed. Hot peppers are used primarily in sauces or in pickles. Today, sweet peppers are pretty much available the year round, but are at their peak during the summer and early fall. Good peppers are fresh, firm, thick-fleshed, and either red or bright green, perhaps with splashes of red. Immature ones are soft, pliable, thin, and pale; stale, they will be shriveled, soft, and dull. Unshapely peppers, if otherwise of good quality, can be used in cooking.

Sautéed peppers are delicious and make an extremely handsome dish when the green and red, or yellow too, are combined.

SAUTÉED PEPPERS

Remove seeds from peppers and slice, crosswise, into ¼-inch slices. Heat a film of olive oil in a heavy pan, add a clove or 2 of garlic—split. Cook the garlic, taking care not to allow it to burn or it will turn bitter, until it has flavored the oil. Remove the garlic, add the peppers, then lower heat and cook over a moderate heat for 10 to 12 minutes, giving an occasional stir, until peppers are tender, but still somewhat crisp when pierced with the point of a small, sharp knife. Season with salt and freshly ground pepper.

How do you slice fresh peppers? Cut off the stem end, then with a small, sharp knife, cut out the ribs and remove all seeds. If you want rings, cut across; if strips, cut pepper in half, then slice lengthwise.

What are pimientos? Mild, spicy red peppers indigenous to the New World. Another one of Columbus' discoveries, which he took back to Spain. The name comes from the Spanish, *pimienta,* meaning pepper. The brilliantly beautiful pimientos, available prepared in cans and jars, are skinned and cored, then packed by hand so as not to damage the heart-shaped pods. Unlike the peppers we grow in our gardens, they are not edible raw. (Despite English and American dictionaries, where it is spelled "pimento," the correct spelling is with a second "i"—pimiento.) Pimento is something else—allspice, the little seeds from the allspice tree.

To store pimientos, after opening, drain off all the liquid in which they are packed, and keep completely covered with cold water, in a covered jar, refrigerated; or add ½ teaspoon of vinegar to the pimiento liquid, cover securely, and refrigerate.

Why can't we get good potatoes? We can, but it's not easy. One of the problems is growers don't label potatoes, nor are we told what potato performs best in a given situation. The principle types of potatoes in the market are: The Russet Burbank which is easily recognized by its long, cylindrical shape, the heavily netted and russeted skin, commonly known as the Idaho (whether it is grown in Idaho or not) which bakes well. My quarrel with the Idaho is the size. It's just too big, although rumor has it a smaller Idaho is being developed. Then we have the round, white Katahdin which is really a "boiling" potato. But it doesn't match that glorious California Long White, often called White Rose. This is truly a great potato, extremely handsome, fawn color, sleek and smooth, with the eyes barely apparent. Available from May 15 through September 12 (spring and summer harvest) and from December 15 through March 15 (winter harvest). Look for them. No, demand them! Another great potato, certainly the equal of the California Long White, is the Dade County Red Nugget (this is the natural color) Brand which Mr. J. Abney Cox (one of the growers) of Princeton, Florida, writes me, is available from the latter part of February to about the middle of April across the country in all the big markets—and the only fresh red potatoes in the U.S. at that particular time. Red Nugget Brand Potatoes are recommended for every use but I found them exceptional for boiling and baking. He further tells me that the word "new" is used to distinguish freshly-dug potatoes from storage potatoes as well as immature potatoes (see Pontiac). The fifth, the red Pontiac which, to most of us, means new baby potatoes, are new only in the sense they are dug before they reach maturity. As a consequence, they are inclined to be expensive, are more perishable than mature potatoes and should be used with dispatch.

How do you slice potatoes or other round vegetables?   As you would onions.

Do you ever use instant potatoes?   Yes, and, in my opinion, one of the really great instant products. In addition to using them as a vegetable, they can be used (as potatoes have been forever) in making cakes, soufflés, doughnuts, dumplings, etc. The great advantage in using them as an ingredient is that they are ready instantly and as smooth as silk.

Why do my scalloped potatoes curdle?   For one, or both, of these reasons: The milk (half cream, half milk is better) was not heated before adding it to the casserole, and your oven temperature was too high. About 325° or 350° F. is the right temperature to forestall curdling.

Are potatoes fattening? Anything is fattening if you eat too much of it. The white potato, one of our best vegetables, which goes with almost anything, has been maligned for years. Actually, one medium-size boiled potato has the same number of calories, 76, as one medium-size apple. Have you ever heard anyone say an apple is fattening?

Why are potatoes sometimes tinged with green? Because they have been "light burned." Potatoes should always be stored away from light, and if the potatoes you see in the market have a green tinge, avoid them like the plague, because the texture of the potato will have changed.

Is the red coloring that comes off new potatoes a dye? Yes. A harmless but nevertheless artificially colored wax used by growers to accentuate the color of the potatoes and, they claim, to inhibit "wilt"—a common problem with new potatoes, which are extremely perishable and, unlike mature potatoes, wither rather quickly. As potato enthusiasts, we find ourselves distressed by the coloring and wax for three reasons: The dye also dyes the cook's hands and takes a good scrubbing with a brush and soap to get it off; the wax and coloring are inclined to make an unattractive ring around the cooking pot; and, further, the dye sometimes stains the flesh of the cooked potatoes pale pink, which is far from appealing. However, the United Fresh Fruit and Vegetable Association reports that research continues and we can, hopefully, look forward to the day when new potatoes will be marketed wearing their own naturally beautiful colors.

Should potatoes be oiled before baking? There is no "should" or "shouldn't." If you like a soft skin, oil or butter well-washed, well-dried potatoes before you put them into the hot oven. On the other hand, if you like a crisp skin (and many do), wash potatoes well and dry very thoroughly, then place in the oven.

Should potatoes be pierced before baking? No one seems in agreement on this. The "piercers" say it allows the steam to escape, forestalls sogginess, makes the potato light and fluffy; the "non-piercers" say it doesn't make one whit of difference.

Should potatoes be wrapped in foil before baking? It's up to you. If you like a soft skin, wrap them. If not, don't. Many people think foil-wrapped potatoes are creamier; others call them "soggy."

Should potatoes be started in cold water or boiling water? Boiling, salted water. Then cook, covered, until they can be pierced easily with the point of a small, sharp knife. Drain immediately, shake the pan over a high heat to dry them quickly, or shake them out the window to accomplish the same thing. Cover lightly with a clean, dry, dish towel to keep them warm. Do not cover with lid, or the potatoes will get soggy.

What are pommes de terre Anna? Potatoes Anna, a French recipe, is essentially a potato cake. Sliced potatoes, sautéed in butter (to the saturation point), browned on one side, pressed together, then flipped over, like a pancake, and browned on the other side. The flipping may make you nervous, but the potatoes are marvelous.

Are sweet potatoes and yams the same thing? Technically, no. The real yam, the *Dioscorea,* which can weight as much as 100 pounds, is rarely seen in this country. Of the hundreds of varieties of sweet potatoes, the two we see in our markets are the soft orange-colored ones that are often mistakenly called yams (yam, from the Senegalese, *nyami,* to eat); and the firmer, lighter sweet potato known as yellow Jersey. Both are members of the morning glory family. Sweet potatoes are available the year round fresh, canned, dehydrated, and frozen.

What's the secret to a good potato salad? There are three: Freshly boiled potatoes; mixing the potatoes with the dressing while they are still warm and allowing the mixture to mellow; never refrigerating the salad. Potato salad can be made with a good, not-too-thick mayonnaise; with mayonnaise mixed with sour cream; with mayonnaise mixed with French mustard; and, one of the best ways, with hot bacon dressing in Pennsylvania potato salad. Eleanor Noderer, my old associate, and now on *Gourmet Magazine*, makes it flawlessly:

PENNSYLVANIA POTATO SALAD

Cut 6 strips of bacon in slivers and fry in a skillet until almost crisp. Pour off all but 2 tablespoons of the drippings, and stir in 2 tablespoons sugar, 1 teaspoon each of flour and salt. Cook over a low heat for several minutes. Add ¼ cup vinegar mixed with ½ cup water, and cook, stirring constantly, until the sauce comes to a boil.

Pour the hot sauce over 2 pounds freshly boiled, peeled, and diced potatoes. Add 1 small onion, chopped, and 1 tablespoon minced parsley, and toss well. Taste and add more salt if necessary. Serve the potato salad warm, garnished with slices of hard-cooked eggs. Serves 6.

What are Saratoga chips? Just the old familiar potato chips. The name comes from the fact they were first "invented" in Saratoga, New York.

Are pumpkin and squash alike? Botanically, they are both known as gourds, and no one seems quite clear as to what constitutes a pumpkin or a squash—to the extent that the U.S. Government permits canners to use the flesh of either vegetable under the name pumpkin. They can be used interchangeably in cooking, and there is a great difference of opinion as to which makes the best eating. In the 1896 edition of Fannie Farmer's *The Boston Cooking School Cook Book*, the recipes for squash and pumpkin are identical. Broadly speaking, we're all inclined to say pumpkin pie (or "Punkin") regardless of which vegetable is used. Pumpkins seem to play their largest role at Halloween time.

For the record, squash is "marrow" in England, and pumpkin in Australia.

How do you make radish fans? Cut each radish crosswise into thin slices, from top to bottom, but not quite to the stem end. Refrigerate in ice water. Pat dry to serve.

How do you make radish roses? Wash and remove all but a nice, little tuft of the leaves; cut off the roots. Then cut 4 thin slices, equidistant, almost down to the leaves; next, cut 4 thin slices of the white flesh between the red slices. Refrigerate in a bowl of ice water until the "roses" open. Pat dry before serving.

Is rhubarb the same thing as pieplant? Yes. Also known as wineplant
(it was once used to make wine). Although we associate rhubarb
with spring, it is actually available almost the year round, if not from
the garden, from the hothouse. Stewed, it is very good, but it is really
best in a pie (perhaps that's how it was first called pieplant) because
it holds its shape better. Unlike other vegetables (and it is a vegetable) such as beets, turnips, etc., the tops are not fit for human
consumption. The leaf blades contain amounts of oxalic acid and
oxalates, sometimes great enough to cause fatal poisoning. In the old
days, rhubarb leaves were used to wrap foods to keep them cold. In
choosing fresh rhubarb, look for fresh, firm, crisp, tender, bright
stalks. Really young rhubarb has immature leaves.

What are the different types of rice and how are they used?
   Regular milled white rice: The hulls, germ, outer bran layers, and
most of the inner bran are removed in the milling process. White rice
comes in three different lengths: long grain, medium grain, and short
grain (sometimes called pearl). All can be used interchangeably in
any recipe calling for white rice. However, the medium and short
grain are less expensive than long grain and are generally used in
puddings and soups, whereas the long grain would be used when rice
plays an important role in the menu.
   Brown rice: The whole unpolished rice with only the outer, in-
edible, fibrous shell removed; it requires more water and longer cooking time than white rice. Its rich, nut-like flavor makes it especially
good as a vegetable, or as a stuffing.
   Parboiled rice: Rice that has been cooked before milling by a special steam-pressure process. It, too, takes longer to cook than regular
milled white rice, but produces fluffy, plump grains.
   Precooked rice: Completely cooked, it is prepared by allowing it
to stand in boiling water only until heated through. These last two
can, of course, be used where you would use regular milled white
rice.

What is wild rice? It is a wild grain, not a true rice at all, with an
unusually interesting texture and—when cooked properly—flavor. Especially delicious with game. Because it is very time-consuming to
harvest, it is rather costly.

What is the best method of cooking rice? Except for long grain rice, the best advice we have to hand out is to follow the manufacturer's instructions. Long grain rice, cooked by the Chinese method, has always seemed to us extremely satisfactory.

To cook long grain rice: Place 2 cups of rice in a bowl and wash under cool running water, rubbing it between your hands, until the water runs clear. Or wash, still rubbing, under a strong spray of cool water. The point here is to get rid of as much of the starch as possible. Drain, place in a large, heavy saucepan with 3 cups of cold water. Bring slowly to a boil, cover, reduce heat to simmer, and cook about 20 minutes or until all the water has been absorbed. Stir well with a fork, while it is still hot, so that it will be flaky and each grain will be separate.

Advice from Dorothy Lee, a splendid Chinese cook: "Too much water in rice cookery is an error; the pot used should never be more than half full."

Can cooked rice be frozen? It certainly can, and most successfully. Place cold, cooked rice in proper containers in the freezer. To serve, thaw, cover with boiling water until hot through—a matter of minutes. Drain thoroughly. Do not cook further.

Are a pilaff and risotto the same? Very much. They are both made with rice. Pilaff (also spelled pilaf, pilaw, pilau) is of Middle Eastern origin and risotto, of Italian. Both call for butter, onions, bouillon, rice, and seasonings. Plain pilaff is served as an accompaniment to meat and chicken dishes, but the basic pilaff is often combined with meat, chicken, chicken livers, vegetables, etc., to make a main dish. A risotto is frequently seasoned with saffron and grated Parmesan cheese. It, too, is used as a base for peas, white truffles, chicken livers, shellfish, etc., and is served as a main course.

Is a chef's salad like a Caesar salad? No. Classically, a chef's salad is a combination of chicken, tongue or ham, and Swiss cheese, in equal proportions, all julienned, tossed in a vinaigrette sauce, and served on greens. However, there are other variations, such as a garnish of quartered tomatoes and hard-cooked eggs.

Is Caesar salad American or Mexican? It's like this. It was created by an Italian restaurateur some years ago in Tijuana, Mexico, and popularized by the famous American tourists who went over the border from California. Essentially, a Caesar salad is this (there are now many variations): romaine, tossed in a bright dressing composed of mustard, lemon juice, Tabasco, olive oil, then sprinkled with Parmesan cheese, with drained anchovies, a "coddled" egg, and croutons added. The salad bowl should be rubbed with salt and a split clove of garlic.

What is a mimosa salad? There are several versions. The one commonly accepted as mimosa is a salad of hearts of lettuce with a garnish of chopped, hard-cooked egg yolks. Another version is hearts of lettuce garnished with orange sections, sliced bananas, grapes, tossed in heavy cream mixed with lemon juice. Small balls of cooked carrots, celeriac, potatoes, asparagus tips, mixed with mayonnaise, on lettuce leaves is also known as mimosa salad.

What is salade niçoise? In *French Provincial Cooking*, Mrs. Elizabeth David describes it thus: "This is always served as an hors d'oeuvre. The ingredients depend on the season and what is available. But hard-boiled eggs, anchovy fillets, black olives, and tomatoes, with garlic in the dressing, are pretty well constant elements in what should be a rough country salad, rather than a fussy chef's concoction. . . . It is up to you to choose the other ingredients: tuna fish, cooked French beans, raw sliced red peppers, beetroot, potatoes, artichoke hearts. It depends what is to come afterwards."

What is salsify? Also known as oyster-plant and vegetable oyster, and colloquially in England, as "John-go-to-bed-at-noon" because its flowers close in the middle of the day. It's a root vegetable, like a carrot in shape, but black in color, half again as long. The flavor resembles that of oysters—hence, the name. To cook, the roots should be scraped, then dropped immediately into acidulated water to prevent discoloring. Cut into pieces, boil, and serve with hot butter, or fry, or turn into fritters, or serve in a well-seasoned Béchamel. Available almost the year round (June to March), look for well-shaped roots of medium size; avoid shriveled and/or large roots.

The young leaves are said to make a delicious spring salad.

What is sorrel? Classified as an herb, it is a hardy perennial that seemingly grows wild all over the world, but is also cultivated. The French braise it, make soups and sauces of it, and some people like a bit chopped up in a green salad. It's rather sour, but the French soup, *potage Germiny*, is something wonderful to eat. Jacques

Pépin, former *chef de cuisine* to President de Gaulle, gave me this recipe.

POTAGE GERMINY

1 small bunch sorrel	3 cups beef or chicken broth,
1 tablespoon fresh chervil	heated
2 tablespoons butter	1 tablespoon arrowroot
4 egg yolks	Salt
1 cup heavy cream	Freshly ground white pepper
	Croutons

Slice the sorrel and fresh chervil into very fine julienne to make about ½ cup. Melt the butter in a heavy pan, add the greens, and cook over a medium heat for 10 minutes. Combine egg yolks and cream in the top of a double boiler and beat together over simmering water with a whip for 10 minutes. This long constant whipping is designed to give you a very creamy liaison, light and fluffy. But, as with Hollandaise, take care not to curdle the eggs.

Take off the heat and combine the liaison with the broth, whipping very hard. Combine the arrowroot with a little broth to make a smooth paste and stir into the mixture thoroughly. Place back over hot water and cook, stirring constantly with a wooden spatula, until the soup begins to stick to the spatula (temperature on a thermometer should not go beyond 175° F.).

Keep warm in a double boiler, over hot water, until serving time, at which time stir in the warm, cooked sorrel. Or chill in the refrigerator and serve cold. Delicious either way. Serve with croutons only if hot. Serves 6.

How can you buy spinach? It is available in almost every way imaginable. You can get it fresh the year round, by the pound: trimmed and washed in transparent bags, canned, frozen (leaf or chopped), creamed frozen—you can even pick up spinach soufflés, frozen.

In choosing fresh spinach, by the pound, look for leaves that are large, fresh, crisp, and a good dark green; avoid those that are crushed, wilted, and show signs of decay. The variety usually available is the Savoy or crumpled leaf, although you may run into some flat leaves.

When you're bored with spinach, what greens do you eat? There's quite a selection to choose from: collards, turnip tops, mustard greens, kale, Swiss chard, dandelions, cabbage sprouts, and beet tops.

All except beet greens and dandelions are available pretty much the year round, and even they come on the market at odd times. In buying, look for greens that are fresh, young, tender, crisp. Avoid all others.

How do you cook spinach and other greens?   Remove any yellow or wilted leaves, twist off any tough stems, then wash in a sink of tepid water. This helps to get rid of the sand. Now give it several good washings under cold running water. Lift out of the water. Don't drain through a colander or you may pick up some of the dirt you washed off. Drain well. If it is necessary to store it, refrigerate in a container and use in a reasonable length of time.

In this country we cook greens with only the water that clings to the leaves, placing them in a heavy kettle or saucepan (not aluminum or iron, which tends to give a metallic taste), cooking them, uncovered, over a moderate heat until just tender—a matter of minutes. Tasting is the best way to test. In France, they cook them the way they do beans, in loads of salted water, refreshing in cold water to stop the cooking and retain the color. By both methods of cooking, they should be squeezed to extract as much water as possible. Cooked greens can be served in innumerable ways, chopped or not: seasoned with salt and pepper, dressed with melted butter; dressed with minced garlic, olive oil, salt, and pepper; creamed and seasoned; mixed with Swiss cheese, bread crumbs, butter, seasonings, and gratined, etc.

Why does spinach turn very dark, almost black, after cooking?   It should be refreshed immediately, under cold water, which stops the cooking. Then all water should be gently squeezed out. To serve hot, reheat in hot, but not boiling, water, then drain.

What is spoon bread?   A famous Southern dish that isn't a bread at all, but a pudding. The name apparently stems from *suppawn,* the Indian name for porridge. Made of cornmeal, milk, eggs, and baking powder, it is baked and served hot, with plenty of butter, as a side dish to the meat course. Southern batter bread is essentially the same thing.

What's the difference between winter and summer squashes?   Actually, the terms "winter" and "summer" are meaningless, because all are available the year round.

Soft-shelled squashes: These are Yellow Crookneck, Straightneck, Zucchini or Italian, and Scallop or Pattypan. With these, no matter how they are prepared, you eat both the skin and seeds.

Mature hard-shelled squashes: The small Acorn, Buttercup (turban-shaped), and Butternut. With the exception of the Acorn, which is usually split, baked, and served in the shell, the others are peeled before cooking, then mashed.

Hard-shelled Hubbard: The big, old familiar squash, with the alligator-like skin. It, too, must be peeled before cooking and is usually served mashed. Although it can be cut into pieces, shell on, and baked like Acorn squash. Quite a production, because the shell is as hard as a rock.

Frozen and canned squash (the hard-shell varieties) are always available the year round.

Is it true you can fry and eat squash blossoms? Yes. Dip the blossoms, fresh from the vine, into a light batter and fry in deep fat until golden. Serve on a napkin-lined plate with salt. The flavor doesn't amount to much—and it's a surprise to look into the heart of the flower—but it's a real conversation piece over cocktails.

What are timbales? A timbale is a food, shaped into a mold, to hold food, or a molded food used as a garnish. For example, macaroni or spaghetti timbales, filled with a chicken or fish forcemeat, served with a compatible sauce; rice timbales served as a garnish, with curried meat. Timbale also means a paper-thin shell made from an egg batter, cooked on a timbale iron (the shapes vary) in deep fat, in or on which to serve creamed foods, such as oysters and chicken. The smaller, more decorative, fried timbales are often sprinkled with confectioners' sugar and served as a confection with tea or coffee.

Do you serve tomatoes in a tossed green salad? No. They are too watery and dilute the dressing. If served when a green salad is served, it's best to slice or quarter them, season, and present on a separate dish. Or forget the green salad.

How do you peel and seed tomatoes? Drop firm, ripe tomatoes into boiling water to cover. Allow to stand briefly or actually boil for 10 seconds. Cut out the stem, peel off the skin, starting from the stem end. Cut in half (peeled or unpeeled) crosswise, and squeeze each half gently to extract seeds and juices from the center. If tomatoes are to be stuffed, sprinkle them with salt to draw out more of the juices and turn them upside down to drain.

What are beefsteak tomatoes? The Department of Agriculture says: "It is an old, large-fruited tomato variety. Few beefsteak types are grown any more because the fruit is rough, crack-and-rot susceptible."

Can cherry tomatoes be cooked? Certainly, and they are marvelous. Very refined cooks peel the little tomatoes. (I don't bother.)

Wash, dry thoroughly, and pull off the stems. Heat some olive oil in a pan with a couple of cloves of garlic, split. Cook together until the cloves have flavored the oil, taking care not to allow them to burn. Lift out of the oil and discard. Add the little tomatoes, a handful of minced parsley, and cook over a moderate heat, shaking the pan, until they just begin to reach the bursting point. Season with salt, freshly ground pepper, and a "hair" of sugar. Serve the next time you have veal scaloppine or a steak.

Is it true tomatoes should be ripened in the dark? Yes. If they are put on a window sill, as so many people are inclined to do, they wither and get pulpy. Light is the culprit. Even fairly green tomatoes will ripen to a rich red if stored away from light. A heavy paper bag is just the ticket. Once ripened, refrigerate them. Here are two good tips from *Food in England,* by Dorothy Hartley. She writes: "To skin (tomatoes) dip them into boiling water 1 minute. Slice with the core to keep in the juices for sandwiches, and against the core to loosen the juices for chopping up and cooking."

What are love apples? An old-fashioned name for tomatoes.

Are green tomatoes edible? Of course. Chowchow or green tomato pickles are classic examples. Here's James Beard's delicious recipe for green tomatoes as a vegetable:

Slice firm tomatoes (1 per person) in thick slices. Dredge in flour and sprinkle lightly with salt and pepper. Sauté in a saucepan with melted butter. Sprinkle each slice with dark brown sugar, before and after turning. Cook slowly so the sugar, butter, and flour blend but do not burn. When tomatoes are lightly browned, add heavy cream. Cook only long enough to heat cream and to thicken the sauce slightly. Pour the sauce over the tomatoes to serve.

What precisely are truffles and how are they used?   Called, "the diamonds of cookery," by Brillat-Savarin, truffles are a fungus fruit, a member of the tuber family, and kin to the famous morel or sponge mushroom. They grow several inches below the surface of the ground under oak, juniper, or hazelnut trees. Temperamental and elusive, truffles cannot be cultivated but must be rooted up by specially trained dogs or pigs. (Pigs are being abandoned because they not only have a nose for truffles but a taste for them, too.) The world's entire crop comes from the Perigord region in France and the Umbria and Piedmont in Italy. Because the harvest cannot be controlled, truffles are scarce and, therefore, very expensive, but if used with finesse, a small quantity goes a long way.

Truffles have a fairly wide color range, from white (really, more cream than white) through shell pink to brown to shiny jet-black, but those most prized, and most used, are the white and black. Truffles are round, wrinkled, sort of "warty" in appearance, ranging in size from a small marble up to a grapefruit (the largest ever found, in Italy, weighed 2 pounds). No one is agreed on what truffles taste like. To one expert, they taste like a mixture of chestnuts and strawberries; another says they are like a combination of filberts and well-aged cheese; the flavor of the whites has been likened to vivid herbs.

Truffles from France, packed in brine, are available in ⅜- to 7-ounce tins; from Italy, peeled and unpeeled black truffles, truffle pieces, peelings in varying size tins from 1-ounce to 16-ounce tins; white truffles, in ½- to 4-ounce tins. (All the Italian imports are packed in natural juice.) Black or white truffle purée, in 2- to 8-ounce tins. Fresh truffles are sometimes available in shops specializing in fine foods in the fall and winter months. Truffles are used in innumerable ways: In *pâtés*—the most famous being *pâté de fois gras*—in omelets, in salads, as a garnish, etc.

Are turnips and rutabagas the same thing?   No. Turnips are a white-fleshed root vegetable that ranges in size from that of an orange up to 40 pounds. Obviously, the best flavor and texture is in the small size. The flavor is milder than, but reminiscent of, the more strongly flavored rutabaga. Housewives often called rutabagas "big yellow turnips" (hence, the confusion) and they are also known as "Canadian turnips" or "Swedes."

Rutabagas, in season from July through April, are usually coated with a thin layer of paraffin to prevent spoilage. For those who think of rutabagas as "cattle food," and many do, I suggest you combine one good-sized rutabaga, cooked and mashed, with a couple of cooked, mashed potatoes, season with salt, pepper, sugar, and butter, then whip in some heavy cream. Great with roast beef, roast pork, chicken or turkey—cattle should have it so good!

Can water chestnuts be preserved once the can is opened? Yes. They are packed in water, and should be kept completely covered with water and refrigerated to keep them firm and crisp.

Is there any way to keep watercress fresh? When you get it home from the market, put only its "feet" in a low bowl or glass of cold water (an Old-Fashioned glass is a good size and depth for one bunch). Wrap the whole thing in a polyethylene bag securely so no air can penetrate. Refrigerate. If the cress was fresh when purchased, it will keep up to a week.

What is Yorkshire pudding? The classic English accompaniment to roast beef, specifically, sirloin. A light, puffy mixture of eggs, milk, flour, and beef drippings, baked, served piping hot, cut in squares.

ACKNOWLEDGMENTS   The author is extremely grateful to the following individuals, organizations, and publications for their generous assistance and cooperation.

A Concise Encyclopedia of Gastronomy
Ac'cent International
Adams, Charlotte
The Aluminum Association
The American Heritage Cookbook
American Home Economics Association
American Institute of Baking
American Lamb Council
American Meat Institute
American Mushroom Institute
American Shrimp Canners Association
American Spice Trade Association
American Sugar Refining Company
America's Table
Ardrey, Robert
Armour and Company
Artichoke Advisory Board
The Art of Fine Baking
The Art of French Cooking
Associated Pimiento Canners
B&M Beans
Bateman, Eleanor
Bazaar de la Cuisine
Beard, James A.
Bird, Kermit
Bordeaux Wine Information Bureau
The Borden Company
The Boston Cooking School Cook Book (1896)
Bourbon Institute
Britt, Helen
Brown, Helen Evans
Brown, Phillip S.
Brownstone, Cecily
Burpee's Seeds 1966

California Almond Growers Exchange
California Avocado Advisory Board
California Olive Advisory Board
California Prune Advisory Board
California Raisin Advisory Board
California Walnut Growers
The Canadian Dept. of Fisheries
Casa Brasil
Cashew Export Council of India
Chamberlain, Narcissa
Chamberlain, Narcisse

Champagne Producers of France
Cheese and Fermented Milk Foods
The Cheese Book
Chenus, Roland
Cherneff, M. N.
Child, Julia
Chocolate Manufacturers Association of the U.S.A.
Chu, Grace Zia
Claiborne, Craig
The Classic French Cuisine
Classic Cooking from India
Cling Peach Advisory Board
The Complete Mexican Cook Book
Cox, J. Abney

David, Elizabeth
Day, Avanelle
deGroot, Roy Andries
Diat, Louis
Dictionnaire de l'Academie des Gastronomes
Donnellon, Sylvia
Donon, Joseph
Dried Fruit Association of California
Dudley, Anderson and Yutzy
Dunham, Ellen-Ann

Economy Gastronomy
The Encyclopedia of Food

Fannie Farmer
Feasts for All Seasons
Filbert/Hazelnut Institute
Filiatreau, Jacques
Fish and Wildlife Service
Fishery Council
Fleischman's Yeast
Florida Citrus Commission
Food in England
Foods of France
The Four Seasons Restaurant
Frank Schoonmaker's Encyclopedia of Wine
French National Association of Cognac Producers
French Provincial Cooking

Garvin, Fernande
Gas Appliance Manufacturers' Association
General Foods Corporation
Glass Container Institute
Grossman, Harold J.
Grossman's Guide to Wines, Spirits, and Beers

Halibut Association of North America

The Handbook of Food Preparation
Harrington, Marie
Hartley, Dorothy
Hecht, Dan
Helma, Dona
Hempstead, Eleanor
Hening, Rachel E.
An Herb and Spice Cook Book
Hering's Dictionary of Classical and Modern Cookery
How to Identify and Prepare Cuts of Lamb
International Milling Company
Italian Food

Joy of Cooking

Kaduson, William
Knox Gelatine
Kosikowski, Frank V., Ph.D.
Kraft Cheese

La Croisette Restaurant
La Cuisiniere
La Popotte Restaurant
Larousse Gastronomique
Lee, Dorothy
Lee, Sarah Tomerlin
Le Pavillon Restaurant
Le Repetoire de la Cuisine
Lianides, Aphrodite
Libby, McNeil and Libby
Liquor Store Magazine
Louisiana Yam Council

Mastering the Art of French Cooking
McIlhenny Company
Morino, Louis

National Apple Institute
National Broiler Council
National Canners Association
National Cherry Growers and Industry Foundation
National Coffee Association
The National Dairy Council
National Fisheries Institute
National Kraut Packers Association
National Livestock and Meat Board
National Macaroni Institute
The Nestlé Company
New Jersey Asparagus Industry Council
The New York Times Cook Book
The New York Times Menu Cook Book
Noderer, Eleanor

Nolle, Jean
Ocean Spray Cranberries, Inc.
The Omelette Book
Ortiz, Elizabeth Lambert

The Paper Cup and Place Industries
Pan American Coffee Bureau
Peck, Paula
Pépin, Jacques
Pet, Inc.
The Pleasures of Chinese Cooking
Popper, Hildegarde
Potato Growers Association of California
Poultry and Egg National Board
Processed Apple Institute

Quality (The Italian Foreign Trade Institute)
Quo Vadis Restaurant

Rice Council
Roquefort Association, Inc.

Scattergood, Leslie W.
Schmidt, Eric
Schoonmaker, Frank
Seelig, R. A.
Seranne, Ann
Shrimp and Shellfish Recipes
The Shrimp Association of the Americas
Singh, Dharam Jit
South African Rock Lobster Service Corporation
Spader, Margaret
Spanish Green Olive Commission
The Spice Cook Book
Staggs, Reba
Stanish, Rudolph
Steindler, Paul
Stillman, Ellen
Stokes, Warren
Stuckey, Lillie
Sturtevant's Notes on Edible Plants
Sumner, Rider and Associates
Sunkist Growers
Swift and Company

The Tart Cook Book
Tea Council of the U.S.A.
The Territorial Imperative
Thompson, J. Walter
Thompson, Sylvia Vaughn

United Fresh Fruit and Vegetable Association
United Fruit Company
U.S. Department of Agriculture
Urbani, Paul A.

Vehling, Joseph
The Virginia Housewife
Von Glahn, John

Washington State Apple Commission
West Coast Cook Book
William Underwood Company
Wine Advisory Board
Wine & Food
Wine Institute

Zum Zum Restaurants

Index